American Government
and Politics

THE UNIVERSITY OF LIVERPOOL
SYDNEY JONES LIBRARY

Please return or renew, on or before the last date below. A fine is payable on late returned items. Items may be recalled after one week for the use of another reader. Items may be renewed by telephone:- 0151 794 - 2678.

For conditions of borrowing, see Library Regulations

American Government and Politics

ALLEN M. POTTER
PETER FOTHERINGHAM
JAMES G. KELLAS
Department of Politics, University of Glasgow

[handwritten annotations: "ALAN ↓ 2nd cousin", "he will sign autographs at 4.00 pm in the lobby"]

FABER AND FABER
London & Boston

First published in 1955
by Faber and Faber Limited
3 Queen Square London WC1
First published in Faber Paperbacks in 1961
Reprinted in 1963, 1966 and 1969
Second edition 1978
This new and revised edition 1981
Printed in Great Britain by
Whitstable Litho Ltd Whitstable Kent

© *Allen M. Potter, Peter Fotheringham, and*
James G. Kellas 1978, 1981

British Library Cataloguing in Publication Data

Potter, Allen M.
American government and politics. – New and revised ed.
1. Civics
2. United States – Constitution
I. Title   II. Fotheringham, Peter
III. Kellas, James G.
320.4′73   JK1759

ISBN 0–571–18044–2
ISBN 0–571–18049–3   Pbk

Contents

Preface to 1981 Edition

The original introduction to this book (pp. 9–17) was written when Jimmy Carter, a Democrat, was taking office as President of the United States. This note is being added as Ronald Reagan, a Republican, is about to succeed him.

An Act of Congress passed shortly before President Nixon's resignation in 1974 required that henceforth the President's appointment of the Director of the Office of Management and Budget obtain senatorial approval (*cf.* p. 231). In 1977 Carter chose a fellow Georgian, Bert Lance, who was approved but who resigned eight months later because of revelations about his previous conduct as a banker. Carter and his 'Georgia Mafia' never found a technique for recovery from their bad start in public relations over the Lance affair.

The mid-term elections of 1978 reduced the Democratic majorities in Congress. (For the results of the 1978 and 1980 Federal elections see the revised Table 5.2 on pp. 150–1.) But the Democrats' hold on the two chambers seemed secure. In an era of disappearing party organization, congressional incumbents appeared to have a decided advantage over opponents in appealing to voters, though since 1968 Senators less so than Representatives.

In 1980 Reagan's lead in the popular vote for President—51 per cent to 41 per cent for Carter and 7 per cent for John Anderson—produced a landslide in the electoral college. Reagan carried forty-four States; Carter, six States (Georgia, Hawaii, Maryland, Minnesota, Rhode Island and West Virginia) and the District of Columbia. The Republicans made twelve gains among thirty-four Senate places at stake, thereby capturing control of the chamber, fifty-three to forty-seven. However, they made a net gain of only thirty-three among the 435 House of Representative seats, leaving the Democrats with a majority there of 243 to 192. (This is the first 'split' Congress since that of 1931–3, when the Republicans, having retained control of both chambers in the 1930 elections, lost their House majority to the Democrats from vacancies arising.) Incumbent Senators have become vulnerable to attack by well-financed and well-organized single-interest (e.g. anti-abortion) and ideological (at present predominantly right-wing) groups, whose media campaigns tend to have relatively more impact in a State-wide senatorial (or gubernatorial) contest than in the typically smaller constituency serviced by a Representative.

In American federalism the 'functional fiefdoms' of governmental agencies, their special-interest clienteles and sympathetic legislators, which extend vertically across the horizontal layers of national, State and local governments and have a preference for categorical intergovernmental grants-in-aid that protect their programmes, have checked the movement of the late sixties and early seventies to 'block grants' and 'general revenue sharing' (cf. pp. 82–3). During Carter's presidency the number of cabinet departments in the national government rose from eleven to thirteen, with the creation of the Department of Energy in 1977 and the division of the Department of Health, Education, and Welfare into the Department of Education and the Department of Health and Human Services in 1979/80.

Carter had no opportunity to appoint to the Supreme Court. The decisions of the 'Burger court' have continued along the lines described in Chapter 10. Congress has extended the period for ratification of the proposed equal-rights-for-the-sexes constitutional amendment (p. 333) to the end of June 1982. In August 1978 it proposed an amendment granting the District of Columbia representation in the two Houses of Congress on the same terms as a State, with a time limit of seven years for the constitutionally-required ratification by three-fourths of the States. In April 1978 the Senate ratified, by one vote more than the necessary two-thirds majority, a treaty providing for the return of the Panama Canal Zone to Panama.

ALLEN M. POTTER

University of Glasgow
January 1981

Preface and Introduction

by Allen M. Potter

We have written this book to replace my *American Government and Politics*, published in 1955. It is an introduction to American political institutions for British readers and others with some knowledge of British government and politics. A book written with such readers in mind is bound to be at least somewhat comparative of the British and American political systems, if only in the selection of features of the American system to which particular attention is drawn. Thus we follow, with diffidence, along the trail of comparison, express and implied, which was blazed by Walter Bagehot in *The English Constitution*, written in 1865–7, and subsequently marked in much greater detail by two distinguished Glasgow graduates, James Bryce and Denis Brogan.

While both political systems are (to use Bagehot's phrase) in their efficient parts representative governments, their constitutions are, according to Bagehot, of 'opposite species', the one concentrating authority and the other dispersing it. In the United Kingdom there is responsible government, ensuring 'the close union, the nearly complete fusion, of the executive and legislative powers'; in the United States there is a separation of powers between independently-constituted executive and legislative branches. In Britain there is a constitutionally unitary state; in America there is a federal system, with a constitutional division of powers between the national or Federal Government and the several (now fifty) States of the Union. The British Parliament is sovereign, with a general competence to make supreme law; the written Constitution of the United States is the supreme law of the land, and the competence of the legislature is circumscribed by judicial construction of that document. However, Bagehot did not mention judicial review. The need for Federal policy makers regularly to consider judicial construction in exercizing the Federal powers began only at about the time he was writing: see Chapter 10 (all references to numbered chapters are to those in this volume).

Bagehot wrote when Americans were still predominantly of British stock and rural dwellers, and when the black slaves had just been freed. Bryce, the first edition of whose *The American Commonwealth* was published in 1888, studied the American political scene—his last account of it was in a section of his *Modern Democracies*, published in 1921—at a time when large-scale immigration from continental Europe and industrialization were turning Americans into a people only a minority of whom are now of British stock and a large majority of whom are urban dwellers. But, the growth of judicial review apart, American political institutions remained largely unchanged. Bryce, like Bagehot, contrasted the dispersal of authority and the absence of a governing class in the United States with the political and social structures of Britain which gave the latter, in their view, more effective government.

When *American Government and Politics* was written in the 1950s its main theme could be the profound changes in American political institutions that had taken place since Bryce wrote. The efficient causes of these were the New Deal of President Franklin D. Roosevelt and the American involvement in World War II and the Cold War. At bottom Bryce's answer to the question in the title of his chapter in *The American Commonwealth* on 'Why Great Men are not chosen Presidents' was that the demands on the President were normally not sufficiently important: 'His main duties are to be prompt and firm in securing the due execution of the laws and maintaining the public peace, careful and upright in the choice of the executive officials of the country.' However, in *Modern Democracies* he observed that a strong President with public opinion behind him 'may prove stronger than both Houses of Congress' and 'draws to himself, as personifying the Nation, something of the reverent regard which monarchs used to inspire in Europe'.

The presidency of Franklin Roosevelt institutionalized the strong presidency. His New Deal produced the latest major realignment of the American political parties: see Chapter 5. It invoked a great expansion in the exercize of Federal governmental regulatory and spending powers. The greater centralization of the governmental and fiscal aspects of American federalism was sanctioned by the Supreme Court after a constitutional crisis in 1937, when Roosevelt, angered by a number of reactionary rulings by a majority of the nine Justices on the Court, attempted to 'pack' it with six new members; although the Court-'packing' plan was defeated, Roosevelt was soon able to fill most of the Justiceships: see Chapter 10. From World War II onwards war and defence needs and foreign affairs further enhanced the power of the Federal Government in the federal system and the position of the President—'the leader of the free world', in the nuclear age.

Twenty years on, what has happened to American political institutions?

In 1939 a White House staff of presidential assistants had formally been established to aid the President in formulating and directing the implementation of executive policies. From the 1950s there was an increasing concentration in the White House of foreign and warmaking policy determination, to the exclusion of the Congress, and of executive policy making and management generally, to the exclusion of most heads of cabinet departments. In the isolation of the White House President Johnson directed the American military intervention in the Vietnamese war while domestic political support for a policy failing to achieve a successful outcome eroded away; President Nixon and his staff engaged in the 'Watergate' and related activities, enough of which came to light to force Nixon's resignation in August 1974.

In 1973 the Congress passed, over Nixon's veto, a War Powers Act restricting the President's pursuit of undeclared wars. In 1974 it passed an Act signed by Nixon in the month before his resignation which provides for legislative oversight of the President's impounding of appropriated funds. But while the Congress can make presidential policy making and management more difficult, it is incapable of offering alternative overall political and administrative leadership: see Chapters 7 and 8. In the balance of the American separation of powers the scales are now tipped permanently in favour of the President.

Under Nixon, White House aides made decisions and issued orders as deputies, engaging in substantive operations which they naturally sought to protect, though the presidential assistantships were originally created to ensure that no operations properly subject to the President's control were protected from his oversight. Nixon's fate is perhaps adequate warning to his successors—this is being written as Jimmy Carter prepares to take office—not to imitate the distinctive features of his régime.

But it is unlikely that there will be a significant shift of influence in executive policy formulation and co-ordination from the White House staff back to the heads of the domestic departments. For, as is pointed out in Chapter 7, the White House assistants are solely the President's men. The heads of departments, though appointed by the President (with senatorial approval), are enmeshed in what McGeorge Bundy, a former member of the White House staff under Presidents Kennedy and Johnson, described in 1968 as 'the network of triangular alliances which unite all sorts of interest groups with their agents in the Congress and their agents in the Executive Branch'.* A President jealous of his prerogatives—and there is every indication that Carter will be that—keeps free of the network. The scope for variation lies in the degree of dialogue between the President and the actors in the network —heads of administrative agencies, members of the Congress, representatives of interests—and also the press and wider public.

We do not consider how American institutions might be reformed to prevent another 'Watergate', since we deal with facts, not fancies. The will-o'-the-wisp that some sort of 'responsible' relationship between the President and the Congress should be established flickers in academic discussions of American government which have British government also in mind.

It is hard to conceive how such a relationship could be maintained other than on party lines. But, whereas the two major parties, Democratic and Republican, have alternated in their control of the Presidency every eight years since 1953, the Democratic party has built up since 1953 a majority in the

* *The Strength of Government* (Harvard U.P., 1968), p. 37.

Congress which presently seems as permanent as the Conservative majority in the existing British House of Lords: see Chapter 5. One of Republican President Ford's most effective arguments in his nearly successful campaign to win the presidential election of 1976 was that, if elected, he would continue to act as a check on a Democratic Congress. The American electorate does not seek 'the close union, the nearly complete fusion, of the executive and legislative powers'.

In any case the American political parties are not instruments for party government. It has been a perennial theme of comparisons of British and American politics that the American parties, unlike the British, are undisciplined in matters of policy: see Chapter 6. However, while American parties have not fitted Burke's definition of a party as 'a body of men united, for promoting by their joint endeavours the national interest, upon some particular principle in which they are all agreed', they could be defined by the common interest of their candidates in securing office.

It can be argued that the two major American parties have since the New Deal maintained consistent differences of approach to policy—the Democrats being more favourable to the exercise of Federal power and public spending than the Republicans—for a longer period than at any time since the Republicans emerged as the chief opponents of the Democrats in the 1850s. (Southern Democrats have to be left out of this generalization about past decades.) But, as is demonstrated in Chapter 5, the factors determining voters' choices in presidential elections since the 1950s have been kaleidoscopic. Each pairing of presidential candidates has produced a new pattern.

Since the 1950s it has become increasingly difficult to describe the Democratic or Republican party as a group of candidates seeking office together, beyond the fact that their names appear in the same column on a ballot or voting machine. Much more than in the past, each candidate can choose how much he wants to associate himself with or dissociate himself from the other candidates on the same party ticket. This trend is accounted for by the greater opportunities candidates have to reach the electorate through the mass media (whose development has undermined attendances at party rallies), the greater openness of nominating primaries and the decline of political patronage. These last two factors reduce the rewards of association with party organizations; the unpopularity of 'professional politicians' rewards independence.

In explaining presidential and congressional election results political scientists refer to a four-party system, distinguishing the presidential and congressional components of each major party. This describes the reality recognized by President Ford in exploiting the expectation of the defeat of the Republican congressional party in 1976 to enhance his own chances of success. Both presidential nominees in 1976 played down their attachments to their parties. It was the 'Ford campaign' versus the 'Carter campaign'. Although 1976 was a year in which regular politics was in special disrepute, the factors operating to weaken organizational ties in the parties have generally made presidential nominations more open to capture by extremists or 'outsiders' with relatively little support among the regular party organizations. Each pairing of presidential candidates has produced a new pattern of voters' choices because each has given the voters a different kind of choice.

American federalism can be said to have become less centralized or more centralized since the 1950s, depending on the indicators used, whereas in the previous two decades all indices recorded a greater centralization: see Chapter 3. There has been an explosive increase in demands on the public services, such as education, provided by State and local governments, with a consequential expansion of State and local government employment. In 1972 there were two and a half times as many employees of State and local governments (10·8 million) as there had been in 1950, but only one and a third times as many civilian employees of the Federal Government (2·8 million) as there had been in 1950. In 1950 the Federal Government raised about two-thirds of the money spent by American governments; in 1972, about three-fifths. In 1972 the Congress enacted a first 'revenue sharing' scheme to turn some money raised by the Federal Government over to the States and localities for spending in a much more general way than had previously been permitted under Federal grants-in-aid programmes.

These are indicators of less centralization. On the other hand, the fraction of State and local government revenue derived from Federal grants-in-aid, always with strings attached and usually requiring at least an element of 'matching' funds from the aided governments, rose from under one-eighth in 1950 to over one-fifth in 1972. The strings do not relate only to the handling of the money or the purposes of particular services receiving support. The Federal Civil Rights Act of 1964 made it a condition of aid to any service that all racially discriminatory practices associated with the service be stopped. In 1965 the Congress enacted the first general programme of Federal aid to elementary and second-ary education. This legislation, rather than the Supreme Court's decisions of the previous decade, broke the system of racial segregation in publicly maintained schools in the South.

When Denis Brogan wrote *The American Political System*, whose preface was dated as at February 1933 (Franklin Roosevelt took office as President in March), he began with chapters on 'The Character of the Constitution' and 'Judicial Review'. When he wrote *An Introduction to American Politics*, whose preface was dated as at February 1954, he began with a chapter on 'The Character of the American Polity' and dealt with judicial review in a final chapter on 'Politics and Law'. By these changes he intended to convey that the Constitution as construed by the Supreme Court had moved from the centre to the periphery of the determinants of policy making. For after 1937 the Court, apart from protecting national concerns from undue State interference, reviewed legisla-tion closely only if it interfered with the freedoms of expression or discriminated against racial or religious minorities.

When Brogan wrote *An Introduction to American Politics* this close review was being exercized with circumspection. In 1951 the Supreme Court had upheld the conviction of Communist party leaders for conspiring to advocate their revolutionary doctrines. In striking down governmental discriminations against blacks it had stayed within the 'separate but equal' formula by which racial segregation had been made compatible with the 'equal protection of the laws' guaranteed by the Fourteenth Amendment to the Constitution. 'That much of the criticism of the Court has died down', Brogan wrote, 'is due, no doubt, to the moderation with which the Court, in recent years, has exercized its functions.'

In May 1954, in a unanimous Opinion delivered by Chief Justice Earl Warren, who had joined the Court in 1953, the Supreme Court repudiated the 'separate but equal' doctrine: racial segregation in publicly-maintained schools was *per se* a violation of the equal protection guarantee. There was no shortage of criticism as the 'Warren Court' shed judicial moderation. In 1957 it made it impossible to convict for mere advocacy of abstract doctrines. In the 1960s it banned school prayers from publicly maintained schools, reformed the electoral system by requiring that the apportionment of seats in legislatures (except the U.S. Senate) be strictly in accordance with population and made the great majority of the procedural safeguards for suspected and accused persons which the Bill of Rights of the Constitution specifies for Federal justice equally and stringently applicable in State and local law enforcement: see Chapters 4 and 10.

Under Earl Warren's successor, Chief Justice Warren Burger, who joined the Court in 1969, the Supreme Court has reduced the stringency of some of the most important—and most controversial —of the Warren Court's rulings on criminal justice. The Court is again, on the whole, exercizing its functions with moderation. But dealing with judicial review in the final chapter of this book is not intended to convey that the Supreme Court of the 1970s is at the periphery of American policy making.

While the British and American constitutions remain of 'opposite species'—American separation of powers, federalism and judicial supremacy contrasting with British responsible government and unitary parliamentary sovereignty—they are of the same genus. Both political systems are genuine representative governments, with free elections under universal suffrage and with respect for the liberties of the individual. Their constitutions, fundamentally so alike while so different in detail, have their common source in English history. Most attention is drawn to the English heritage in Chapter 2 on the American Constitutions and Chapter 9 on the judiciary.

The recent activity of the Supreme Court in enhancing the rights of persons through the exercize of a judicial constitutional authority absent in present-day Britain is nevertheless, as Louis

Heren of *The Times*, the most perceptive of contemporary reporters on American government and politics, pointed out in the 1960s, a manifestation of what the two societies have in common: 'remembrance of things past, of the long struggle for human liberty. . . . Magna Carta, common law, and the English Bill of Rights of 1689 are part of that living past which the Court helps to keep alive. Modern America has many origins and its sources of inspiration are certainly not only English, but the Constitution was written by Englishmen and in interpreting it the Court more often than not returns to the English past.'*

Chapter 1 of this book is wholly, and Chapter 2 largely, introductory to the other chapters. Chapter 1 contains a selection of information about the origins and nature of modern America, and Chapter 2 a general account of the theory and practice of American constitutional government. In the final part of Chapter 1 the geographical sections and regions of the United States are defined in a way used throughout the book. Otherwise, the several chapters are intended to be self-contained treatments of their subjects, with few cross-references among them. Mr. Fotheringham wrote Chapters 4, 5, 6 and 8; Dr. Kellas wrote Chapter 3; and I wrote Chapters 1, 2, 7, 9 and 10.

We are grateful to the Nuffield Foundation and the University of Glasgow for small grants-in-aid. We thank the secretaries who typed draft chapters: Mrs. Charlotte Logan, Miss Sheila Hamilton, Mrs. Jean Beverly and Mrs. Elspeth Shaw. Miss Elizabeth Potter helped prepare the index.

University of Glasgow,
January 1977

---

* *The New American Commonwealth* (Weidenfeld & Nicolson, 1968), p. 101.

1: The American Scene

A: THE GROWTH OF THE AMERICAN DEMOCRACY

'We hold these truths to be self-evident;' read the American Declaration of Independence from Great Britain in 1776, 'that all men are created equal; that they are endowed by their Creator with certain unalienable rights; that among these are life, liberty, and the pursuit of happiness; that to secure these rights, governments are instituted among men, deriving their just powers from the consent of the governed; that whenever any form of government becomes destructive of these ends, it is the right of the people to alter or abolish it, and to institute new government, laying its foundation on such principles, and organizing its power in such form as to them shall seem most likely to effect their safety and happiness.'

The Declaration 'was intended', its chief author, Thomas Jefferson, wrote later, 'to be an expression of the American mind. . . . All its authority rests then on the harmonizing sentiments of the day, whether expressed in conversation, in letters, printed essays, or the elementary books of public right, as Aristotle, Cicero, Locke, Sidney, etc.'—especially among those books, Locke's second Treatise of Government. The American experience of establishing communities in the New World, under compacts and charters, confirmed the settlers' belief that governments are instituted to serve their subjects' needs.

From 1775 to 1777 the thirteen colonies rebelling against Great Britain adapted their old charters or adopted new constitutions to accord with their new status as States. The first written national constitution, the Articles of Confederation and perpetual

Union, was approved in 1777 by the Continental Congress which directed the struggle for independence, but was not ratified by every State until 1781. The Articles provided for the continuance of a unicameral Congress, composed of delegates chosen annually and recallable by the State legislatures, each State's delegation having one vote. The Congress was granted powers to conduct foreign affairs, declare and conduct war and regulate weights and measures, but not to regulate commerce among the States. It had to rely for its resources on the States' complying with requests for soldiers and funds and on its powers to issue bills of credit and borrow money, unsupported by a power to tax.

The Articles of Confederation were superseded in 1789 by the Constitution of the United States, which had been drafted in 1787 at a convention in Philadelphia, Pennsylvania, convened by spokesmen of those dissatisfied with the weakness of the national government and the susceptibility of States to debtors' pressures, and presided over by George Washington, who had been Commander-in-Chief of the Continental Army during the War of Independence (1775–83). The new Constitution granted the Congress the powers to raise armies, to tax and to regulate inter-state commerce. The Congress was made bicameral. Members of the House of Representatives (Congressmen), apportioned among the States according to their populations, were to be directly elected for a two-year term. Members of the Senate (Senators), two per State, were to be elected by the State legislatures (an amendment to the Constitution in 1913 provided for direct election) for a six-year term, one-third of them retiring every two years, and, like Congressmen, were to vote as individuals.

Table 1.1:
Presidents of the United States

President	Year took Office	Party
1. George Washington	1789	Non-Party (Federalist)
2. John Adams	1797	Federalist

President	Year took Office	Party
3. Thomas Jefferson	1801	Democratic-Republican
4. James Madison	1809	Democratic-Republican
5. James Monroe	1817	Democratic-Republican
6. John Quincy Adams	1825	(Dem.-Rep. faction)
7. Andrew Jackson	1829	Democratic
8. Martin Van Buren	1837	Democratic
9. William H. Harrison	1841	Whig
10. John Tyler	1841*	Whig
11. James K. Polk	1845	Democratic
12. Zachary Taylor	1849	Whig
13. Millard Fillmore	1850*	Whig
14. Franklin Pierce	1853	Democratic
15. James Buchanan	1857	Democratic
16. Abraham Lincoln	1861	Republican
17. Andrew Johnson	1865*	†
18. Ulysses S. Grant	1869	Republican
19. Rutherford B. Hayes	1877	Republican
20. James A. Garfield	1881	Republican
21. Chester A. Arthur	1881*	Republican
22. Grover Cleveland	1885	Democratic
23. Benjamin Harrison	1889	Republican
24. Grover Cleveland	1893	Democratic
25. William McKinley	1897	Republican
26. Theodore Roosevelt	1901*	Republican
27. William H. Taft	1909	Republican
28. Woodrow Wilson	1913	Democratic
29. Warren G. Harding	1921	Republican
30. Calvin Coolidge	1923*	Republican
31. Herbert Hoover	1929	Republican
32. Franklin D. Roosevelt	1933	Democratic
33. Harry S. Truman	1945*	Democratic
34. Dwight D. Eisenhower	1953	Republican
35. John F. Kennedy	1961	Democratic
36. Lyndon B. Johnson	1963*	Democratic
37. Richard M. Nixon	1969	Republican
38. Gerald R. Ford	1974*	Republican
39. Jimmy Carter	1977	Democratic

* Vice-President succeeding President who died in or (in 1974 only) resigned from office.

† Democrat elected with Lincoln on 'National Union' ticket in 1864.

The new Constitution also provided for a President of the United States, to be chosen by a special electoral college for a four-year term, and for a Supreme Court of the United States. In 1789 Washington became the first of several American war heroes to become President.

When Washington took office, there were 3·2 million white Americans with 700,000 Negro slaves; there were 60,000 free blacks. More than three-quarters of the whites were of British stock. The population was overwhelmingly Protestant Christian. Only one in twenty people lived in communities with 2,500 or more inhabitants.

The impetus to strong national government favourable to mercantile interests was sustained for a time by the policies of Alexander Hamilton (Secretary of the Treasury, 1789–95), who acted as 'Federalist' party prime minister in President Washington's non-party administration. However, the opposing 'Democratic-Republican' party put together by Thomas Jefferson (Secretary of State, 1789–93), who became President in 1801, appealed to the predominant agrarian and artisan interests of the country so effectively that by 1820 the Federalists allowed the then Democratic-Republican President, James Monroe, to be re-elected unopposed.

In 1824 several factions sponsored presidential candidates. Andrew Jackson, a war hero of the second war with Great Britain (1812–15), proved the most popular, but failed to obtain the requisite absolute majority of votes in the electoral college. Under the Constitution, members of the House of Representatives, voting as State delegations, had to choose among the three candidates with the highest number of electoral votes: they elected John Quincy Adams, who had received the second highest number. In 1828 and 1832 Jackson won as 'Democratic' candidate against a 'National' Republican opponent.

The Democrats also won four of the next six presidential elections. From 1834 their chief opponents called themselves 'Whigs', winning the presidential elections of 1840 and 1848. In 1856 the 'Republicans' displaced the Whig party as one of the two main parties.

In the eras of Jeffersonian and Jacksonian Democracy—the

first six decades of the nineteenth century—the United States expanded across the North American continent, and democracy expanded in the United States. In 1803 Jefferson nearly doubled the size of the country by purchasing from France the Louisiana Territory—seventeen times the size of the present State of Louisiana. By other purchases, by the demarcation with Great Britain of the United States boundary with Canada, and through annexation and the Mexican War (1846–8), all the present United States territory coterminous with that of the original country was obtained by 1853. In 1860 the population of this continental domain was 31 million, of whom nearly 4 million were Negro slaves and nearly 500,000 free blacks. Alaska was purchased from Russia in 1867.

The lands acquired by the national government were opened for settlement on increasingly liberal terms. From 1830 Acts of Congress gave legal recognition to 'preemption': the right of a squatting homesteader to buy 'his' land at the minimum price when its sale was authorized; from 1862 homesteading alone could give title. As lands outside the States were settled, the settlements were organized as Territories, which upon admission to the Union became States equal to the rest.

New States led in the removal of all property qualifications for voting. In the Jacksonian era, adult white male suffrage became almost universal. At the State and local levels of government a large number of administrative and judicial as well as legislative offices were made elective. The 'spoils system' of appointing and removing non-elective office holders on partisan grounds, which was perfected at all levels of government, was defended by President Jackson as a democratic means of preventing the formation of a privileged office-holding class.

Jeffersonians and Jacksonians believed on the whole in little government, and in local rather than national government. Individualism and localism were manifested in religion as well as politics. The Baptists and Methodists, the fastest-growing denominations, were highly subject to schisms. New sects were continually being formed. The Protestant tradition of secular education fostered the establishment outside the South of tax-supported, free local schools. 'The little white church, the little red schoolhouse, the quarter-section preemption—these were the mainsprings that fed American equalitarianism.'*

The country divided over the black slave. The main issue between North and South, from 1820 to the outbreak of the Civil War (1861–5), was the extent to which new lands and States were to be 'free' (for white preemptors) or 'slave'. Southern slave owners became increasingly intransigent, partly as the result of minority agitation in the North for the total abolition of slavery. The election in 1860 of Abraham Lincoln, a former Whig, as the first Republican President, on a platform opposing any extension of slavery, precipitated the Southern attempt to leave the Union.

The defeat of the South was followed by a decade of political 'Reconstruction' by the Republicans of the eleven 'Confederate States' which had tried to secede. During the period of Reconstruction, three amendments to the national Constitution were adopted, prohibiting slavery, forbidding States to infringe due process of law or deny any person the equal protection of the laws, and prohibiting discrimination in the suffrage on account of race, colour or previous condition of servitude. After Reconstruction, however, all the organs of the national government allowed Southern whites to frustrate the recognition of racial equality, until the Supreme Court began in the 1910s to apply the constitutional provisions more stringently against laws and practices with discriminatory effects.

B: THE MAKING OF PRESENT-DAY AMERICA

Prior to the Civil War the mountain chains and Mississippi River system of the North American continent had made North-South internal transport predominant. The large American merchant fleet under sail linked the two sides of the continent together, as well to Europe and Asia. Railway construction, aided by land grants, began before the war to create an East–West system of transport. In the postwar years the Mississippi River

* Louis M. Hacker, *The Shaping of the American Tradition* (New York, Columbia University Press, 1947), p. 338.

steamboat yielded to the iron horse; and Yankee Clippers to the steamships of other countries.

The entrepreneurs who were leading the United States to become the chief industrial producer among the states of the world concentrated on an expanding home market protected by high tariffs enacted by the Republican Party. During the second half of the nineteenth century both major parties, Republican and Democratic, and the Supreme Court in its interpretation of the Constitution, allowed the railway kings like Cornelius Vanderbilt and James J. Hill, and captains of industry and finance like John D. Rockefeller, Andrew Carnegie, and J. P. Morgan, to create the structure of a new industrial economy with little governmental interference.

The growth of industry accelerated the growth of cities. In 1860 one-fifth of the American people lived in communities with 2,500 or more inhabitants; in 1890, more than one-third; and in 1920, over half. However, twice as many Americans lived in communities with fewer than 2,500 inhabitants in 1920 as had done in 1860, because the total population had more than trebled—from 31 to 106 million.

Immigrants from Europe poured into the United States, reaching in 1882 a peak annual entry for the nineteenth century of 640,000, including 251,000 Germans, 179,000 from Great Britain and Ireland and 105,000 Scandinavians. Many of the incomers, attracted by the advertisements in Europe of Western railways, land companies and States, went to the farming areas outside the South. After a fall-off in the 1880s and 1890s, immigration rose to new heights in the first years of the twentieth century; between 1901 and 1914 nearly 12 million immigrants from Europe entered the United States, most of them from eastern and southern Europe: Poles, Russians and other Slavs, Italians. Far more of these new immigrants stayed in the ports and other cities.

Farmers felt themselves the victims of the rise of industry and the urban society. Until 1896 their protests produced third-party movements for inflationary monetary policies, governmental regulation or ownership of railways, and other attacks on the corporate 'trusts'. The third-party Populist presidential candidate received a twelfth of the popular vote in 1892. In Populism there were strands of agrarian socialism, which persisted, as in the Progressivism of the La Follettes of Wisconsin, until the large agricultural subsidies initiated in the 1930s made farmers once more staunch defenders of 'free enterprise'; of the 'Bible Belt' morality that later achieved the national constitutional prohibition of alcoholic beverages from 1919 to 1933; and of resentments against the cosmopolitanism of Eastern 'plutocrats', which can be traced through and beyond the manipulation of such feelings by Senator Joseph McCarthy of Wisconsin in the 1950s.

In 1896, and again in 1900 and 1908, the Democrats nominated William Jennings Bryan as their presidential candidate. Bryan's first claim to national attention was as the most eloquent advocate of the unlimited coinage of silver ('you shall not crucify mankind upon a cross of gold') and his last, a few days before his death in 1925, as the chief prosecution witness in the trial of John Thomas Scopes for teaching the theory of evolution to Tennessee schoolchildren. Bryanism absorbed Populism, creating the Democratic 'Solid South', in which Populists had previously competed for poor white votes.

The over-all effect of the political realignment of 1896 was to replace close presidential contests between the two major parties by Republican landslides. In 1912 the Democratic candidate, Woodrow Wilson, won (with only 42 per cent of the popular vote) when the Republicans split in their support for their incumbent President William H. Taft (23 per cent) and their former President Theodore Roosevelt (27 per cent), who, denied nomination by the party's national convention, ran as a Progressive. The Socialist candidate, Eugene Debs, received 6 per cent of the popular vote that year, the highest percentage ever obtained by a socialist in an American presidential election. In 1916 Wilson was barely re-elected. Otherwise the Republicans won every presidential election decisively from 1896 through that of 1928. In that year, however, the Democrats recognized the sources of electoral support upon which their victories in most presidential elections since 1932 have largely been based, when they nominated as their candidate Alfred E. Smith, a Roman Catholic who had risen to the governorship of his State from 'the sidewalks of New York'.

Theodore Roosevelt's, Taft's and Wilson's presidencies were all associated with the Progressive movement. This had started at the local and State levels of governments as a reaction, especially on the part of middle-class, older-stock Americans, against 'machine politics'. The growth of the cities furnished the local and State party organizations with many opportunities for corruption, especially with businessmen seeking contracts, franchises and freedom from or lax enforcement of regulations. The new immigrants were especially susceptible to guidance in voting from party precinct captains who understood their feelings better than did the charitable organizations, run by middle-class, older-stock people: there were almost no official social services.

Revelations of corruption fed reform movements that defeated individual 'bosses', introduced forms of 'non-partisan' government in many small cities, required candidates for at least some offices in almost all States to be nominated in direct 'primary' elections, and extended the use among the States of voters' initiatives (petitions) and referenda in the legislature process. The social needs served by 'machine politics', as well as the weaknesses of human nature, enabled the system to survive the attacks upon it, especially in the large cities, though there has been, especially since the development of official social services from the 1930s, a lessening of the cruder forms of corruption and political manipulation.

The Progressives enacted legislation to protect workers, especially women and children, from exploitation, though both State and national acts were often declared invalid by the courts. Nationally the Progressive administrations enforced and strengthened 'anti-trust' legislation, which is still based on the earlier Sherman Anti-Trust Act of 1890. In their willingness to assume national governmental responsibility for policing the economy the Progressive presidents set precedents for the New Deal of Franklin D. Roosevelt, Theodore Roosevelt's Democratic kinsman, who became President in 1933.

By 1890 the frontier within the territory coterminous with the original United States had disappeared. Americans had fulfilled their 'manifest destiny': they had settled a vast continental domain. At the end of the century there was a burst of outright overseas imperialism. The Hawaiian Islands were annexed. After the Spanish-American war of 1898—in which the United States secured the independence of Cuba from Spain—Puerto Rico in the Caribbean, and Guam and the Philippine Islands in the Pacific, became American possessions. The Samoan Islands were divided with Great Britain and Germany in 1899.

Thereafter American influence in the Caribbean and Central America was extended mainly through the 'dollar imperialism' of investments protected by police actions on the part of the United States Marines, though in 1904 the Panama Canal Zone was leased from a Panama whose independence from Colombia had just been achieved with American naval aid, and in 1917 the Virgin Islands were purchased from Denmark. After the Second World War the Philippines became independent; and the Pacific Islands previously governed by Japan under League of Nations mandate became strategic trusteeship territories of the United States under the United Nations.

From the late nineteenth century the spread of industry, improvements in transport (the motor car and aeroplane) and in communications (telephone, cinema, radio and television) have lessened differences among the regions of the country and among rural, small town and metropolitan ways of life. The great depression of the 1930s demonstrated the unity of the national economy in disaster. Since then it has increasingly been recognized that the national government has a responsibility for the nation's economic and social well-being. Although most Americans tried to forget the First World War (for the United States 1917-8) except as a lesson against foreign entanglements, after the Second World War (for the United States 1941-5) they were inescapably drawn into a concern for the state of the world. The responsibility for policy again rests on the national government, and in particular on the President of the United States.

After an interruption of heavy immigration by the First World War, from 1914 to 1918, the flow of immigrants resumed; but Acts of Congress in 1921 and 1924 put severe restrictions on the total number allowed to enter in a year, with quotas for countries of origin calculated in favour of the older immigrant stocks. The restrictions were somewhat relaxed after the Second World War; and quotas are no longer based on the composition of the

American population. Time, prosperity and comparatively higher birth-rates have helped other ethnic groups to obtain more equality with the 'WASPS' (white Anglo-Saxon Protestants)—socially, economically and politically.

Irish Roman Catholics were the first of that faith to come to America in large numbers. In 1960 their acceptance in the highest levels of American society was recorded in the election of the Democratic party candidate for President, John F. Kennedy, a wealthy, Irish-descended, Catholic graduate and overseer of Harvard University. The Democrats had been bolder in nominating Alfred E. Smith thirty-two years earlier; but Kennedy's election as the first President of the Catholic faith was taken as demonstrating that the bounds of 'availability' for the highest political office now included all the white stocks. In 1964 the Republicans nominated Barry Goldwater, a Protestant of part-Jewish extraction, and William Miller, a Roman Catholic, as their presidential and vice-presidential candidates.

Black people, the first of whom were brought to English North America by 1619, remain the people with least equality. Discrimination against blacks is now less than it has ever been. However, they are much more impatient than in the past about a situation ill becoming a nation founded on the self-evident truth that all men are created equal.

C: THE NATION

The Constitution of the United States requires an enumeration of the population to be made every ten years, primarily to provide information for apportioning seats in the House of Representatives among the States. The decennial censuses, which together with other governmental inquiries produce a wide range of official statistics, are carried out in years whose dates end in a nought.

In 1970 the population of the United States—the fifty States and the Federal capital (District of Columbia)—was over 203 million: 178 million whites; 22·5 million blacks; 800,000 American Indians; and two million others (mainly Asiatics). There were, in addition, about one million members of the American armed forces and 370,000 of their dependants overseas.

The area of the United States is 3·6 million square miles. The population density in 1970 was one-tenth that of the United Kingdom, which then had 55 million people in 94,000 square miles. Ten States have each a larger area than the whole United Kingdom. In 1970 forty-six of the States were less densely populated.

The annual rate of entry of immigrants per thousand population has been under two in recent decades, as compared with over ten in the first decade of this century. In 1970 400,000 entered the United States. The overall net increase in the population that year was 2·2 million: eleven per thousand population at the start of the year.

In 1970 only one-twentieth of the American population lived on farms. More than two-thirds of the population lived in urbanized areas with at least one central city of 50,000 or more inhabitants. Between 1960 and 1970 the balance of population in such metropolitan areas tipped decisively in favour of their suburbs over the central cities: the whole increase in the number of white metropolitan dwellers in the 1960s was accounted for by the increase in white suburbanites, while the central cities became more black. A smaller proportion of the total population than in the United Kingdom live in very large conurbations.

More than one-sixth of the American people moved house during 1970. Of the movers, three-fifths stayed in the same county, four-fifths in the same State; 7 million moved between States. Both whites and blacks have left the farming areas in recent decades. The decline in farm population has been absolute as well as relative. The movement of blacks from rural shanties to urban 'ghettos' was substantially under-recorded. The Bureau of the Census has estimated on the basis of evaluation studies that the 1970 census missed about 5·3 million persons, of whom about 1·9 million were blacks. For every twelve blacks recorded, one was missed. (The census statistics are not adjusted for under-enumeration.)

In ethnic composition the white population is now less than half British, even including the Irish element. No questions about religious affiliation are asked in the decennial censuses. Probably about two-thirds of adult Americans are Protestant in religious identification or background, one-quarter Roman Catholic and 3 per cent Jewish. In urbanized areas with 250,000 or more inhabitants fewer than half of the people are Protestants, about two-fifths Roman Catholic and nearly one-twelfth Jewish. In 1960 about one in seven elementary schoolchildren were enrolled in Catholic schools; in 1973, about one in eleven.

In 1970, 86 per cent of adults aged twenty-five years or older had completed eight or more years of schooling; 55 per cent had completed twelve or more years: that is to say, had 'graduated from high school'. More than one-fifth had had some further education: one in nine were 'college graduates' with four or more years of further education. The proportion of women high-school graduates was about the same as for men; but about one-sixth of women compared to about one-quarter of men had had further education. Blacks, especially black men, had generally had less education than whites.

In recent decades education through high school has become nearly universal (at least among the enumerated population). Further education has expanded enormously for men and women, whites and blacks. In 1970 48 per cent of all people aged eighteen and nineteen and 22 per cent of those aged twenty to twenty-four were enrolled for education.

Among employed persons in 1970, 51 per cent of whites and 28 per cent of non-whites were 'white-collar' workers; 34 per cent of whites and 42 per cent of non-whites, 'blue-collar' workers; 11 per cent of whites and 26 per cent of non-whites, domestic and similar service workers; and 4 per cent of both whites and non-whites, farmers or farm labourers. In the late 1960s the differences between the occupational distributions of employed whites and non-whites had markedly diminished. However, the unemployment rate of non-whites tends to remain about twice that of whites.

In 1950 about one in ten of the employed population were public employees, in 1970 nearly one in six. In 1950 about three in ten of the employed population were women, in 1970 about three in eight. In 1970 23 per cent of the employed population —

27 per cent of those in non-agricultural establishments—were in trade unions. More than three-quarters of trade unionists were in unions in the American Federation of Labour-Congress of Industrial Organizations (AFL-CIO).

In 1970 the American gross national product—the output of goods and services for the year—was approximately $4,800 per capita as compared with approximately $2,200 per capita in the United Kingdom. Comparisons between the economies of the two countries run into many difficulties over differing definitions. The information in Table 1.2 is at best a rough guide.

Table 1.2:

United States (United Kingdom) expenditure accounts, 1970

in standardized units of expenditure
(+ or — = less than ½ unit)

Defence *and*		8 (5)		
Non-defence		2 (21)		
Federal Government purchases *and*		10		
State and local government purchases *make up*		13		
PUBLIC SECTOR PURCHASES OF GOODS AND SERVICES,			(26)	23 (26)
which with transfers, interest and subsidies	9 (18)			
account for total public expenditure.	32 (44)			
Personal consumption *and*		64 (62)		
business investment *make up*		13 (10)		
PRIVATE SECTOR PURCHASES OF GOODS AND SERVICES.				77 (72)
Exports *less*	6 (22)			
Imports *equal*	6 (21)			
Net Exports of goods and services, *which with*		+ (1)		
Net Transfers from foreigners *make up*		— (1)		
NET FOREIGN INVESTMENT.				+ (2)
GROSS NATIONAL PRODUCT			100 (100)	100 (100)

It indicates that considerably more of the country's income passed through the public sector in the United Kingdom than in the United States. British public authorities re-allocated more purchasing power among the people by tax-supported insurance schemes and other 'transfer payments', and with their nationalized industries accounted for a much greater share of the country's fixed capital investment. Americans spent more of the gross national product on defence. It should also be noted how relatively unimportant foreign trade is in the American economy.

The American, like the British, private economy is dominated by large industrial, merchandizing and financial corporations. In 1972 the hundred biggest industrial corporations controlled about half the country's corporate manufacturing assets, a greater share than had been controlled by the 200 biggest twenty years before.

The organization of the mass-communication industries is of special interest in a book on government and politics. Three 'network' companies predominate in effecting links among the 750 (as at 1973) commercial television stations and, with a fourth network, are involved in a relatively minor way among the 7,000 commercial radio stations. (Non-commercial stations play a small part in mass communications.) In 1973 about three-quarters of the revenue of radio stations reporting on their finances came from local sales of advertising, one-quarter from national sales. Three-quarters of the revenue of television stations came from sales to national advertisers and sponsors of programmes. American television is paid for mainly by large corporations advertising to the mass consumer market. Both radio and television stations are licensed and regulated by the Federal Communications Commission of the national government.

Because there are both nationwide networks and a large number of stations across the country, television is a medium for both national and local newscasts and political advertisements. However, political advertising must be paid for and is also constrained by the time segments offered. For presidential elections the networks reduce the length of some of their major programmes shown by stations at prime times, so as to make five-minute segments available. Otherwise, only thirty- or sixty-second advertising 'spots' are for sale at prime times: 'candidates are forced . . . to tailor their material to meet the time segments the stations will sell them.'*

In 1973 there were about 1,800 daily and 600 Sunday newspapers in the United States. Newspaper pages per issue averaged 59 for dailies and 182 for Sundays. There are national newspaper columnists, but no national newspapers. There are newspaper chains; and local monopolies of press ownership are the rule. But there is less over-all concentration of entrepreneurial control of newspapers than of broadcasting or the periodical press. Much the greater part of newspaper income comes from advertising; the remainder from subscriptions and sales. The press is unlicensed. In its coverage of public affairs the American press is much less affected than the British by libel laws and other constraints.

D: THE STATES

In the rest of this book references to parts of the United States that include more than one State accord with the groupings in Table 1.3. Like official census regions and divisions, to which the sections and regions of the Table more or less correspond, most of the groupings are geographically compact areas—in the case of the Pacific States as compact as their locations allow—that were differentiated from one another in the acquisition and settlement of the territories now part of the United States. However, the social uniqueness of the South is recognized by assigning labels to States in that section and most of the States next to it which imply distances from a central core of 'Southernness': the Deep South, the Outer South and the Border States. The last are defined solely in relation to the South. They have nothing else in common distinguishing them from their neighbours in other sections.

The District of Columbia, the Federal capital comprising the city of Washington, is listed with the Middle-Atlantic States. It

* Joseph Napolitan, 'Media Costs and Effects on Political Campaigns', *The Annals of the American Academy of Political and Social Science*, Vol. 427 (September 1976), p. 120.

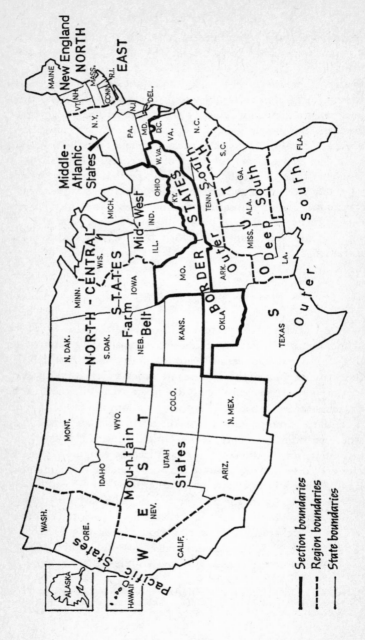

The United States of America

Section boundaries
Region boundaries
State boundaries

occupies land taken from Maryland in 1790. The land across the Potomac River taken from Virginia at the same time was returned to that State in 1846.

Table 1.3 provides data about the several States which are most readily presented in tabular form, and which cannot be simply summarized in general references to the groupings. Thus, while it is true in general that the American continent has been

Table 1.3: the States

Section	Region	STATE	Year entered Union	Population Total in thousands (1970)	Population % increase 1960–70	% of population Urban (1970)	% of population Black (1970)	Median family money income in $000 (1969)
NORTHEAST	New England	Connecticut	1788*	3,032	20	77	6·0	11·8
		Massachusetts	1788*	5,689	10	85	3·1	10·8
		New Hampshire	1788*	738	22	56	0·3	9·7
		Rhode Island	1790*	947	10	87	2·7	9·7
		Vermont	1791	444	14	32	0·2	8·9
		Maine	1820	992	2	51	0·3	8·2
	Middle-Atlantic States	Delaware	1787*	548	23	72	14·3	10·2
		Pennsylvania	1787*	11,794	4	72	8·6	9·6
		New Jersey	1787*	7,168	18	89	10·7	11·4
		Maryland	1788*	3,922	26	77	17·8	11·1
		New York	1788*	18,237	9	86	11·9	10·6
		District of Columbia	Non-State	757	—1	100	71·1	9·6
NORTH-CENTRAL STATES	Midwest	Ohio	1803	10,652	10	75	9·1	10·3
		Indiana	1816	5,194	11	65	6·9	10·0
		Illinois	1818	11,114	10	83	12·8	11·0
		Michigan	1837	8,875	13	74	11·2	11·0
		Wisconsin	1848	4,418	12	66	2·9	10·1
	Farm Belt	Iowa	1846	2,824	2	57	1·2	9·0
		Minnesota	1858	3,805	12	66	0·9	9·9
		Kansas	1861	2,247	3	66	4·8	8·7
		Nebraska	1867	1,483	5	62	2·7	8·6
		North Dakota	1889	618	—2	44	0·4	7·8
		South Dakota	1889	666	—2	45	0·2	7·5

* 13 original States (year ratified Constitution of the United States).

Section	Region	STATE	Year entered Union	Population Total in thousands (1970)	Population % increase 1969–70	% of population Urban (1970)	% of population Black (1970)	Median family money income in $000 (1969)
SOUTH	Deep South	Georgia	1788*	4,590	16	60	25·9	8·2
		South Carolina	1788*	2,591	9	48	30·5	7·6
		Louisiana	1812	3,641	12	66	29·8	7·5
		Mississippi	1817	2,217	2	44	36·8	6·1
		Alabama	1819	3,444	5	58	26·2	7·3
	Outer South	Virginia	1788*	4,648	17	63	18·5	9·0
		North Carolina	1789*	5,082	12	45	22·2	7·8
		Tennessee	1796	3,924	10	59	15·8	7·4
		Arkansas	1836	1,923	8	50	18·3	6·3
		Florida	1845	6,789	37	80	15·3	8·3
		Texas	1845	11,197	17	80	12·5	8·5
	Border States	Kentucky	1792	3,219	6	52	7·2	7·4
		Missouri	1821	4,677	8	70	10·3	8·9
		West Virginia	1863	1,744	—6	39	3·9	7·4
		Oklahoma	1907	2,559	10	68	6·7	7·7
WEST	Mountain States	Nevada	1864	489	71	81	5·7	10·7
		Colorado	1876	2,207	26	78	3·0	9·6
		Montana	1889	694	3	53	0·3	8·5
		Idaho	1890	713	7	54	0·3	8·4
		Wyoming	1890	332	1	60	0·8	8·9
		Utah	1896	1,059	19	80	0·6	9·3
		New Mexico	1912	1,016	7	70	1·9	7·8
		Arizona	1912	1,771	36	80	3·0	9·2
	Pacific States	California	1850	19,953	27	91	7·0	10·7
		Oregon	1859	2,091	18	67	1·3	9·5
		Washington	1889	3,409	20	73	2·1	10·4
		Alaska	1959	300	33	48	3·0	12·4
		Hawaii	1959	769	22	83	1·0	11·6
UNITED STATES				203,212	13	74	11·1	9·6

settled from east to west and that there is still a westward movement of population in the United States, the data about the year
in which each State entered the Union and about the growth of
its population in the 1960s as a percentage of its total population

* 13 original States (year ratified Constitution of the United States).

at the start of the decade indicate more complicated patterns of settlement and recent internal migration.

Likewise, it may be said that the Middle-Atlantic States (with lower New England) and California are the most urbanized parts of the country. However, the information in Table 1.3 shows the range and variations in the degree to which the populations in the several States are urban. (The urban population is defined in the census as people living in places with 2,500 or more inhabitants and in the fringes of urbanized areas.)

The last column in Table 1.3 lists the median money income of families. That is to say, the figure for a State is the annual money income that divides the number of families in the State's population into two equal parts, one-half of the families having an income below and one-half above the indicated figure. This set of figures is the best single indicator of the general standard of living from one State to another.

Northeast

Much the most populous urbanized belt in the country runs from Portland, Maine, through Washington, D.C., as far as Richmond, Virginia. The part from Boston, Massachusetts, to Baltimore, Maryland, has included all the main ports of entry for European immigrants throughout the nation's history. The populations of most of the States in that part of America have the highest proportions of the new immigrant stocks of the late nineteenth and early twentieth centuries. However, the historically low rate of immigration in recent decades and the movement of people within the United States have made the populations of the industrialized, highly urbanized States of the Northeast, Midwest and Pacific States more similar to one another now in their ethnic and religious compositions than half a century ago.

New England: Boston, the most populous place in New England since its founding by English Puritans in the 1630s, was the cultural capital of the nation in the middle years of the nineteenth century. The prosperity of the region long rested on its maritime commerce, and from the early nineteenth century also on textiles and other manufactures. After the Civil War, the American

merchant navy declined precipitously. New York City became the nation's cultural capital. By the turn of the century
the textile industry was shifting to the South to be near cotton
and cheap labour. Connecticut, owing to its proximity to New
York City, escaped from New England's decline in relative prosperity.

In 1775 Edmund Burke said that 'the religion most prevalent
in our Northern Colonies is . . . the protestantism of the Protestant
religion.' Today New England, with its Boston Irish, French
Canadian, Italian and Polish stocks, is the region with the highest
proportion of Roman Catholics in its population.

Middle-Atlantic States: The Middle-Atlantic States have had a
mixture of peoples from the earliest European colonization. New
York City, the chief port of entry for immigrants and the largest
American city, with in 1970 eight million inhabitants in a metropolitan area containing another four million, is the city of ethnic
superlatives: with far more Jews (two million), and far more
people of Irish extraction, than any other city in the world. Many
New Yorkers are of Italian extraction. The Harlem district of
Manhattan Island is the largest black 'ghetto' in the country.
Since World War II there has been an influx of Puerto Ricans. In
1960 21·5 per cent of the pupils in the New York City school
system were black, 15·6 per cent Puerto Rican; in 1974 36·6 per
cent were black, 28·0 per cent Puerto Rican. (The changes in the
percentages are partly accounted for by an increased use of
private education by whites staying in the city.)

'Wall Street' is the American financial capital, centred on the
New York Stock Exchange. 'Madison Avenue' is the capital of
the advertising industry of the mass-consumption society. But
increasingly, in the New York metropolitan area, as in others, the
full citizens of that society reside in the suburbs, leaving the central
city for living to the absolutely and relatively deprived. In 1960
slightly more than 10 per cent of the pupils in the New York City
school system were eligible to receive free lunches because they
were in low-income families; in 1974, 51 per cent.

New York State and Pennsylvania extend across (and Maryland into) the Appalachian mountain chains which lie west of the
coastal plain that runs along the Atlantic coast south of New

England. Buffalo, New York, and Pittsburgh, Pennsylvania, are Midwestern cities.

North-Central States

Between the Appalachian mountains and the Rockies of the Mountain States lies a land of plains and plateaux, 1,500 miles in breadth, drained largely by the Mississippi River system. The Mississippi rises in northern Minnesota and flows 2,348 miles to the Gulf of Mexico. From the point at which it reaches the western boundary of Wisconsin to Cairo, Illinois, where the Ohio River (which runs along the southern boundary of the Midwest) joins it, the Mississippi forms the dividing line first between the Midwest and Farm Belt and then between the Midwest and the Border State of Missouri. Thus, on the whole, except for the areas draining to the Great Lakes, the Midwest is drained by the eastern and the Farm Belt by the western part of the Mississippi River system.

The vast arable lands of the North-Central States were tilled on family farms and became the prime setting for the 'Main Street' America of small towns, where back doors were left unlocked, all parents sent their children to the local school, the ambitious and industrious 'got on' (and often out to the big cities) and the 'shiftless' remained deservedly poor. This was the America of the older-stock white, middle-class people who set the country's standards until the present age.

The North-Central section still leads the nation in farm output. The Midwest leads in dairy products, the Farm Belt in livestock products and both regions in field crops.

Midwest: The Midwestern States lie entirely in territory that was part of the original United States but outside the original States. Between 1781 and 1802 the States ceded their individual claims to western lands to the national government. In two Ordinances in 1785 and 1787 the Congress under the Articles of Confederation organized the Midwestern region as the Northwest Territory, setting the pattern for the settlement of the continental domain: the land was to be surveyed in six-mile-square townships and one-mile-square sections (hence the earlier reference to the 'quarter-section preemption'); when the Territory was sufficiently settled, a legislature was to be formed in it, whose acts would be subject to veto by the governor appointed by the national government; and when enough further settlement had taken place, States were to be created in the Territory and admitted to the Union on equal terms.

The most industrialized, urban parts of the Midwest are along the Great Lakes, which were made a single system of waterways by canals completed in the 1850s and opened to ocean-going vessels from the Atlantic by the St. Lawrence Seaway in Canada, completed as a joint United States–Canadian project in the 1950s. Chicago, Illinois, on the southern shore of Lake Michigan (and connected by river and canal to the Mississippi River system), is the hub of the nation's railway network and the centre of its second most populous urbanized belt.

Farm Belt: Except for some territory along the Canadian border which was part of the original United States, the Farm Belt lies in the Louisiana Territory purchased from France in 1803. The sequence of admission of the Farm Belt States to the Union, especially the twenty-two-year gap between the admission of Nebraska in 1867 and North and South Dakota in 1889 (more or less simultaneously with four more Territories to their west), is a clue to the presence of a geographical barrier in the smooth, gently sloping landscape of the region. All of Iowa and Minnesota and more than half of Kansas and Nebraska, but less than half of North and South Dakota lie east of the 100th meridian of west longitude, which coincides approximately with the 20-inch per annum average rainfall line and the 2,000-feet above sea level contour line. To the west the rainfall is lower and the land higher: the rainfall is often inadequate for intensive agriculture, especially to the south; the winters are severe on the higher ground, especially to the north.

Family farming fared well in the western part of the Farm Belt only when good crops coincided with world demand for them. Otherwise in fine weather, crops were good and prices low; in bad weather, crops were poor. Kansas gained no population and Nebraska and the Dakotas all lost population in the 1930s, the decade of the 'dustbowl' and the great depression, when weather, crops and demand were poor. Since then the family has yielded, here as elsewhere in the country, to large-scale, mechanized farming.

South

When Lincoln was elected President in 1860 there were eighteen free and fifteen slave States. Seven of the latter—South Carolina, Mississippi, Florida, Alabama, Georgia, Louisiana and Texas—seceded from the Union before Lincoln took office in March 1861. These contained most of the major cotton, rice and sugar-cane producing areas, where slave labour was used in large-scale operations on plantations. Four more States—Virginia, Arkansas, North Carolina and Tennessee—seceded after the first shots were fired in April in the war between the States. The eleven seceding States joined together in the Confederate States of America. They had seven-eighths of the slave population and five-sixths of the total black population of the country. Political manoeuvring and military intervention by Union forces ensured that none of the four remaining slave States—Delaware, Maryland, Kentucky and Missouri—seceded.

The Civil War and its aftermath created further differences between the eleven seceding States—the South—and the slave States that did not secede. The Confederate States were devastated in their defeat. During Reconstruction, governments including blacks and northern 'carpetbaggers', who had come South to obtain the victors' spoils, were maintained in the conquered States by Union armies. As the troops withdrew, white supremacy was ruthlessly restored. The Southern States have a shared history of their own without counterpart in any other section of the country.

The whites in the South and the Border States are predominantly English-speaking old-stock Protestants, with substantial numbers of Catholics of French extraction in Louisiana and of Mexican origin in Texas (as well as in the States to its west). These are all peoples of the early European settlements. On the whole, later white immigrants avoided areas where they might have to compete with black labour, slave or free. However, they came into the urban areas of Delaware and Maryland in sufficient numbers to assimilate in this century these former slave States with the Middle-Atlantic States north of the Mason and Dixon line (drawn in 1767 to determine the northern boundary of Maryland, and from which the South derived the name 'Dixie').

Deep South: The five States labelled the Deep South were 'plantation States' which seceded upon Lincoln's election. Their populations were then more than half black: Mississippi's population was still more than half black in 1940. Although black people are now much more spread about the country than in 1860, or in 1940, the States of the Deep South remain those with the highest proportions of blacks in their populations.

Outer South: At the time of the Civil War Texas was fully settled only in its east and Florida only in its north. Further settlement has made each less 'Southern': Texas more 'Western' —its livestock products are more valuable than its cotton; and, later, Florida more 'Northern'—it is a place of retirement for people from regions to the north. By the time of the Civil War the tobacco-plantation economy of Virginia had been largely destroyed by soil erosion, and the chief interest of the State in the slave economy was as an exporter of slaves to cotton-producing areas. It has become more 'Northern' since, owing to the growth of the suburbs of Washington, D.C. Only relatively small areas of North Carolina, Tennessee and Arkansas were in the plantation economy; their larger parts were, and are, mountainous areas farmed by non-slaveholding whites, who have generally been hostile to Negroes but distrustful, too, of the Southern 'plantation gentry' and their successors, the so-called 'Bourbons', of the post-Reconstruction South.

Border States: Kentucky, Missouri and western Virginia were also slave areas most of whose farmers were non-slaveholding whites. This was so overwhelmingly the case in western Virginia, that when Virginia seceded from the Union, its West left it and became a separate State in 1863. Oklahoma was reserved for the American Indians until some of the land in this Indian Territory, as it was then called, was taken from it in the late nineteenth century and opened to general settlement, in the event mainly by poor whites from the South and the older Border States. The settlements and the remaining Indian Territory were rejoined for admission as a single state in 1907.

'Poor-white' country is in particular the mountain and plateau areas—hill country—extending southward from the Border States to the northern parts of the States in the Deep South. This is also the core of the 'Bible Belt'.

West

The United States established old claims or acquired new titles to most of the Western section in the coterminous United States in the 1840s. Gold was discovered in California in 1848 and it was a State by 1850. The last frontier of the coterminous United States —the frontier of the 'Westerns'—lay between the Pacific States and the Farm Belt.

Mountain States: The easternmost parts of the most eastern Mountain States are among the lands west of the 100th meridian described under the *Farm Belt* above. Next, farther west, are the Rocky Mountains. Between them and the mountain ranges of the Pacific States is mainly desert, rich in minerals but where intensive farming depends on irrigation. The Mormons (members of the Church of Jesus Christ of Latter-day Saints) who left Illinois in the United States for Utah outside it in the 1840s—almost immediately to be brought back under American jurisdiction as a result of the Mexican War—were the first to make the desert bloom, in the only successful communitarian settlement of the frontier. Today the Mountain States with the most rapidly growing populations, like Nevada and Arizona, owe much of their recent development to the construction of great public dams. Senator Barry Goldwater of Arizona ran as the Republican candidate for President in 1964 appealing to the tradition of frontier individualism.

Pacific States: Peopled in the main by migrants from other States, Northern and Southern, the Pacific States create the new, standard, homogenized white Americans.

This is the only region with a sizeable Asiatic population. In 1970 there were about 215,000 people of Japanese and 170,000 of Chinese origin in California, where they together constituted about one-fiftieth of the population. In 1970 there were a like number of people of Japanese origin in Hawaii, where they and those of Chinese origin constituted more than one-third of the population; with native Hawaiians and Filipinos added, the non-white, non-Negro peoples made up about three-fifths of the population. The racial mixture (and mixing) of Hawaii worked against its admission as a State, until the entry of Alaska—with a much smaller population and much nearer the Soviet Union—removed all the alleged grounds why it was inappropriate or dangerous to bring in a Territory outside the coterminous United States.

In the 1960s California became the most populous State in the Union. The greatest growth occurs in its southern part. The gold is now in the sunshine. 'Hollywood' in Los Angeles has conveyed to the world, on big and small screens, perhaps an exaggerated picture of the American mass-consumption society. But in Los Angeles, where there are more motor cars—the prime symbol of the mass-consumption society—per head than in any other metropolis, life most nearly imitates the mass media. The riots in a black 'ghetto' of the city in 1965 made 'Watts' the symbol for other features of contemporary American society.

2: The Constitutions

A: WHAT AMERICANS MEAN
BY A CONSTITUTION

At the outbreak of the American War of Independence several of the colonies had charters which, like the present Constitutions of the United States and the fifty States, defined the structures and limits of government. In every colony there was a separation of powers between the executive (the Governor was chosen for eight colonies by the Crown, for the three proprietary colonies of Maryland, Pennsylvania and Delaware by the proprietors and in Connecticut and Rhode Island by the colonial legislatures) and the legislative assembly (elected on the basis of a restricted suffrage). Like the present States, the colonies exercized powers within a more general system of government of superior legal status. In judicial proceedings an act of a colonial government was set aside if judged to be beyond the powers of the colony or in conflict with superior law.

Along with English political habits, the colonists had taken the philosophy of natural rights and the institution of government by consent to the New World. This philosophy found legal expression in enactments which were declared to be beyond the reach of ordinary legislation, and which defined the liberties of persons, their procedural rights in law, and the principles of government and public policy considered most germane to the rights and privileges of subjects. Thus the Body of Liberties promulgated by the legislature of the Massachusetts Bay Colony in 1641 (after its circulation to the towns of the Colony for comment) listed the rights of persons in the Colony (including the right to leave it), stipulations about elections and a prohibition of monopolies (excluding those for new inventions).

In some of the first Constitutions adopted by the rebellious colonies the articles relating to the form of government were appended to those setting forth a declaration or bill of rights. Thus the revolutionary convention of Virginia approved a Declaration of Rights and a Constitution or Form of Government in June 1776. The Declaration of Rights expressed the ideas of natural rights and government by consent in phrases much like those of the Declaration of Independence adopted by the Continental Congress in July. The Virginia Constitution laid down that 'the legislature, executive, and judiciary departments shall be separate and distinct, so that neither exercize the power properly belonging to the other.' In practice the first State Constitutions strengthened the legislature, especially against the executive, in reaction against the experience of dealing with royal and proprietary governors. In most States, including Virginia, the Constitution bestowed on the legislature the power to elect the Governor or other chief executive for a short, fixed term.

New York provided for a directly elected Governor in 1777; and the Massachusetts Declaration of Rights and Frame of Government of 1780, which did likewise, gave more impetus to the view of the separation of powers which, reinforced by the Constitution of the United States drafted in 1787, came to prevail in all the States. Although put, like other views of the separation, in terms of distinct powers, its essence lies in the independence of the three branches of government from one another.

The Massachusetts Constitution of 1780 was the first to be drafted by a convention elected solely for that purpose and to be ratified directly by the electorate. The constitutional convention and referendum became the standard devices by which a State adopted a new Constitution.

To Americans, then, a Constitution is the instrument by which a people establishes its framework of government. It is a written document which is adopted and amended by processes different from, and more difficult to operate, than those of ordinary legislation. It forms a code of higher law, in the sense that the courts refuse to give effect to the acts of the government established by the Constitution which the courts consider to be in conflict with it. It prescribes in more or less detail the composition of the organs of government and the distribution of powers among them. It defines substantive and procedural rights of persons to be protected from infringement by government. It also gives certain public policies protected status.

Those specifications of a Constitution need still to be set in the context of the ideas about government to which Americans have always been sensitive. Operationally, an American Constitution limits government because the courts may declare acts of government unconstitutional; but the courts vindicate their supremacy in constitutional interpretation because of the belief that government ought to be limited by a Constitution guaranteeing—in the words of the Massachusetts Constitution of 1780—'a government of laws and not of men'. The phrases of the Declaration of Independence and other documents about all men or people being created equal and instituting government by consent have frequently been dismissed, as by the defenders of Negro slavery before the Civil War, as mere 'glittering . . . generalities'.* It is true that in the late eighteenth century the 'men' or 'people' of the body politic tended not to include blacks, women and people who owned no property or paid no taxes. However, the phrases have aided the extension of their meaning to all those groups. The generalities still glitter.

B: THE CONSTITUTION OF
THE UNITED STATES†

The Constitution of 1787

The Articles of Confederation and perpetual Union which came into effect in 1781 were based upon 'a firm league of friendship' among the thirteen original States listed by name in the full title of the Articles. Those political and social leaders who contrived to replace them by a Constitution establishing a much stronger central government took advantage of a meeting of delegates

* Rufus Choate, quoted in Carl Becker, *The Declaration of Independence* (Knopf, 1956), p. 244. The last sentence of the paragraph is Becker's.
† See the Appendix for a copy of the Constitution.

from five States in 1786 to call upon all of the States to appoint commissioners to a convention in Philadelphia, Pennsylvania, the next year: 'to devise such further provisions as shall appear to them necessary to render the constitution of the Federal Government adequate to the exigencies of the Union; and to report such an Act for that purpose to the United States in Congress assembled, as, when agreed to by them, and afterwards confirmed by the legislatures of every State, will effectually provide for the same.' The arrangements for approving the report were the procedures for amending the Articles of Confederation. Twelve States—all but Rhode Island—appointed delegates to the Philadelphia Convention.

The framers of the Constitution knew that some of the State legislatures would be hostile to their proposals. Despite the undertaking to follow the procedures for amending the Articles, they provided that the new Constitution should come into effect when ratified by special conventions in nine States. Not knowing which States would thus join the 'more perfect Union'—it started in 1789 with eleven States; North Carolina entered later that year and Rhode Island in 1790—they made virtue of necessity by declaring the source of the new Constitution to be, not the adhering States, but 'the People of the United States'. A compact of States became, almost inadvertently, a government of the people.

In 1787 Americans believed that they had a federal system of government under the Articles and that the United States in Congress assembled was a Federal Government. The Congress determined policy in respect of the powers 'expressly delegated' to it, though the exercise of the more important powers required the assent of nine of the State delegations. All other powers of government were reserved to the States. Thus, like the subsequent Constitution of the United States, the Articles of Confederation provided the most distinctive feature of a federal system of government: a constitutional division of powers between the whole and the parts of the system. Under the Articles, however, the Federal Congress was constituted by State delegations and was ultimately dependent on the States for the enforcement of its policies.

The framers of the Constitution augmented the powers of the

Federal Government. They omitted the declaration in the Articles that the powers not expressly delegated were reserved to the States. They made the Federal Government a government derived in part from the people and, like the State governments, acting directly on them. The framers took the name 'Federalists' so as to make their opponents, as 'Anti-Federalists', appear to oppose the continuance of the Union. They succeeded in redefining federalism, then and ever since, by reference to the system of dual government they created.

Among the sources of the new Constitution were, most immediately, the Articles of Confederation. There are many common phrases. By far the greater part of new material in the Constitution of 1787 concerns the separation of powers. For while the Articles established only a unicameral Congress, Article I of the Constitution established a bicameral Congress in which are vested all the legislative powers of the Federal Government, Article II the office of the President of the United States in which is vested the executive power and Article III a Supreme Court in which (and in such inferior courts as the Congress establishes) is vested the judicial power of the United States. However, almost all the clauses defining the federal division of powers—limits on the powers of the United States and the States in the interests of the other level of government, as well as grants of powers to the Federal Government—are in Article I relating to the Congress: thus the arrangement of the Constitution shows its provenance as a revision of the Articles of Confederation.

The English inheritance is also apparent. Even the provision whose application characterizes the American separation of powers—'no Person holding any Office under the United States shall be a Member of either House' of the Congress—derives from the Place clause in the English Act of Settlement of 1701, whose failure to prevent ministers sitting in the House of Commons characterizes British responsible government. The American observance is stricter than required. The Constitution does not bar heads of departments from the floor of the Houses, though in practice they appear instead before congressional committees.

The English inheritance was so much a part of colonial and State political practice that it is impossible to isolate its direct influence. The phrases of the Constitution often echo English—but also New World—documents.

The framers sought to protect and promote the interests of the propertied, commercial and creditor classes to which they belonged. They safeguarded the interests of southern planters by providing that the African slave trade could not be prohibited by the Congress before 1808 and that no taxes could be laid on exports. They adopted a familiar formula for counting slaves as three-fifths of free persons in providing for the apportionment among the States by population of their representation in the new House of Representatives of the Congress. Northern merchants were expected to benefit from the virtual prohibition of State taxes on interstate and foreign commerce, and generally from the establishment of a strong Federal Government able to enforce the Constitution in the States and to negotiate more effectively with other countries.

Several States had made conditions easier for debtors, directly by law and indirectly by issuing paper money as legal tender. The framers prohibited the States from impairing the obligation of contracts, coining money, emitting bills of credit, or making anything but gold and silver legal tender. The only power of the Congress under the Articles of Confederation which they did not expressly grant to the new Federal Government was the power to 'emit bills on the credit of the United States'.

Although the framers of the Constitution were men of substance, so were most of those who took the lead in opposing ratification: it is an exaggeration to treat the Constitution as the outcome of a 'counter-revolution' against the 'revolution' represented by the Declaration of Independence. The latter's 'glittering . . . generalities' seem, especially in the light of later history, more democratic. They declared that a people may in the pursuit of their happiness set aside a government that has forfeited their consent. The clauses of the Constitution of 1787 protected commerce and contracts and provided for direct election of only one-half of one of three branches of the Federal Government. Yet the Constitution reaffirmed the commitment to the 'republican form of government', in which all political authority ultimately derives from the 'people'.

Once ratified, the Constitution was generally accepted. Thomas Jefferson, chief author of the Declaration of Independence, became Secretary of State under President Washington. Then, as the leader of the first modern political party organizing support among a fairly widespread electorate, he helped start the process, while himself becoming Vice-President and then President of the United States, of developing the republican form of government into the American democracy.

The Bill of Rights and other amendments

Article V of the Constitution specifies two procedures for proposing amendments and two for ratifying them. The Congress shall, by a two-thirds majority in each House, propose amendments or, on the application of two-thirds of the State legislatures, call a convention for that purpose. The Congress shall determine whether ratification is to be by the legislatures or special conventions in the States; in either case the assent of three-fourths of the States is required.

In practice all proposals for amendments have come from the Congress. The Philadelphia Convention has been a warning of what a convention to propose amendments might get up to. Of the twenty-six amendments adopted by 1971 all but one have been ratified by the State legislatures. In 1933 the Congress determined that what became in the same year the Twenty-first Amendment should be considered by conventions in the States, which would represent the balance of opinion on the issue more accurately than the State legislatures with their then gross over-representation of rural areas. The Twenty-first repealed the Eighteenth Amendment, adopted in 1919, which had prohibited the manufacture and sale of intoxicating beverages.

Like the Articles of Confederation, the Constitution of 1787 did not contain an extensive bill of rights. For, like the Articles, it established a Federal Government of delegated powers, leaving to the States (though perhaps more ambiguously than the Articles) general responsibility for the health, morals, safety and welfare of the people. The framers foresaw, on the whole accurately, that the discharge of that responsibility rather than the exercise of the

Federal powers would give rise to conflicts with the freedom of individuals. Likewise, most cases in law, especially criminal cases, would be tried in State courts under State law. The bills of rights in State Constitutions protected liberties and procedural rights in law where protection seemed to be needed.

However, in securing ratification of the Constitution, its supporters averted a call for another general convention to draft a Federal bill of rights only by promising that the first Congress would submit appropriate amendments to the States. The first ten amendments, known as the Bill of Rights, were added to the Constitution before the end of 1791. They are generally regarded as part of the original Constitution of the United States.

Some of their clauses go back to Magna Carta, whose 'by the law of the land' became 'due process of law' in a confirmation of the charters in 1354, in which form it appears in the Fifth Amendment (and in the Fourteenth Amendment to the Constitution adopted in 1868). The Bill of Rights has provisions in common with, for instance, the Massachusetts Body of Liberties, the English Bill of Rights of 1689, and the Virginia and Massachusetts Declarations of Rights—all of which, for example, protect against cruel and unusual punishments. That these were rights to be safeguarded from infringement by governments had not been in dispute: they gave concrete content to 'the harmonizing sentiments of the day' about the natural rights of men.

Most of the substantive effects of the subsequent amendments to the Constitution are referred to in Section C. These sixteen amendments may be grouped by years of adoption as follows: 1798–1804: two; 1865–70: three; 1913–20: four; 1933: two; 1951: one; 1961–71: four. After two early amendments, there were none until Reconstruction. There was another long gap until well into the Progressive era. There has been a sprinkling of amendments since. The last four were added at invervals of three or four years.

Six of the sixteen may be characterized as tidying-up amendments: the Eleventh (1798), Twelfth (1804), Twentieth (1933), Twenty-second (1951), Twenty-third (1961), and Twenty-fifth (1967). This underrates the political significance of the Twenty-second Amendment's restricting the President to two terms. Like the first clause of the Twenty-fifth, which confirms that on the death of the President the Vice President becomes President (instead of merely discharging the powers and duties of the office—see Article II, Section 1, of the original Constitution), the Twenty-second Amendment puts a custom into the Constitution. But the two-term tradition had recently been broken for the first time by Franklin Roosevelt (and the American electorate); and one of the motives for the Amendment was the hostility of Congressmen and State legislators to the growing independent political strength of the Presidency.

Two amendments may have been unnecessary because by the time they were adopted the Supreme Court could probably have been persuaded to alter its previous interpretation of the existing Constitution: the Sixteenth (1913) and Twenty-fourth (1964). Three may have been largely unnecessary because political action was achieving the same result: the Seventeenth (1913), Nineteenth (1920) and Twenty-sixth (1971). Prohibition was also spreading by legislation when the Eighteenth (1919) Amendment was adopted. Because it was adopted, the Twenty-first (1933) was adopted to repeal it.

That leaves the Thirteenth (1865), Fourteenth (1868) and Fifteenth (1870) Amendments. The ending of slavery, in the Thirteenth, required a Civil War. The adoption of the Fourteenth and Fifteenth Amendments, for the purpose of protecting the civil rights of blacks in general and their voting rights in particular, also depended upon coercion: of the defeated Southern States in the Reconstruction era. The Fourteenth Amendment has had a general importance as the prime basis of the Supreme Court's oversight of the exercise and enforcement of the general power to govern reserved to the States.

The law and custom of the Constitution

While the foregoing summary may err on the side of minimizing the contribution of the amendments, there is fair margin for concluding that the important sources of constitutional change must lie outside the amending process. The most substantial amendment, the Fourteenth, was, like the Constitution of 1787, adopted through a manipulation of amendment procedures. The other sources of constitutional change are: the law made by judicial decisions, statutes and administrative actions; and custom. These implement and supplement the written Constitution (as amended) to produce the 'living constitution' of the United States.

Judicial decisions as a source of the 'living constitution' are referred to at many points below. It suffices here to point out their authority, by quoting from a fairly recent statement by the Supreme Court of 'the American doctrine of judicial supremacy':

In August and September 1958 the Supreme Court met in special session to deal with a case arising from the efforts of the Governor (Orval Faubus) and Legislature of the State of Arkansas to prevent the desegregation of schools in Little Rock. Their actions were a direct challenge to the ruling of the Supreme Court in 1954 that the public maintenance of racially segregated schools was contrary to the Constitution of the United States. Speaking for the unanimous Court in the case of Cooper *v.* Aaron, Chief Justice Warren said that 'we should answer the premise of the actions of the Governor and Legislature that they are not bound by our holding. . . . It is necessary only to recall some basic constitutional propositions which are settled doctrine.

'Article VI of the Constitution makes the Constitution the "supreme Law of the Land". In 1803, Chief Justice Marshall, speaking for a unanimous Court, referring to the Constitution as "the fundamental and paramount law of the nation", declared in the notable case of Marbury *v.* Madison . . ., that "It is emphatically the province and duty of the judicial department to say what the law is." This decision declared the basic principle that the federal judiciary is supreme in the exposition of the law of the Constitution, and that principle has ever since been respected by this Court and the Country as a permanent and indispensable feature of our constitutional system. It follows that the interpretation . . . enunciated by this Court . . . is the supreme law of the land.'

Statutes and administrative actions fill out provisions of the Constitution. The Constitution, for example, left to the Congress the decision whether there should be any Federal courts other than the Supreme Court. The first Congress determined, in the

Judiciary Act of 1789, that there should be a full set of Federal courts along with the State judicial systems.

Moreover, until statutes and administrative actions exercise constitutional grants of powers, cases giving rise to their interpretation do not reach the courts. In the early nineteenth century Chief Justice Marshall gave a very broad interpretation of the Federal power to regulate interstate commerce, but at a time when it was scarcely exercised. By the time the Federal Government began to exercise it substantially—the creation in 1887 of the Interstate Commerce Commission to regulate railways and the passage in 1890 of the Sherman Anti-Trust Act mark the start of this development—the Supreme Court had enunciated some limits to the Federal commerce and taxing powers on behalf of States' rights. There followed a half century of intermittent pressure from the political branches against the limits imposed, somewhat erratically, by the Court.

An Act of Congress of 1916, for example, banned goods made by child labour from interstate commerce. In the case of Hammer v. Dagenhart in 1918 the Supreme Court held the Act to be an unconstitutional invasion of States' rights over the regulation of manufacturing. In the Revenue Act of 1919 the Congress taxed the employers of child labour. Although a majority of the Court had upheld a destructive Federal tax on margarine coloured to look like butter and a Federal tax law which was used to prohibit the sale of opium except for medical purposes, in the case of Bailey v. Drexel Furniture Company in 1922 the Justices of the Court with one dissentient invalidated the child labour tax as a misuse of the taxing power of the Congress to accomplish what was beyond the Federal regulatory powers.

In the 1930s the pressure from the political branches became overwhelming. From 1937 the restrictions on the Federal powers on behalf of States' rights were swept aside by judicial decisions that cited the opinions of Chief Justice Marshall in very different contexts from those in which they were written. The main lines defining the reach of the Federal powers in the federal system are now largely set by statutes, as implemented by administrative actions and interpreted by the courts.

Custom is not so easily distinguished from the law of the Constitution in the United States as in the United Kingdom, owing to the tendency in the United States to appeal to the courts as the final interpreters of the Constitution in all matters. The courts refuse to rule on what they regard as 'political questions' (such as which territories belong to the United States); but they decide what are 'political questions'. In the 1960s the Supreme Court decided that the apportionment of seats in State legislatures and the definition of the constituencies of members of the United States House of Representatives must provide for constituencies of equal population to the satisfaction of the Federal courts; previously it had appeared to regard such issues as 'political questions'. No constitutional matter is with certainty beyond the reach of the law.

Moreover, there are no agreed meanings for terms like 'practices' and 'conventions' of the Constitution, which are used here to distinguish two sorts of customs:

Practices of the Constitution are customs not breached by failure to observe them. Thus conference committees are used in the Congress to provide a common version of bills passed by the two Houses in somewhat different forms. The reports of conference committees are submitted for approval to the two chambers, which are almost invariably constrained to accept them. However, the two Houses are free to reconcile their differences by less formal means if they can.

Conventions of the Constitution are customs that (like laws) are breached if not observed. Serious breaches either end the convention or lead to its conversion into a legal requirement (as in the case of the two-term tradition for Presidents). The most important conventions are those applying to the selection of the President and Vice-President, especially that the electors who choose them are themselves chosen under State laws by the people and pledge themselves to particular candidates. Some of the inter-relations of the practices of the presidential nominating procedures, the conventions of presidential electoral procedures and the relevant provisions of the original Constitution and its amendments are referred to in the next section.

C: THE PRINCIPLES OF THE
CONSTITUTION OF THE UNITED STATES

The Constitution of the United States provides for the republican
form of government, the separation of powers, federalism and the
protection of personal rights. These four principles define a system
of limited government. The first two purport to prevent the
exercise of absolute, arbitrary power in the Federal Government
by subjecting those exercising political authority to election and
by apportioning the power to govern among branches of government independent of one another. The second two purport to
limit the scope of governments by dividing the power to govern
between two independent levels of government and by setting
certain subjects beyond the reach of the Federal Government, the
States or both.

The republican form of government

The republican form of government is guaranteed for the United
States by the requirements that the members of the two Houses of
the Congress and the President and Vice-President be elected for
limited periods of office, either directly by the qualified voters
among the people or indirectly by others chosen by the electorate.
The Constitution also provides, in Article IV, Section 4, that 'the
United States shall guarantee to every State in this Union a
Republican Form of Government.' Nothing in the Constitution or
statutes of a State, including provision for a considerably larger
measure of direct participation by the electorate than in the
Federal Government, has ever been held to be in conflict with this
clause. It has been invoked by the President and the Congress—
the Supreme Court so far claiming no competence in this
'political question'—to settle disputes among rival State governments, in Rhode Island in 1842 and in the Reconstruction South.

The great compromise in the Philadelphia convention between the delegates from large and small States resulted in a
bicameral Congress of the United States consisting of the House
of Representatives, in which each State is represented according

to population, and the Senate, in which each state is equally represented by two Senators. Under the original Constitution Senators were chosen by the State legislatures. The Seventeenth Amendment adopted in 1913 made Senators, like Representatives (Congressmen) under the original Constitution, directly elected by the voters in each State with the qualifications for electing the most numerous branch of the State legislature. The significance of that way of specifying the electorate is that it leaves the precise definition of the suffrage to the several States. Universal adult (over 21) white male suffrage was substantially achieved in the Jacksonian era.

Article II, Section 1, of the Constitution provides that the President and Vice President be chosen by electors appointed as the State legislatures determine, each State having as many electors as it has Senators and Representatives. The electors ballot in their respective States, sending their returns to the Congress; the so-called electoral college never meets as a body. With the almost immediate emergence of party politics under the Constitution, the electors have (with a few exceptions) surrendered their discretion. The Twelfth Amendment adopted in 1804 took account of what had already happened to the extent of recognizing that the electors voted for 'tickets' of presidential and vice-presidential candidates, but it left the electoral college intact.

By 1804 the majority of State legislatures provided for the popular election of presidential electors; by 1828, almost all. Shortly thereafter the practice was established of nominating presidential and vice-presidential candidates in national party conventions composed of delegates from the States. Starting in the Progressive era, most of the States have provided 'presidential primary' elections for testing the popularity of prospective nominees and choosing delegates. In the general election for choosing the members of the electoral college, the States have almost invariably provided since 1836 that the winning ticket in a State-wide election gains all the State's places.]In most States the ballot contains only the names of the presidential and vice-presidential candidates with their party labels, without the names of the electors pledged to them for whom the voters are technically voting.

While changing the starting dates of the terms of the elective offices and of the regular annual sessions of the Congress, so as to do away with the 'lame-duck' session of a Congress which met after the election of its successor in November but before the latter's term began, the Twentieth Amendment adopted in 1933 provided for a failure to choose or for the death of a President-elect before he was due to take office. The Twenty-third Amendment adopted in 1961 added electors from the District of Columbia to the electoral college. The Twenty-fourth adopted in 1964 referred to 'the right of citizens of the United States to vote in any primary or other election for President or Vice President, for electors for President or Vice President, or for Senator or Representative in Congress' but did not create that right; 'any primary or other election for President' in which citizens of the United States vote is otherwise unknown to the Constitution. In their essentials the Constitutional provisions for electing a President are still those of Article II, Section 1, as altered by the Twelfth Amendment.

For election by the electoral college a presidential candidate needs an absolute majority of electoral votes. In a number of recent presidential elections Southern white-supremacists sought to prevent the election by popular vote in November of an absolute majority of electors pledged to one candidate, in order to create opportunities for bargaining in connection with either the balloting of electors in December or (if the electors fail to elect) the choice of President by an absolute majority of State delegations in the House of Representatives in January. Although the manoeuvres have failed, they have drawn attention to the dangers in the present discrepancy between constitutional form and reality. There is widespread support for an amendment to end the discrepancy but as yet insufficient agreement about what precisely to do.

The power of the States to determine the qualifications for voting has been limited by the Fifteenth Amendment adopted in 1870, the Nineteenth in 1920 and the Twenty-sixth in 1971, prohibiting discrimination on grounds of race, sex and age over eighteen in elections for any level of government, and by the Twenty-fourth Amendment adopted in 1964, prohibiting any poll or other tax requirement for voting in Federal elections. In the case of Harper *v.* Virginia State Board of Elections in 1966 the Supreme Court held poll-tax requirements to be unconstitutional in other elections, too. The Fourteenth Amendment adopted in 1868 contains a penalty clause reducing the representation in the House of Representatives of a State which restricts adult male suffrage, but it has never been invoked. All amendments relating to the suffrage grant to the Congress the power to enforce their provisions by appropriate legislation. The Voting Rights Acts of 1965 and 1970, suspending State literacy tests which had been used severely to restrict the suffrage and setting a requirement of only thirty days' residence at the present address for voting in presidential elections, went a long way towards superseding the definitions of the suffrage by the States.

The separation of powers

The separation of powers in the Federal Government is ensured by the independence of the President and the two Houses of the Congress from one another. Every fourth year the electors for the President, one-third of the Senators and all of the Representatives are elected at the same time; but the President serves a fixed term of four years, the Senators six years and the Representatives two years. In the 'mid-term' contests two years later, another third of the Senators and all of the Representatives are elected. One consequence of the staggering of terms of office (and the two-term limit on the presidency) is that a President and the Senators (running for full terms) elected together never run together again for re-election to their offices.

Article I, Section 5, of the Constitution makes each House of the Congress the judge of the qualifications of its own members. But in 1969 in the case of Powell *v.* McCormack the Supreme Court set aside the practice of a century by ruling that 'the House is without power to exclude any member-elect who meets the Constitution's requirements for membership.' Each House may expel a member by a two-thirds majority.

The President may be removed during the term for which he is elected only by conviction, by a two-thirds majority of Senators present for the vote, on an impeachment by the House of Representatives. In 1868 President Andrew Johnson was impeached by the House as a political move of the Reconstruction Congress, but the Senate vote for conviction was one short of the two-thirds majority required. In 1974 President Nixon resigned to forestall impeachment and probable conviction for obstruction of justice in the Watergate affair. The Twenty-fifth Amendment adopted in 1967 lays down procedures for determining whether a President is for the time being unable to discharge his powers and duties.

That Amendment also provides for filling a vacancy in the office of Vice President by presidential nomination with the consent of both Houses of the Congress. In 1973 Gerald R. Ford was so chosen to succeed Vice-President Spiro Agnew, who had resigned on admitting some of the charges of financial irregularities made against him. Ford succeeded Nixon as President in August 1974; his nominee, Nelson Rockefeller, was confirmed as Vice President in December. Before the adoption of the Twenty-fifth Amendment casual vacancies in the Vice Presidency had remained unfilled.

Appointments of Supreme Court Justices are made for life on nomination by the President with the consent of the Senate. The Chief Justice (mentioned only incidentally in the Constitution as presiding over the Senate when it tries a President on impeachment) is appointed as such and not (as in some State courts) chosen by his colleagues. The requirements for the removal of a Justice by impeachment are the same as for the President.

By involving the Senate in presidential appointments and foreign negotiations—the advice and consent of the Senate is required for major appointments, and for lesser appointments unless the Congress provides otherwise; and 'two-thirds of the Senators present' must concur to make a treaty—the framers of the Constitution intended that the Senate should, like similar bodies in colonial and some State governments, act as an advisory council to the President. While negotiating an Indian treaty, President Washington appeared in the Senate chamber to ask the Senators' advice. The President left the chamber on the second day of consultation muttering that 'he would be damned if he ever went there again.' Written consultation broke down in 1794 during the negotiations leading to a treaty with Great Britain. That ended the history of the Senate as an advisory council.

Whatever is done in advance to ease the reception of a treaty, the President usually sends it to the Senate only after the negotiations have ended. Likewise, although the President is required by 'senatorial courtesy' to clear most appointments involving senatorial consent and party political considerations—such as appointments to the lower Federal courts—with the Senators of his party from the States in which the appointees are to serve or from which they come, the President sends a single nomination for each post to the Senate. In this, as in much else, both the form and the practice of the American constitutional separation of powers involve a sharing of functions in which the reciprocal independence of the executive and legislature is maintained by checks and balances.

Although all revenue bills must originate in the House of Representatives, every bill to become law must be passed by both Houses of the Congress in the same form before presentation to the President. This equal legislative power of the two Houses is a more important fact about them than all of their differences. They balance each other in the legislative process. The President's veto over legislation acts as a check, for its regular use may be overriden by two-thirds majorities of both Houses.

While the Constitution vests in the Congress the powers to declare war and to establish armed services and requires the consent of a two-thirds majority of the Senate to treaties, the President is made 'Commander in Chief' of the armed services, 'he shall receive Ambassadors' (which entails the power to grant or withhold recognition of foreign governments) and he may conclude executive agreements with foreign powers without senatorial approval. Such agreements are not mentioned in the Constitution but have been held by the Supreme Court to have the force of treaties. In the Opinion of the Court in the case of United States v. Curtiss-Wright Export Corporation in 1936 Justice Sutherland referred to 'the very delicate, plenary and exclusive power of the President as the sole organ . . . in the field of international relations'.

Article II of the Constitution vests 'the executive Power' in the President and charges him to 'take Care that the Laws be faithfully executed'. These broad phrases, like that of Article III vesting 'the judicial Power' in the Supreme Court and the inferior Federal courts, have been generously interpreted by the Supreme Court. The emphasis has, on the whole, been on the need for presidential discretion in the exercise of executive authority.

There have, however, been comparatively few decisions of the Supreme Court relating to the principle of the separation of powers. Moreover, no amendment has altered the distribution of powers among the organs of the Federal Government provided for in the original Constitution. The history of the separation of powers since 1787 lies, more exclusively than that of any of the other Federal constitutional principles, in political practice.

Federalism

The three most important of the delegated or enumerated powers of the Federal Government are the powers to tax and spend for the general welfare, to regulate commerce with foreign nations and 'among the several States' (interstate commerce), and to declare war (with which the powers relating to the armed forces may be bracketed). These are all in the list of powers conferred on the Congress in Article I, Section 8, of the Constitution, which ends with the power 'to make all Laws which shall be necessary and proper for carrying into Execution the foregoing Powers, and all other Powers vested by this Constitution in the Government of the United States, or in any Department or Officer thereof'. In Article VI the Constitution, laws of the Federal Government made in pursuance thereof and 'all Treaties made, or which shall be made, under the Authority of the United States' (a wording intended to preserve the validity of treaties entered into by the United States before the adoption of the Constitution of 1787) are declared 'the supreme Law of the Land . . . any Thing in any Constitution or Laws of any State to the Contrary notwithstanding'. The Tenth Amendment in the Bill of Rights confirmed that the powers not delegated to the Federal Government were reserved to the States or the people, but the word 'expressly' before 'delegated' in the equivalent declaration in the Articles of Confederation was omitted.

The Sixteenth Amendment adopted in 1913 made it practicable for the Federal Government to levy an income tax, after the Supreme Court in 1895 held parts of an income tax to be direct taxes which must, according to Article I, Section 9, of the original Constitution, be apportioned among the States by population. The Twenty-first Amendment adopted in 1933, while repealing the prohibition of intoxicating liquors, forbade their importation into any State in violation of its laws. This enables a State to prohibit or regulate the liquor trade in the State without regard to the effects on interstate or foreign commerce. (Mississippi repealed the last State-wide prohibition law in 1966: the State had been 'legally dry, revenue-wet', taxing the prohibited trade.) No amendment to the Constitution of 1787 has redistributed the substantive powers to govern so as to increase those originally granted to the Federal Government.

A great expansion in the reach of the Federal powers has been brought about, especially since 1933, by their exercise, sustained, especially since 1937, by the Supreme Court. In 1819 in the case of McCulloch v. Maryland, Chief Justice Marshall held for the Court that the Congress, in exercising its *express* power to tax and spend, had by virtue of the necessary and proper clause the *implied* power to charter a Bank of the United States. The omission of 'expressly' from the Tenth Amendment provided Marshall with an argument for adopting this 'loose construction' of the Federal powers which had been propounded in Washington's cabinet by Alexander Hamilton in contrast to the 'strict construction' of Thomas Jefferson. Although later the Supreme Court held, for example, that the Tenth Amendment reserved manufacturing and agriculture from the reach of the Federal commerce power unless in the flow of interstate or foreign commerce, it never formally reversed this 'loose construction' and in a line of cases from 1937 returned to Marshall's view that if a Federal action was otherwise lawful it overrode, as 'the supreme Law of the Land', any reserved power of the States.

In the Legal Tender Cases in 1871 Justice Strong held for the majority of the Court that the Federal Government could issue paper money as legal tender, as a power *resulting* 'from more than one of the substantive powers expressly defined, or from them all combined'. With respect to foreign relations the Court has read a good deal into the wording of the 'supreme Law of the Land' clause that, while Federal laws must be made in pursuance of the Constitution, treaties are made under the authority of the United States. In 1936 in United States *v.* Curtiss-Wright Export Corporation, Justice Sutherland declared that 'the investment of the Federal government with the powers of external sovereignty did not depend upon the affirmative grants of the Constitution': but was *inherent* 'from the conception of nationality'. However, in 1957 in Reid *v.* Covert, Justice Black, writing the Opinion of the Court, insisted that 'the United States is entirely a creature of the Constitution. Its power and authority have no other source.'

Under the present interpretation of the express, implied, resulting and inherent powers of the Federal Government, the question in cases involving the federal division of powers is rarely whether a subject is within the reach of the Federal Government, but often what scope the States have left in its regulation. Federal powers are constitutionally *exclusive* of State action in three circumstances. First, the Constitution grants an exclusive power to the Federal Government in so many words: for example, 'to exercise exclusive Legislation in all Cases whatsoever' over the District of Columbia. Second, the Constitution grants a power to the Federal Government and denies it to the States: for example, to coin money. Third, the Constitution grants a power to the Federal Government which, according to the Supreme Court, requires exclusivity. The Court has held that some of the activities reached by the interstate commerce power require uniform treatment, by Federal action or inaction, to the exclusion of the States.

Conversely, Federal and State powers are constitutionally *concurrent* when the Constitution more or less explicitly says so—the phrase 'concurrent power' appears only in the Eighteenth Amendment, adopted in 1919 and repealed in 1933; but the Constitution refers, for example, to both Federal and State taxing powers—or when the Constitution grants a power to the Federal

Government which, according to the Supreme Court, allows concurrent regulation by the States. This is true in part of the interstate commerce power: the Court first enunciated the rule that while some of the subjects of the power require uniform, exclusive treatment, others do not, in the case of Cooley v. Board of Wardens in 1851, involving pilotage in ports. The Congress may supersede State action in a field previously held by the Supreme Court to allow concurrent action, by express legislation or by acting in such a way as to lead the Supreme Court to decide that supersession has taken place. The Congress may then act to restore the position if it disapproves of the decision.

Without restricting the ultimate power of the Congress, the Supreme Court allows the States to exercise power over much of commerce. Indeed, the controls of a State over a subject of the commerce power not requiring completely uniform treatment, such as limitations on commercial motor vehicles allowed to operate in the State, sometimes act as trade restrictions in the generally free-trading area created by the Constitution. The Court has increasingly allowed State regulation and taxation that touch interstate as well as intrastate commerce generally in a non-discriminatory way; but some fine lines are drawn in determining whether or not a State has burdened interstate commerce unconstitutionally.

Obviously the judicial umpiring of the federal system is a complicated business. As well as the problems of Federal-State relations, there are those which arise among the several States. Article IV, Section 1, of the Constitution of the United States requires each State to give 'full faith and credit' to the acts, records and judicial proceedings of the other States. However, the Supreme Court has held that a State is not necessarily required to accept as conclusive the rulings in divorce proceedings undertaken in another State by a person domiciled in the first State. Thus a little care has to be exercised in using Nevada's divorce mill. No simple summaries are possible about such points in the constitutional law of American federalism.

The last forty years of judicial precedents permit one sweeping generalization. The federal division of powers in the Constitution of the United States does not now prevent the Federal Government from regulating any private activity which it regards as of national concern.

The protection of personal rights

The Constitution of 1787 specified some protections of personal rights. Under its provisions the Federal Government may not suspend the privilege of the writ of habeas corpus unless in cases of rebellion or invasion the public safety requires it. A person accused of a Federal crime has the right to insist on a trial by jury. No religious test can be required for any Federal office. Neither the Federal nor a State government may enact a bill of attainder or *ex post facto* law. A State may not impair the obligation of contracts.

The Bill of Rights—the first ten amendments, adopted in 1791 —added protections of the substantive freedoms of religion, speech and the press (First Amendment), such procedural safeguards as prohibitions of unreasonable searches and seizures (Fourth Amendment) and self-incrimination (Fifth Amendment) and further requirements for the use of juries in the Federal courts. The Fifth Amendment provides that no person shall 'be deprived of life, liberty or property, without due process of law'. The Bill of Rights applies only to the Federal Government.

The protection of personal rights provided in Section 1 of the Fourteenth Amendment, adopted in 1868, applies to the States: 'No State shall make or enforce any law which shall abridge the privileges or immunities of citizens of the United States; nor shall any State deprive any person of life, liberty, or property, without due process of law; nor deny to any person within its jurisdiction the equal protection of the laws.' It has been argued that the privileges and immunities clause was intended by the Reconstruction Congress to impose all of the protections of personal rights in the Bill of Rights on the States. A majority of the Justices of the Supreme Court have never accepted that argument.

Prior to the adoption of the Fourteenth Amendment the chief protection of personal rights against the States was the clause forbidding them to impair the obligation of contracts. From the 1880s and 1890s the Supreme Court interpreted the due process clause as a limitation on economic regulation of persons (including business corporations). It held that 'the general right to make a contract in relation to his business is part of the liberty of the individual protected by the Fourteenth Amendment of the Federal Constitution.'

Those words are from the Opinion of the Court by Justice Peckham in the case of Lochner v. New York in 1905, in which a State law limiting the hours a baker might contract to work to ten hours a day and sixty hours a week was declared contrary to the 'liberty of contract': 'We do not believe in the soundness of the views which uphold this law. . . . Statutes of the nature under review . . . are mere meddlesome interferences with the rights of the individual.' In such circumstances no process could be due process.

Justice Holmes, dissenting, wrote that it was not the duty of the Court to agree or disagree with an economic theory. 'The Fourteenth Amendment does not enact Mr. Herbert Spencer's Social Statics. . . . a Constitution is not intended to embody a particular economic theory, whether of paternalism . . . or of laissez faire.' The statute did not obviously 'infringe fundamental principles as they have been understood by the traditions of our people and our law'; and, therefore, whatever the Justices thought of its merits, it should be allowed.

After 1937 the latter judicial attitude to economic regulation, Federal or State, prevailed; but from 1925 the Supreme Court interpreted the due process clause of the Fourteenth Amendment so as to apply to the States protections of civil liberties specified in the Federal Bill of Rights. This interpretation has come to embrace almost all such protections.

Despite clauses like 'Congress shall make no law . . . abridging the freedom of speech' (in the First Amendment), none of the constitutional protections as applied by the courts is absolute. However, unusual justification—the showing of a 'compelling' public interest—is required for a government to be allowed to regulate the freedom of speech or other protected liberties, confine the procedural rights of accused persons, or deny the equal protection of the laws (whether in regulating private activities or in bestowing the favours of government on persons) in fields subject to exacting judicial scrutiny.

Judicial enforcement of the equal protection clause of the Fourteenth Amendment has been especially associated with the civil rights of blacks, as in the case of Brown *v*. Board of Education of Topeka in 1954 declaring the segregation of races in publicly maintained schools to be *per se* unconstitutional. Since there is no equivalent explicit clause applying to the Federal Government, the due process clause of the Fifth Amendment has been interpreted as including the requirement of 'equal protection'. In the case of Bolling *v*. Sharpe in 1954, involving the District of Columbia, Chief Justice Warren wrote for the unanimous court that 'we have this day held that the equal protection clause of the Fourteenth Amendment prohibits the States from maintaining racially segregated public schools. . . . it would be unthinkable that the same Constitution would impose a lesser duty on the Federal Government. We hold that racial segregation in the public schools of the District of Columbia is a denial of the due process of law guaranteed by the Fifth Amendment to the Constitution.'

Thus, one way or another, the due process clauses of the Fifth and Fourteenth Amendments have been held to protect from both the Federal and State levels of government most of the personal rights otherwise explicitly protected in the Constitution from only one or the other of the levels. In the federal system the State level includes all local government, too.

D: THE STATE CONSTITUTIONS

The Constitution of the United States, including its amendments, runs to between 7,000 and 8,000 words. At the end of 1975 (to which time, unless otherwise indicated, all the data in this section refer) the median length of the 50 State Constitutions was over 21,000 words. Only two were shorter than or as short as the Federal Constitution. When replaced by a new Constitution of 26,300 words in 1974, the Louisiana Constitution was estimated to run to 256,500 words. At the end of 1975 the Georgia Constitution was estimated to run to 600,000.

The greater length of the typical State Constitution, as compared with the Federal Constitution, is basically due to the greater detail about the framework of government and many more definitions of public policies contained in it. Its text expands by much more frequent amendment, though the increase in length is sometimes temporarily reversed by the adoption of a new Constitution consolidating the text as well as making changes of substance.

Whatever its length, a State Constitution establishes a more complex structure of government than does the Federal Constitution. Paradoxically, this has been a consequence of its starting from a simpler political principle. Within the federal system established by the United States Constitution, that Constitution has to enumerate the powers of the Congress. There is no need for a State Constitution to confer powers on the State legislature, which simply possesses the general power to legislate, within the limits set by the Federal Constitution, subject only to such additional restrictions as are imposed by the State Constitution.

However, a general tendency to distrust government and pressures to protect particular interests have multiplied the restrictions. The State Constitutions contain lists of what State legislatures may not do, or do only in prescribed ways. Just as judicial interpretation by the Federal courts has expanded the grants of powers to the Congress by expanding their implications, so State courts have tended to expand the restrictions on State legislatures. In reaction, provision is made in the State Constitutions to confirm powers that have been or might otherwise be put in doubt by judicial interpretation. The over-all effect is to make State legislators more conscious than Congressmen of constitutionally defined limits on their powers.

The history of the provisions in the State Constitutions about the executive and judicial branches likewise reflects more concern with preventing abuses of government than with establishing effective authority. During the first 100 years and more of American independence, while the independence of the Governor and his veto powers were strengthened in many States as checks on the originally predominant legislature, executive authority was diffused among a number of elective offices and autonomous administrative boards. From the late nineteenth century until recently, Progressive reformers regarded the courts as enemies of social legislation and administrative agencies, and sought to protect the policies and agencies from adverse judicial action. On the other hand, in this century there has been some strengthening of State Governors as the chief executives in the States. In recent decades there has been some simplification of judicial systems.

In general, State Constitutions are documents full of prohibitions and prescriptions designed to restrict the discretion of governmental organs. They limit the taxing and borrowing powers of State and local government, earmark revenues, establish executive departments and independent commissions and define their duties and powers, sometimes set the salaries and hours of work of public officials, regulate school systems, and restrict or prohibit the granting of special charters and other special or private legislation.

Most States have adopted a new Constitution to replace their old one at least once. Comparisons among the States about the number of Constitutions which they have had since entering the Union can be misleading, since a major revision may be a more substantial change than a formal replacement. Nonetheless, Louisiana and Georgia are again extreme cases: Louisiana has had 11 Constitutions since entering the Union in 1812; Georgia has had eight Constitutions since 1777, the most recent dating from 1945. By the end of 1975, 832 amendments had been added to the present Georgia Constitution, 685 of them a species of local legislation that must use the constitutional process. Provisions of the Georgia Constitution of general Statewide applicability accounted for about 64,500 of its 600,000 words.

Popularly elected constitutional conventions whose recommendations are submitted to the voters for ratification have been the principal means for effecting replacements and extensive revisions of State Constitutions. The conventions are usually called by the State legislatures with the approval of the voters. (In fourteen States the question of holding a constitutional convention must periodically be submitted to the electorate.) State legislatures have increasingly sought to control the outputs of the conventions by restricting their terms of reference. They have also increasingly made use of constitutional commissions, composed of appointed and *ex officio* members, for replacing and making major or minor changes in Constitutions. The commissions' proposals are reported to the legislatures for approval before submission to the voters. However, the Florida Constitution of 1968 provides for the periodic establishment of a commission, whose proposals, like those of conventions, go straight on the ballot.

In sixteen States sufficient numbers of voters may put amendments straight on the ballot by initiative (petition), though in Illinois only for changes in the Article on the legislature. By far the largest numbers of amendments, however, are proposed by the State legislatures. All amendments must be approved by the voters, except in Delaware, where they need only to be approved by two-thirds majorities of both Houses of the State legislature in two successive sessions. Most States require unusual majorities (most commonly, two-thirds majorities) and some States approval in two sessions before legislative proposals for constitutional change are submitted for popular ratification.

The proposals usually appear on the ballot for a general election along with the candidates for the numerous offices being filled. Many voters may vote only for candidates for the major offices at stake. Therefore, it is of importance whether the requirement for the voters' approval of a proposal means that it has to be supported only by a majority of those voting on the proposal, or also by a majority or some lesser proportion of all those casting ballots in the election. In most States a simple majority vote for the proposal suffices.

Typically, then, an amendment is initiated by the State legislature and ratified in a referendum in which perhaps only a minority of those casting ballots in the election of which the referendum is a part have voted for the amendment. It may have received little public attention. Once adopted, it may arouse adverse criticism but, typically again, a demand for a repealing amendment looks to legislative initiative. Interests with influence in State legislatures are often able almost unnoticed to put into the Constitutions definitions of public policies or restrictions on governmental action favourable to them. Thereafter, so long as the interests maintain their influence over a sufficient number of legislators—one-third plus one of them in one House where two-thirds majorities are required for proposing an amendment—they can block repeal. Observation has confirmed that the States in which interest groups have most influence over legislators are the States in which the most amendments are proposed and adopted. Their Constitutions are replete with detailed specifications of policies and protections of particular interests.

The public policies defined in constitutional provisions range as widely in subject matter as those in statutes. Privately owned public utilities, insurance companies and other businesses that have been especially subject to State regulation promote amendments to secure favourable regulation of their rates and responsibilities. Churches and ex-servicemen's organizations secure constitutional tax exemptions. Depending on the balance of political forces or, for the pressures to be most effective, imbalance of political forces from State to State, Constitutions may protect the rights of trade unions or the 'right to work' (prohibiting the closed shop). They define various restrictions or privileges relating to the sale of intoxicating beverages. The Missouri Constitution prescribes a tax in aid of the deserving blind. The Oklahoma Constitution requires schools to teach the 'elements of agriculture, horticulture, stockfeeding, and domestic science'.

There is a law and custom of the Constitution in each State; but the law tends to predominate even more than at the Federal level, because the State Constitutions are more detailed and frequently amended and because as a consequence of the greater detail there is much more scope for closer judicial supervision of political practices. Three of the principles of the Constitution of the United States, which were present in State Constitutions before 1787, are incorporated in the Constitutions of the fifty States: the republican form of government, the separation of powers, and the protection of personal rights.

The republican form of government in the States is usually associated with many opportunities for the electorate to act. In most States there are a number of directly elected executive officers besides the Governor. In most States, too, at least some judges are elected. The large number of elective offices dates from the era of Jacksonian democracy. In recent decades the efforts to improve executive and judicial administration have produced a slight reaction.

In thirty-eight States there are constitutional provisions for referenda on laws submitted to the electorate by the legislature or challenged by petition or both. Twenty-one State Constitutions allow voters to initiate legislation by petition. Usually an initiated proposal must be submitted directly to the electorate, but in some States the legislature is given a chance to enact it first. Thirteen States permit the electors to petition and then vote for the recall of any of the elective officials, except for judges in five of these. Seventeen other States have a recall process available only in local government. Initiative, referendum and recall are devices especially associated with the Progressive reformers' attacks on 'machine politics'. Recall is little used and rarely successful.

The separation of powers in the States, as in the Federal Government, means that the legislative, executive and judicial branches are independent of one another. Nebraska has had a unicameral legislature since 1937. The other State legislatures are bicameral. Until the United States Supreme Court's decisions of the 1960s required that the apportionment for all State legislative chambers be according to population, one of the two Houses was typically a 'little Senate', mainly representing the counties or towns of the State, though the apportionment usually took some account of population: urban centres were grossly under-represented. Because of a failure to re-apportion to adjust to changes in population, the other House also under-represented the cities.

The Governor, as has already been mentioned, is usually only one of several elective executive officers. He is elected for a two-year term in four States, for a four-year term in forty-six. But in eight of these forty-six he may not succeed himself, and in nineteen he can serve no more than two consecutive terms. There are usually constitutional restrictions on the Governor's power to appoint and remove officials, and constitutional provisions establishing departments and agencies that are more or less independent of his control. In three States the Governor acts with a legislative body or as chairman of a board of executive and legislative members in budget making. But the trend has been to strengthen his budgetary powers. In all but a few States the

Governor has the power to veto items in an appropriation bill. In North Carolina, on the other hand, he has no veto power at all. Generally, the separation of powers in the States is characterized by a more intricate set of checks and balances than in the Federal Government.

The protection of personal rights is provided for in State Constitutions by Declarations or Bills of Rights, which are usually much longer than the comparable provisions of the Federal Constitution. Besides substantive freedoms and procedural rights of accused persons, the rights protected may include that of fraternal organizations to sell alcoholic beverages or that of citizens to fish in public waters.

There is *no federal division of powers* in the States, though in most of them there has been a strong tradition of local government. The State Constitution may provide, or authorize the State legislature to provide, opportunities for local communities to exercise a measure of 'home rule' in defining their forms of government. However, constitutional provisions restrict the taxing, borrowing, spending and regulatory powers of local government. Moreover, the powers are usually divided among a variety of overlapping local authorities. Once again the over-all effect is to restrict and disperse the power to govern.

FOR FURTHER READING:

Duane Lockard, *The Politics of State and Local Government*, 2nd ed. (Collier-Macmillan, 1969).

C. Herman Pritchett, *The American Constitutional System*, 4th ed. (McGraw-Hill, 1976).

Martin Shapiro and Rocco J. Tresolini, *American Constitutional Law*, 4th ed. (Macmillan, 1975).

Carl Brent Swisher, *American Constitutional Development*, 2nd ed. (Houghton Mifflin, 1954).

3: Federalism

A: INTERGOVERNMENTAL RELATIONS

The American federal system is designed to give the States making up the Union the maximum amount of independence compatible with the general welfare and constitutional rights of all its citizens. Americans are subject to the laws of the Federal Government and to State laws. Moreover, they come under the authority of a variety of local governments, which exercise important powers under the Constitutions of the States.

What binds these three levels of government together is a set of constitutional and legal rules, financial and political interdependence, and a general belief in decentralized government. All these date back to the origins of the Federal Union in 1789, when the thirteen colonies established a common government on the basis of a compromise between a centralized system and a loose confederation of virtually independent governments. Such a compromise is still in force, but the character of the federal bargain has been adapted to suit the needs of the present day. It is now immensely complex, since the vast growth of governmental powers has been shared between the Federal, State and local governments in a way undreamt of by the Founding Fathers.

These developments have been seen by some as upsetting the balance of the federal system, so that in recent years attempts have been made to reverse this process of centralization. But despite the changes over the years, the system of government in the United States is still considered by observers throughout the world to be a model of 'true' federalism, in which the central government and the States have real independence of one another, and where the Constitution as interpreted by the Supreme Court is the final authority above them all.

Federalism today

The Constitution gives some indication of the relative powers of the Federal and State levels of government, but it is not a complete guide to the operation of these powers today. For this, it is necessary to look at the range of modern governmental functions and how these are shared between the different levels. For example, such clauses in the Constitution as those relating to the federal power to provide for 'the general welfare' (Art. I, sec. 8) and to 'the equal protection of the laws' (Fourteenth Amendment, sec. 1) have come to include 'the welfare state' and 'civil rights' in modern politics. In both cases, the Federal Government has gained powers in practice, while apparently staying where it is in constitutional terms.

The States, similarly, have had to face up to the new meaning given to the constitutional limits on their powers. They can no longer escape Federal regulation in manufacturing, labour relations, education and elections. But they have also taken on a vastly increased burden of government, as the demands of citizens for more and more services have grown. It is perhaps paradoxical that during a period of increasing Federal power and centralization, State and local budgets have grown more than the Federal budget in domestic affairs, and civilian employment in government has increased more at State and local level than at Federal level.

State and local expenditures increased sevenfold between 1950 and 1972, while Federal expenditures increased fourfold. In the late 1960s, half of the Federal budget went on defence, though by the mid-1970s this was down to below one-third. Of just under 3 million civilian employees in the Federal Government, around half are in activities related to defence and foreign policy. Another quarter are in the Post Office, so that three-quarters of the civilian employees of the Federal Government are still involved in the two traditional functions of the Federal branch: national security and the postal services.

In contrast, most domestic functions are in the hands of the States, and under them, the local authorities. Together these employ over 11 million people, a total which more than doubled between 1950 and 1972, while Federal civilian employment rose only slightly. Local authorities employ three times as many people (most of whom are in education) as the States. Schools are locally administered, while the States employ university and college staffs (there are also a large number of private universities and colleges). One in ten State and local employees is in health services, and roads and police take up another tenth. Nine-tenths of the police are working for local government, with employment on health and roads shared equally between the States and localities.

These figures stress the growing importance of the States and local governments. But there is another side which is not evident from State expenditures and employment, and that is the growing dependence on Federal finance and the greater degree of policy direction from Washington.

Since the 1930s, the proportion of total government expenditures derived from Federal Government revenues has overtaken that of the States and localities, and is now about three-fifths. Much of this money is not spent by the Federal Government itself but by the States and local governments, in the form of Federal grants-in-aid. These amount to about a quarter of State and local expenditures today, and take up a fifth of Federal outlays. As recently as 1965, only 15 per cent of State and local spending was Federally subsidized, and ten years before that, 10 per cent. In 1972, local governments were dependent on the States for 36 per cent of their expenditures, much of it ultimately financed by Federal grants-in-aid, and received another 3 per cent direct from the Federal Government.

These developments are the result of the demand for more government services, and the stronger financial capability of the higher levels of government. There was a large expansion of 'welfare' legislation during President F. D. Roosevelt's New Deal of the 1930s, and President L. B. Johnson's 'Great Society' of the 1960s. Both these programmes of reform were extremely expensive to operate, and the Federal Government had to shoulder much of the burden in policy areas which were previously the responsibility of the States.

The taxing power under the Constitution is a concurrent one, shared between the Federal Government and the States, and the Federal Government has been able to draw on the entire wealth of the United States for its revenue. Individual States are limited by their own resources, and may be unable or unwilling to raise taxes to a high level. In any case, the Federal tax cannot be avoided, and States must shape their own taxes in the light of Federal demands.

Nearly three-fifths of all taxes are raised by the Federal Government, mostly in the form of income tax, corporation tax and customs, but also in earmarked social security taxes. The remainder is raised by the States and local governments in equal proportions. The States rely primarily on income and sales taxes (including motor fuel, tobacco and alcohol taxes), while local governments depend principally on property taxes (i.e. rates). But there are some local sales and income taxes (notably in New York City). Nearly a third of State and local revenues derive from non-tax sources such as income from insurance trust funds, public utilities and charges for a wide variety of services. Licences for oil, gas and coal exploration, and revenues from natural resources production fell to the States (except offshore beyond the 'tidelands').

Federal grants-in-aid

The system of Federal grants-in-aid is one of the hallmarks of American federalism, and distinguishes it from federalism in Australia, Canada, and West Germany, in which countries there are more rigid and centralized arrangements for sharing revenues. The U.S. system has preserved more freedom for the States, and they are still not so dependent on central government for finance.

The first major economic resource of the United States government to be expended partly as intergovernmental aid was the public land of the United States. The Morrill Land Grant Act of 1862 provided States with Federal land, the proceeds from which had to be used to establish 'land-grant' colleges and universities. In this century, Federal money, largely derived from Federal income taxes, which were made feasible again by the adoption of the Sixteenth Amendment to the U.S. Constitution in 1913, replaced Federal land. Unlike its resource of land, the Federal Government's resource of money is replenished each year, providing the basis for continuous penetration by the Federal Government downwards into State and local governments. Congress provided for a regular programme of grants-in-aid for highway construction in 1916. Grants for highways made up by far the largest programme of grants to the States until overtaken by public welfare grants after 1933. By 1970, the Federal Government was paying for about three-tenths of public highway expenditure and three-fifths of public welfare expenditure.

The 'New Deal' and 'Great Society' policies of the Federal Government set Federal standards in welfare and civil rights which all the States had to follow, or (in the case of welfare) could ignore only at great cost to their citizens. A typical example of New Deal legislation is the Social Security Act of 1935. This inaugurated Federal old age pensions and survivors' insurance; Federal-State systems of unemployment insurance; aid to States in public assistance for needy persons; and aid to States for maternal and child welfare. Only the first of these programmes is totally Federal, and the others require the voluntary co-operation of the States.

This is somewhat theoretical, however, since the Federal Government can impose a tax and then promise to remit most of it when a State introduces a welfare scheme which conforms to Federal standards. For example, Federal unemployment insurance is financed by the 'tax offset' method, whereby 90 per cent of a Federal payroll tax is remitted when an approved State unemployment insurance scheme is introduced. This does not mean that all States pay the same unemployment benefits, but minimum levels and conditions are laid down by Washington.

More variation occurs in other welfare programmes which are Federally inspired, and financed in part by the Federal Government. Several hundred schemes are financed by Federal 'categorical' or conditional grants, many of which were introduced in the period of the 'Great Society' legislation (1964–8). These relate typically to public assistance, education and urban redevelopment, and are paid by the Federal Government not only to the States, but also to local governments and some voluntary organizations. The grants usually contain conditions which require such bodies to match the Federal financial contribution with a contribution of their own. This imposes more of a burden on poor authorities than on rich, and in the 1960s and 1970s, such conditions were eased in many cases, so that the Federal contribution rose. This now varies between a half and nine-tenths of the money. In 1970, on average, one-third of the money had to be put up by the authority receiving the grant, that is $1 for every $2 of Federal money.

The matching formula may take account of the States' differing abilities to pay. In 1973 the taxpayers of twenty-two States paid more in Federal taxes than their States and localities received in Federal grants. Those in twenty-eight States and the District of Columbia paid less. The grants tend to deal with urban and poverty problems, and this, together with the formula used in allocating funds, redistributes resources from rich to poor authorities.

All these categorical grants carry strings related to the substantive purposes of the programme. But there are also general conditions applying to all Federal grants. The requirement that the officials of State and local agencies receiving Federal aid must be in civil service merit systems (as opposed to 'spoils' patronage appointments) has been the chief means by which such systems have been extended in most States. In some States about the only personnel in merit systems are those in agencies financed by Federal grants. Another requirement is that there should be no racial or ethnic discrimination among State and local personnel administering Federally-financed programmes.

Nevertheless, State and local civil servants are never the subordinates of Federal administrators. They are not 'hired and fired' by Federal Departments, and the sanctions against them are lawsuits, which are cumbersome, or the withholding of grants, which is likely to inflict most damage on the innocent beneficiaries of the services. The latter sanction is so severe that it can sometimes be threatened but only very rarely used—and then only temporarily in order to produce some sort of accommodation in programmes the Federal Government wants carried out as much as the States and localities.

New forms of Federal grant have been introduced. In 1968, the Partnership for Health Act and the Safe Streets legislation introduced 'block grants', giving wider discretion to States and local governments in the use of Federal money, within the scope of specific programmes. Most States already had legislation in the areas covered by Federal programmes, and the use of grants-in-aid shows that the Federal Government does not wish to supplant the responsibilities of the States and local governments, rather to help them to perform services felt desirable by the Federal Government. This, however, has meant that national objectives have come to replace State objectives, and that the States have come to depend on Federal finance for their own political well-being.

Revenue sharing

In 1972, the State and Local Fiscal Assistance Act established 'general revenue sharing' for an initial five-year period. A proportion of grants now came with few strings attached. This proportion was 13 per cent of total Federal grants in 1975, compared with 87 per cent in categorical and block grants. Congress laid down a strict formula for the distribution of 'revenue sharing' grants to States and local governments, which took account of population, tax effort by State and local governments, and the income level of the population. One-third of the grant goes to the State, and two-thirds to the local government in that State. About 37,000 local governments are in receipt of revenue sharing money, but this amounts to no more than 10 per cent of their direct expenditure. The 'tax-effort' clause of the formula (i.e. local tax level as a percentage of potential tax level) is hardest to enlarge for the poorest cities, and so the annual allocation often dropped each year for those most hard pressed.

Revenue sharing marks a major departure, in political terms, for Federal relations. It represents a shift away from Federal controls to State and local autonomy. As we have seen, however, it can be claimed that the funds are not being directed primarily to the areas of greatest need. Instead, they are also subsidizing local governments which are already well off. This seems to be the result of aiming at a politically acceptable 'share-out' of Federal funds, and the relaxation of Federal controls. Revenue sharing is described as 'handing back power to the States'. It may be a turning point in American federalism, or it may be an unsuccessful attempt to stem the tide towards centralization and uniformity in social policy.

The Federal Government has also penetrated downwards into the traditional concerns of the States and localities by mandatory laws as well as with conditional grants of money. Under the Federal 'interstate commerce' power, food is inspected, wages, hours of work and collective bargaining regulated, and racial discrimination in public accommodations prohibited. Federal laws strike at narcotics peddling and organized crime.

The politics of federalism

Various labels have been attached to the successive phases in American federalism, and they indicate the growing interdependence of the levels of government. The classical interpretation of the Constitution was one of 'dual federalism', which meant that the Federal Government and the States were each sovereign authorities within their own constitutional spheres. Neither level could dictate to the other or destroy its existence. Thus the Federal Government could not alter the boundaries of States without the consent of the legislature of the States concerned (Art. IV, sec. 3). Nor could the States destroy the Federal Union, or impair the functioning of the Federal Government under the Constitution (Art. VI). Of more practical significance, it implied that while the Federal Government was concerned with foreign affairs and commerce moving across State lines, the States were to be left to regulate their internal economies and social (including race) relations.

This doctrine of federalism seemed to match the nineteenth-century practice of American government, although it was never strictly adhered to. For example, there were many 'concurrent' powers, such as taxation and the regulation of commerce, shared between the Federal Government and States. This sharing of power within the same spheres of authority led to the development of the idea of 'co-operative federalism', a phrase that became current during the New Deal period and afterwards. It was especially appropriate to the practice of Federal grants to the States, and State administration of Federal policy discussed before.

President L. B. Johnson (1963–9) talked of 'Creative Federalism', which encompassed not only the States but the local governments as well. Under his 'Great Society' programme, grants were paid direct to local governments, as well as through the States. Thus, 'Creative Federalism' meant a direct relationship between the Federal Government and local authorities (including voluntary organizations and private bodies). After Johnson, President Nixon introduced his 'New Federalism', the principal feature of which was the revenue sharing legislation of 1972.

Apart from 'welfare state' policies, Federal-State relations have been powerfully affected by the civil rights court decisions and legislation of the 1950s and 1960s. These have limited the scope of State independence, and strengthened the Federal Government. It is no longer possible for States to pursue race discrimination policies in education, employment, housing or public facilities. State laws relating to voting rights are now not only unconstitutional if they discriminate on racial or sex grounds: the constituencies must be as equal as possible in size. All this adds up to a considerable diminution in State independence, as compared with the period before the 1950s.

Americans have been prepared to give the Federal Government general legitimacy in setting national standards and goals. But in granting such legitimacy to the Federal authority, Americans still hark back to 'limited government' and decentralization. The Federal Government can go only so far in taking over the functions previously managed by the States, and it will usually do so carefully through 'co-operative' devices. Only in times of real emergency will it act decisively and against the clearly stated wishes of the elected representatives of the States and local governments.

The position of the States in the Federal system is further safeguarded by the many constitutional provisions which preserve their power. In the Senate each State has two Senators, irrespective of size. The electoral college for the President gives extra weighting to the small States. No constitutional amendment may be passed without three-quarters of the States consenting. The Constitution enumerates the Federal powers, while leaving the remainder to the States 'or to the people'. In the crucial area of revenue, the Federal Government cannot force the States to adopt any particular taxation policy, and its control over the national economy is subject to the constitutional freedom of the States to tax, borrow and lend as they wish. They may not, however, increase the money supply by printing banknotes. That is a power possessed solely by the Federal Government.

The extra-constitutional parts of the political process also enhance the States' position. The parties are highly decentralized, and operate most effectively at State and local level. The States determine the nominating procedures for U.S. Senators and Representatives as well as State and local elective officeholders. They set up the presidential primaries. The four-yearly party conventions to nominate presidential candidates give great power to State delegations, who bargain their votes for political favours. National issues are intermingled with local issues, and presidential election campaigns have had to deal with schools, law and order, and the distribution of public welfare relief, which are primarily the administrative responsibility of State and local governments. Similarly, Presidents must cultivate support in the State parties. President Kennedy was assassinated in November 1963 on a trip to Texas to try to patch up a quarrel in the State Democratic Party which might have hurt his prospects in the State in the 1964 presidential election.

U.S. Congressmen pay more attention to constituency considerations than they do to party discipline or national politics. State delegations are formed in Congress to press for favourable Federal policies towards their States. If a large administrative apparatus is required to implement a new Federal programme, it is often as convenient and as politically acceptable to look to State and local governments as to the established Federal agencies.

In part, this is because Congress is more uneasy about any growth of a Federal bureaucracy than it is about the growth of State and local administration. But even the Federal bureaucracy is relatively decentralized from Washington, and career officials tend to identify with their regions rather than with Washington, and with their programmes and agencies rather than with the Federal Government as such. This involves them with a wide variety of State and local officials, whose co-operation is essential to the success of their agencies. They are also closely connected with Congressional committees and, of course, with the clients of the services themselves. Shifting more power to Washington in this 'clientele politics' would be a largely bogus centralization, and one which would produce few political gains.

On the other hand, the attempts to return functions entirely to the States have failed. For when proposals for such decentralization begin to move from talk to reality, the States are political losers. Decentralization would result in fewer public programmes —which is why conservatives want to remove the Federal elements—or heavy increases in State taxes, or both. But State taxes are based less on a progressive income tax than are Federal taxes. It is politically less painful for Congress to hold tax rates steady, and take in more with the rise in incomes, during periods of growing prosperity (or inflation) than it is for States to raise their tax rates. This truth prompted the proposals for 'revenue sharing'. Moreover, the policy makers of individual States and localities fear that raising their taxes would drive industry and wealthier people elsewhere, while raising their welfare services would draw poorer people in from less generous authorities, in the free market of goods and movement of people in the United States. All these factors give 'co-operative federalism' great political strength, and made it resistant to anything more than minor changes.

Interstate relations

The relationship among the States themselves is a further aspect of federalism. The Constitution states that 'Full Faith and Credit shall be given in each State to the public Acts, Records, and judicial Proceedings of every other State' (Art. IV, sec. 1). The citizens of each State are entitled to the 'Privileges and Immunities of Citizens in the several States', and criminals fleeing from one State into another ought to be returned to the State in which the crime was committed, if the government of that State so demands (Art. IV, sec. 2).

These clauses have not been strictly adhered to. Divorces granted in Nevada or Florida may not be recognized in other States unless a bona fide residence is established in the State where the divorce took place. Similar cases arise over alimony payments and the custody of children. State licences are issued to doctors, lawyers and teachers, and the licences of other States may not be considered valid. Students who are residents of a State are usually charged lower fees at their state university than those who are not residents. Extradition of criminals is rarely refused, but the Supreme Court has not tried to compel any State which has refused to do so. It is, however, against Federal law for anyone to move from State to State in order to avoid arrest, and most States have agreed among themselves a uniform extradition law.

'Uniform laws' and 'interstate compacts' are a significant feature of modern American federalism. They indicate a growing co-operation among the States, similar to that of Federal-State 'co-operative federalism', but by no means as well developed, or as important politically. Uniform laws tend to deal with commercial matters, such as stock transfer or negotiable instruments. Interstate compacts are more important, and are allowed under the Constitution, if Congress consents. In practice, this consent is not necessary, unless Federal power is affected. There are now over 160 of these compacts, comprising agreements on matters ranging from water, pollution, and conservation to social welfare. Two of the best known are the compact which set up the Port Authority of New York (1921) and the Delaware Basin River Compact (1961). The Port Authority was established by New York State and New Jersey, and the Delaware Compact includes not only the States of Delaware, New York, New Jersey and Pennsylvania, but also the Federal Government itself. It is concerned with water resource problems in the Delaware River.

The States come together in a variety of organizations. The

most prominent is the annual National Governors' Conference, in which the Governors of the fifty States meet to discuss State interests. They have been vocal in recent years in their support of Federal revenue sharing. Other important conferences are the Council of State Governments and the National Legislative Conference. At local government level, there is the U.S. Conference of Mayors, the National Association of Counties, the National League of Cities, and the International City Management Association.

B: STATE AND LOCAL GOVERNMENTS

The full dimension of intergovernmental relations in the United States is seen in the number of governments in the country. There are today over 78,000 such governments, although twenty-five years ago there were as many as 102,000.

Table 3.1:
governments of the United States

	1957	1975
Federal	I	I
States	48	50
Local Governments	102,341	78,218
Counties	3,050	3,044
Municipalities	17,215	18,517
Townships	17,198	16,991
School districts	50,424	15,781
Special districts	14,424	23,885

Local Governments have declined numerically, but this has been almost entirely due to the drop in school districts. Special districts, on the other hand, have risen considerably, with other local governments remaining much the same.

The States

What do these governments do, and how are they run? Each

State has its own Constitution, almost always a much longer document than the Federal Constitution, and typically containing a long list of things which the State legislature and other institutions may or may not do (see Chapter 2, Section D). Unlike the broad delineation of governmental powers in the U.S. Constitution, a State Constitution usually gives in minute detail what is legally permissible. For example, the form of State taxation and the limits of State borrowing are laid out. When a State wishes to borrow money by issuing bonds, it may require to amend its Constitution or to consult the people in a referendum. State Constitutions establish the local government system, including the administration and content of education through school boards.

Quite often, a State Constitution reflects a particular party or interest group domination, and battles are frequently waged by aggrieved citizens to amend the Constitution. Taxpayers' groups, businessmen, war veterans and farmers are often responsible for writing clauses in State Constitutions to their own benefit. Trade unions and central city populations, on the other hand, are frequently disadvantaged. This gives a somewhat conservative character to State government, in marked contrast to some city governments, such as that of New York, where generous social welfare and free and open university education have been in operation. Yet there are States whose laws have been more progressive or innovatory than those of the Federal Government, and have served as a model for Federal legislation. Modern income tax, for example, began in the United States in Wisconsin and Mississippi in 1911, before the Federal Government's tax in 1913. Retail sales tax and value-added tax also began in the States, as did unemployment and health insurance.

The most telling indication of State power is control over education. Federal involvement in education is essentially through assistance to the States and local governments in the form of grants, rather than the prescription of a national system of education. Even this aid amounts to under 8 per cent of school revenues, with the remainder being split equally between State and local sources. Including higher education, Federal involvement is now about one-seventh of public expenditure on education. It provided, as we have seen, land grants for agricultural and technical colleges. To ease the burden on States where Federal defence establishments increase school enrolments, it gives grants to such schools. It subsidizes courses and provides loans and fellowships to university students. To assist the 'Anti-Poverty Program' it subsidizes schools whose enrolments include a high proportion of poor children. To maintain civil rights it requires desegregation and 'busing'.

All other aspects of education are very much in the hands of the States. States lay down the system of education to be adopted; whether schooling is compulsory or not (since 1918 all States have had compulsory education), and to what age. They prescribe the qualifications of the teachers and may set minimum salaries; they can determine the courses and exams, and even in some cases, the textbooks. Most university students attend State universities, which are financially maintained by the State governments; about 30 per cent attend private institutions. There is no central government direction of higher education, as there is in Britain or France.

Education is the domestic function most completely retained by the States, but civil and criminal law follow closely on. Each State has its own system of law, subject only to Federal law and the U.S. Constitution. This leaves such matters as murder, theft, and traffic offences as part of State jurisdiction. In civil law, marriage and divorce and most forms of property law, including the charters for business corporations, are virtually untouched by Federal legislation. State and local governments deal with the vast mass of litigation, employ nearly all police, and maintain nearly all prisons. Considerable variety exists between the States in their legal systems, their prosecuting practices, and their prison populations.

The structure of government in the States reproduces the principle of 'separation of powers' which is found at Federal level. The chief executive is the Governor. Unlike the President of the United States, the Governor is hamstrung by the direct election of other executive officials, who may not be inclined to co-operate in his policies. Such elective officials are the Attorney General (in forty-two States), the State Treasurer (thirty-nine

States), State Auditor (twenty-five States), and the more formal posts of Lieutenant Governor (rather similar to Vice-President, forty-one States), and Secretary of State (keeper of State records and State electoral officer, thirty-eight States). Other elected officials in certain States include Superintendents of Education, Public Utilities Commissioners and Agriculture Commissioners.

In most States, appointments by the Governor require confirmation by the Senate of the State legislature. There are many boards and commissions to be appointed, and the Governor is limited in his choice of members by the frequent requirement that they should possess some technical or geographic qualifications. The terms of appointment quite often run for several years, with overlapping expiry dates. Dismissals are difficult, and may require impeachment. These 'buffer boards' were created in order to take their activities out of politics in an era when the spoils system was prevalent. But today, they tend to weaken the power of the Governor to initiate policy changes.

The State legislature is also weak in comparison with the Federal Congress. Sessions are short. In seventeen States the State legislature sits only every second year. There is more 'direct democracy' in the States. Nearly half give the people the right to initiate legislation by petition, or challenge its enactment. The use of referendums has already been mentioned. In twelve States the Governor and other State officials can be 'recalled' by popular vote before their term of office expires. Only one Governor, however, has been recalled, in 1921, and he was quickly elected to the U.S. Senate.

Despite its weaknesses, a State legislature can oppose a Governor effectively, and it is not unusual for a deadlock to persist, to the detriment of the State. The Governor is the one political figure who clearly represents the whole State, and not sectional interests. He will probably have to stand up for the central cities in their battles for State aid and welfare legislation, while the legislature will favour the suburbs and rural areas. The re-apportionment of seats in State legislatures in the 1960s merely emphasized this division. For, while removing rural dominance, it increased suburban representation, and provided a new alliance between suburbs and rural areas.

The Governor is responsible for the State budget in forty-six States (three others have budget boards or committees, and Arkansas uses a legislative council), and, with the exception of North Carolina, he possesses the power of veto over bills, and in four-fifths of States over clauses of bills. This latter power is not possessed by the U.S. President. On the other hand, a simple majority in the State legislature may overrule the Governor's veto in some States, although most copy the Federal Congress's two-thirds requirement.

States vary according to whether their constitutions provide for 'strong' or 'weak' Governors, but in comparison with the President of the United States the Governor is not a powerful executive, and his weakness limits the effectiveness of State governments. Yet a State governorship continues to provide a power base for securing recognition in national affairs. Perhaps to compensate for their difficulties at home, some State Governors seek recognition as national politicians. Governor Nelson Rockefeller of New York, Governor George Wallace of Alabama, Governor Ronald Reagan of California and Governor Jimmy Carter of Georgia are recent examples of State-based politicians who have achieved prominence in national politics. A Governor of a State, like the President of the United States, is looked to to deal with major crises, whatever his formal powers in relation to them. In 1975, Governor Hugh Carey of New York State was largely responsible for 'bailing out' New York City from its insolvency.

The localities

A further limitation on State government is its fragmentation through the system of devolution to local authorities. There are around 78,000 local authorities in the United States, ranging from those of the great cities of New York and Los Angeles to those of the tiny New England townships. There are 16,000 school boards, alongside the municipalities, township and county authorities. These are all separately elected bodies. In addition, there are 24,000 'special district' authorities, which are typically set up to run public utilities such as bridges, ports, tunnels, roads, and refuse collection, or to administer grant programmes. Americans live under a 'two-tier' or 'multi-tier' system of local government.

All the powers of local government come to them from the States, as they are creatures of the States. But in practice many have been granted 'home rule' or are politically immune to State interference. This is most clearly seen in the failure to reform local government through reorganization and the creation of larger authorities. While reorganization is technically within the power of the State, it has nearly always proved unacceptable to public opinion, and to the vested interests of the existing authorities. The exceptions are independent school districts, which have declined from 127,000 in 1932 to 16,000 in 1972.

Many traditions of American local government derive from an essentially rural or small-town environment. In most of the West and South the county is the basic unit, while in the New England States the town—a community with its surrounding countryside —is commonly found. Most municipalities in the United States are small villages, boroughs or cities. In 1970 only about a third of them (6,000) were cities with more than 2,500 inhabitants, and only 400 had 50,000 or more.

Nevertheless, over 70 per cent of the American population live in 'metropolitan areas', which are typically old cities ('central cities') with a vast suburban hinterland. In 1972, there were 264 'standard metropolitan statistical areas', which contained within them 440 counties, 5,500 municipalities and over 16,000 other local governments—a grand total of over 22,000 units. Thirty-two metropolitan areas, with over a fifth of the American population, contained parts of more than one State.

Urban problems have come to dominate American social and political life since the 1960s. Yet many of these problems are not necessarily 'urban' at all. They are often facets of more general developments, albeit concentrated within the cities. Some show themselves as aspects of race relations, arising from the movement of blacks and Puerto Ricans to northern cities, with the consequent alarm of the white citizens. Others are economic, such as the level of unemployment, and are related to the economies of regions as well as cities. The general problem of inequalities in tax burdens between citizens of different communities is especially seen in the cities and suburbs. The cities find it difficult to sustain adequate public services, even when taxing their citizens heavily. The suburbs, with fewer demands for public expenditure, are also the most able to pay, since they are largely middle-class.

On top of this there is the general complexity of American government, with its divisions of powers and its multiplicity of authorities. In the urban context, there are so many different bodies with competing and overlapping jurisdictions that the result has been virtual administrative chaos. The line of responsibility which runs from the people to the agencies which 'deliver' the services is in many cases totally obscured. This is because so many are joint authorities or non-elected boards. But even this is not a peculiarly 'urban' problem, since it is reproduced, admittedly to a lesser degree, throughout the system of government. What makes it most inappropriate in the context of the cities is the fact that the combination of pressing problems of various kinds points to the need for a controlling authority with wide powers, which is at the same time accountable to the electorate. Such a body is usually conspicuously absent in American cities.

Perhaps as a reaction to the failure of city governments to cope with their problems, these problems have been redefined as 'national' ones. The President and Congress have introduced numerous programmes designed to deal with housing, local employment, social welfare, law and order, race relations, urban transportation, pollution, and so on. Most of these programmes date from the 1960s. Unfortunately, their implementation has been subject to so many obstacles that the end result has often seemed to be paralysis.

It could be said that many of the 'needs' of the cities point to 'solutions' which are particularly difficult to realize in the United States. This is not just a matter of the structure of government, but of the acceptable content of politics. For example, the creation of municipal housing on a large scale has not taken place, but instead it is more usual to offer financial aid to prospective house buyers or renters. This means that the poorest citizens tend to remain in the slums. Public transportation services are difficult to provide on a comprehensive and profitable basis when so many own cars. The ideal of equal opportunity in education, probably only attainable through national standards and centralized finance, is almost impossible to achieve in a decentralized system. Wealthy suburban districts can afford to pay their teachers more and provide better buildings and teaching materials than can the poor districts in the cities. Finally, urban renewal depends on a degree of planning and direction which will not be achieved so long as there is a strong desire to avoid centralization and the break-up of existing authorities.

Nevertheless, the decade from 1964 saw strenuous efforts at all levels of government to tackle these difficulties. The Federal Government established hundreds of programmes, with generous funds attached, which could be taken up by the States and local governments if they wished. Acts were passed on Model Cities (1966), Housing and Urban Development (1968), Urban Mass Transportation (1964 and 1970), and numerous other subjects, each spawning grants-in-aid and administrative agencies. Local governments were encouraged by the Federal Government to come together in regional Councils of Government (COGs) to co-ordinate their plans with those of the Federal Government Departments.

Behind all this activity there was the constant fear that society was breaking down in the cities, and indeed for a time in the 1960s this seemed to be the case, with race riots across the country. Great strains were caused by the movements of population—the blacks to the north, the middle class to the suburbs. Business was shifting out of the centres of the cities to be near the homes of middle-class employees. Thus, while the Federal Government moved into the cities, the old inhabitants were moving out.

It could be that the system of government in the urban and suburban areas has reached a new 'equilibrium' as a result. Increasingly, the picture is one of impoverished central city authorities propped up by the Federal (and to some extent State) Government, and a ring of prosperous middle-class suburbs surrounding them. The equilibrium is, however, based more on the segregation of social classes than was the old system, which was along urban-rural lines. This makes it just as difficult to reform local government in order to create 'metropolitan' authorities with executive rather than just 'co-ordinating' powers. Such reforms are resisted not only by the privileged suburban dwellers, but by many of the city dwellers as well. Blacks, for example, who are concentrated in many central cities, resist the merging of city authorities in metropolitan ones, since they might lose political control through the addition of white suburban voters. City officials are also reluctant to exchange the patronage system which nurtured them for an entirely different power structure. The same can be said about the interests of the suburbs. In this way, the force of inertia is maintained in American local government, at some considerable cost to the condition of the cities.

The structure of government at the local level varies with the size and type of community. Most large cities adopt the 'strong Mayor' and Council system, which resembles the 'separation of powers' at Federal and State levels. The city councils are not large bodies, with New York City council having under forty councillors, and Los Angeles, a city of 3 million people, only fifteen. The Mayor is directly elected, and can be a figure of considerable importance. Former Mayor John Lindsay of New-York, for example, was a politician of national stature, and was considered as a potential Presidential candidate. Mayor Richard Daley of Chicago, besides running his own city as a political 'boss' of the Democratic Party, was influential in determining the course of events at the Democratic National Convention in Chicago in 1968.

But these 'strong Mayors' are often tarnished and weakened by the web of corruption and poverty that surrounds American city administration. The Knapp Commission on the police of New York City (1971) uncovered a network of bribery and illegal practices in all sections of the police force, which Mayor Lindsay seemed powerless to tackle effectively. Much the same can be said of the failures of the cities to deal with crime, the slums, refuse collection and public transport. Because these problems are concentrated in the urban areas, the record of local government appears much worse than that of the States or Federal Government. Yet this record comes from a combination of lack of resources and governmental inefficiency. The cities need more money (which they cannot raise themselves), and they need better forms of government. Subsidies from the States and Federal Government can alleviate the former deficiency, but structural reform is the answer to the latter.

The financial collapse of New York City in 1975 was an extreme case of the big city problem. New York had suffered for many years from its position as a port for immigrants and a magnet for the poor, who were attracted in part by the city's generous welfare provision. Successive Mayors and city councils built up political support through cultivating a clientele among the underprivileged poor and privileged city employees. The latter enjoyed high wages and pensions, while staying immune from tight administrative controls because of the multiplicity of separate boards and commissions under which they worked. The collapse of the city led to the transfer of effective financial control to independent bodies under the supervision of the State Government, and also brought in Federal support to prevent financial bankruptcy. Reforms of the structure and powers of local government in the city will be needed in the long term, and this points to a more effective State interest in the problems of the city. Since 'upstate' interests in New York are often hostile to the central city, this requires a political as well as a constitutional change.

Cities with under 500,000 inhabitants have tended to avoid the 'strong mayor' pattern of government, and half of the cities from 25,000 to 500,000 have a 'city manager' administration. The aim here is to establish non-partisan government, with a business-type executive in charge of running the affairs of the city. A small council, usually between five and nine councillors, elected on a non-party basis, appoints the manager and determines the main lines of policy to be adopted. The manager prepares the budget, and may himself initiate policy proposals.

This type of local government first attracted attention in Dayton, Ohio in 1914, and was seen as the way to avoid the traditional corruption of the 'party boss' city administration. Its applicability is, however, limited to small or medium-sized cities with a cohesive social structure. In such localities (usually predominantly middle-class), party politics are not deemed necessary, and a strong consensus prevails. The same holds true for many county governments, where elected boards of commissioners take on the combined functions of a council and executive. Such types of local government present stark contrasts to the turbulent politics of the large cities, and illustrate a duality in American life which is growing more marked with time. On the one hand, conflict and corruption, and on the other, consensus and business efficiency.

This brief account of the States and local authorities has indicated the diversity which these bodies present, historically, socially and in their governmental structures. Americans value a decentralized form of government, in part because they consider that all forms of government are a 'necessary evil', and that 'Big Government' in Washington is more to be feared than the more accessible forms at State and local level. At the same time, they are reluctant to give up any of the benefits of Federal programmes as a result of 'returning powers to the States'. Thus Goldwater's anti-centralist campaign in 1964, and Nixon's pruning of Federal grants in 1973 did not gain much popular support.

Federalism, in old-fashioned language, divides power between the central government and the 'sovereign States'. The cities, counties and townships typify 'local self-rule', and the education of Americans is dominated by 'grassroots democracy' in the school boards. But nationalism is also a potent force, and no State commands the emotional ties which the citizen feels for the United States as a whole. However locally administered a school may be, it supports the 'nationalizing' process through its curriculum and its use of the flag as a symbol of patriotism. The President of the United States is the most salient (if not today always the most revered) political figure throughout the fifty States. The Supreme Court remains the most trusted body in the land. These institutions bind together the nation of 215 million people (1976) and 78,000 governments in a Federal Union of great strength.

FOR FURTHER READING:

Thomas R. Dye: *Politics in States and Communities*, 2nd ed. (Prentice-Hall, New Jersey, 1973).

Daniel R. Grant and H. C. Nixon: *State and Local Government in America*, 3rd ed. (Allyn and Bacon, Boston, 1975).

R. P. Nathan, A. D. Manvel, S. E. Calkins: *Monitoring Revenue Sharing*. (Brookings Institution, New York, 1975).

Ira Sharkansky: *The Maligned States: their accomplishments, problems, and opportunities* (McGraw-Hill, New York, 1972).

4: The Electoral System

The electoral system as outlined in the Constitution has been enlarged and changed by Federal and State legislation and made operational by political parties. It has contributed profoundly to the development and maintenance of several characteristic features of party systems in the nation and in the States. Many critical aspects of the electoral system came within the sphere of State legislation and administration until the middle of the twentieth century. In the 1950s and 1960s the system became the subject of intense legal and political controversy as individual citizens, the Federal Government and the Supreme Court were involved in attempts to change such elements as the qualification and disqualification of voters, the apportionment of national and State legislative districts, access of minor parties to the ballot in presidential elections and the regulation of the financial aspects of election campaigns. The discretion of the States has been considerably reduced as a substantial nationalization of the electoral process took place.

The changes have, moreover, had considerable political impact: for example, black voter registration, previously greatly restricted by discriminatory laws in most Southern States, doubled between 1965 and 1970; and the number of blacks elected to public office throughout the United States increased from under 200 in 1960 to 3,503 in 1970. The topics discussed below include the size of the electoral system, the operation of the electoral college and its effects upon the party system, the apportionment 'revolution', and regulations governing the right to vote, access to the ballot and the financing of campaigns.

A: SIZE AND COMPLEXITY
OF THE ELECTORAL SYSTEM

There were over 522,000 elected public officials in the United States in 1967, 521,758 at State and local government levels. The American electorate is required to vote more frequently and to fill many more public offices than its British counterpart. This fact, the product of federalism, the complicated structures of State and local governments, the separation of executive and legislature, and a preference for electing lesser officials, has had important effects on the parties, contributing to their decentralization, to their concern with winning elections at the expense of policy making, and to the development of 'machine politics'. The demand for popular participation in the selection of government officials, one result of the democratization of politics associated with the Jacksonian era, was extended to the selection of party officials and the nomination of party candidates for national and State offices when the Progressives called for State regulation of political parties. As a result State laws now regulate the structures of political parties and require party primary elections which are run by State officials, thus placing further demands on the voter.

At the national level voters now elect the President (and Vice-President), 100 Senators and 435 Representatives. At State level, there are fifty Governors, about 8,000 legislators and about 5,000 other State officials from the important offices of Attorney General and State Treasurer down to University regents and State printer. The members of many State administrative agencies are elected, but these are mainly agencies initiated in the nineteenth century; nowadays State agencies dealing with health, welfare and highways tend not to be elected. Within the States, there were, in 1972, 3,044 counties, 18,517 municipalities, 16,991 townships, 15,781 school districts and 23,885 special districts, electing about half a million local government officials.

The relatively short tenure of some national and State officials and the timing of elections to prevent the coincidence of State and presidential elections increase the frequency of elections. A two-year term is common to the national House of Representatives, four Governors and the lower house in most States. Senators alone enjoy a six-year term but elections are staggered so that one-third of the Senate is also elected every two years. The President, forty-six Governors and the upper house in most States have a four-year term. Thus there are important Federal and State elections at least once every two years in every State.

Five States (Kentucky, Mississippi, New Jersey, Virginia and Louisiana) opt for a complete separation of national and State elections by holding the latter in odd-numbered years, thus avoiding national campaigns influencing voting behaviour in State elections. In contrast, ten States with gubernatorial four-year terms hold State elections simultaneously with presidential elections. Thirty-one States hold their gubernatorial elections to coincide with mid-term congressional elections. The four States (Arkansas, New Hampshire, Rhode Island and Vermont) with two-year gubernatorial terms hold their State elections at the same time as presidential elections and mid-term congressional elections.

The timing of State elections can have political consequences. Turn-out in congressional and in State elections is higher in presidential years. Gubernatorial candidates of the party winning the Presidency tend to fare better in presidential election years than candidates of the same party in mid-term election years. Presidential elections attract the most media attention and the highest turnout. In 1972, 55 per cent of the voting age population participated in the presidential election, while 50·9 per cent participated in the elections for Representatives. In 1974 turn-out in elections for Representatives dropped to 36·2 per cent.

The number and frequency of electoral contests require that parties concentrate on winning elections instead of formulating policy, and reinforce the tendency towards decentralized national parties by encouraging strong State or local parties. The frequency of elections allied to the separation of institutions increases the opportunities for divided party control of State institutions. Following the 1970 State elections, control of the legislative and executive branches was shared by the parties in twenty-one of the forty-eight States permitting party competition (Minnesota and Nebraska require that candidates for their State legislatures be non-partisan).

B: PRESIDENTIAL ELECTIONS

The electoral college

The concentration of Federal executive powers in one elected office, and the presidential electoral system, have been major constitutional forces in the development and maintenance of a national party system dominated by two decentralized, non-ideological parties. The constitutional provisions regulating the election of the President remain substantially as they were written in 1787, but their application has been radically altered. Four basic rules, derived from the Constitution, State law and custom, govern the operations of the electoral college which, in form, still provides for the election of the President by electors chosen by the people in the fifty States and in the District of Columbia.

The first rule, stated in Article II, Section 1 of the Constitution, assigns to each State as many electors as it has representatives in Congress, i.e. the number of Representatives from the State, based on population, plus two based on the system of representation in the Senate. The District of Columbia has been treated as a State for electoral college purposes since the adoption of the Twenty-third Amendment in March 1961. The size of the electoral college remained at 531 electors from 1912, following the admission to the union of Arizona and New Mexico, until 1960 when it was increased to 537 electors in response to the grant of Statehood to Alaska and Hawaii. There have been 538 electors since the 1964 election, as a result of decisions to maintain the size of the House of Representatives at 435 seats and to give the inhabitants of the District of Columbia a voice in the election of the President.

The relative weight of each State in the electoral college is largely based on population, qualified slightly by the allocation of two electors per State irrespective of population. The smaller

States benefit disproportionately from this provision. In 1968 the eight Mountain States occupied almost 4 per cent of the House seats but received 6 per cent of electoral college votes. Yet together they cast fewer electoral votes than either New York or California. The smaller States tend to oppose reform of this aspect of presidential elections.

The re-allocation of House seats and electoral votes in response to shifts in population among the States is implemented every ten years, based on the results of the national census. In the 1968 election the number of electoral votes ranged from forty-three (New York) to three (Alaska, Delaware, District of Columbia, Nevada, Vermont and Wyoming). Five of the fifty States—New York, California, Pennsylvania, Illinois and Ohio—occupied over 30 per cent of the electoral college. Three States, California, Florida and Texas, have enjoyed increased representation in accordance with the census results of 1950, 1960 and 1970, whereas New York and Pennsylvania have lost ground each time. California, with forty-five electoral votes, is the largest State in the electoral college for the 1972, 1976 and 1980 elections followed by New York (forty-one), Pennsylvania (twenty-seven), Texas and Illinois (twenty-six), and Ohio (twenty-five). The winning margin in California has been particularly close in some recent elections; Truman (1948) and Nixon (1960) carried the State by margins of less than 1 per cent of the popular vote. In 1916 Wilson carried California by 1,983 votes; the loss of California would have meant a Republican victory despite Wilson's nation-wide lead of nearly 600,000 votes.

The second rule, based mainly on custom, provides for the direct election of the President by requiring that the electors who are formally chosen under party labels in the November election every four years cast their votes in December for the candidate to whom they are pledged in advance. This rule is seldom broken; only three out of 3,206 electors have voted contrary to instructions since 1948. This custom, which was established by 1820, frustrated the intentions of the Founding Fathers, who expected the electors to act both independently and judiciously when they met in their respective States to elect a President and Vice-President. Although it is open to the States to determine how electors are to be chosen, since 1836 they have been elected in a popular election in all States except South Carolina. The true state of affairs is accurately reflected in the form of the ballot in most States. Thirty-five States now use the presidential short ballot on which the names of the elector candidates do not appear; only Alabama uses a ballot on which the names of the presidential candidates do not appear. The remaining States use the presidential long ballot on which appear the names of both the presidential and elector candidates.

Attempts have been made to ensure that electors act according to the pledge exacted from them by their party. In 1952 the Supreme Court ruled, in Roy v. Blair, that political parties were entitled to require a pledge to a particular presidential candidate before nominating an individual as an elector. But it was not made clear that such a pledge would be legally enforceable. In 1960 a Republican elector in Oklahoma cast his vote for Senator Byrd, instead of Richard Nixon, to whom he was pledged. Subsequently Oklahoma passed a law requiring an elector candidate to take an oath to support his party's presidential candidate; if the oath is broken the elector would be open to a fine up to $1,000. In 1968 Senator Muskie (Maine) and Representative O'Hara (Michigan) challenged the vote cast for Wallace by a North Carolina elector pledged to Nixon. The House and the Senate both rejected the challenge. It would appear that custom remains the only force binding an elector to his pledge. And since the Constitution implied that electors cast their votes in a secret ballot it is doubtful if pledges are enforceable by law, though there may be a political remedy in the form of congressional action. It is possible to produce unpledged electors. In 1960 the Democratic party in Alabama and Mississippi secured the election of unpledged electors who voted for Senator Byrd in protest against the anti-segregation stand of the Democratic Party nationally.

The third rule, the unit rule or general ticket system, assigns all the electoral college votes of each State to the presidential candidate receiving the most popular votes, be it an overall majority or merely a simple majority, in the State. The unit rule, which is applied by all fifty States and the District of Columbia, strengthens the forces making for a two-party system by making it difficult for minor party candidates to win electoral votes. The unit rule also places a heavy premium on winning the most heavily populated States. In 1968 the eleven largest States in terms of population (California, New York, Pennsylvania, Illinois, Texas, Ohio, Michigan, New Jersey, Florida, Massachussets and Indiana) disposed of 272 electoral votes, slightly more than half of the electoral college.

Campaigning is usually most intense in the largest States and in the marginal States. Richard Nixon's defeat in 1960 has been partly attributed to his decision to campaign personally in all fifty States while his rival concentrated on nine key States, seven of which he won. Because of the importance of the populous States with their broad spectra of interests, presidential candidates of the two major parties tend to belong to the centre of American politics. In particular, Republican candidates normally come from the liberal wing of the party, a custom which Goldwater successfully challenged in 1964, but with disastrous electoral consequences.

The unit rule was established in all States except South Carolina by 1836, despite the support in some States for a district system in which electors would be chosen in political subdivisions within a State, thereby permitting the electoral votes of each State to be shared by the parties. But the district system worked against the stronger political party in States using this system as soon as other States opted for the unit rule. Major party candidates usually attract more than 90 per cent of the popular vote. The only exceptions to this tendency since 1896 occurred in 1912 when Theodore Roosevelt won 27·4 per cent of the vote, in 1924 when Robert La Follette won 16·6 per cent and in 1968 when George Wallace won 13·5 per cent.

The fourth rule, stated in the Twelfth Amendment, requires that the winning presidential candidate receives a majority of electoral votes in the electoral college. If such a majority is lacking the election is to be decided in the House of Representatives, where each State delegation has one vote to be cast for one of the three leading candidates in the electoral college. Two-thirds of the States must vote and a majority of States voting is required in order to win. Each State delegation's vote is decided by a simple majority among its members.

The electoral college met with increasing criticism in the 1960s as other aspects of the electoral system were reformed. In addition the candidacy of George Wallace, firmly based in the Deep South States and an unknown but feared quantity elsewhere, raised the possibility of the electoral college failing to produce a winner. The election would then have been decided either by a deal between Wallace and one of the major party candidates before the electoral college voted, or in the House of Representatives. Either way the Southern States might have been able to exact policy promises relating to civil rights in return for votes in the electoral college or in the House. The threat did not materialize in 1968 and the electoral college system has not been altered. Other aspects of the electoral system, notably campaign financing and the apportionment of House districts, have been substantially reformed.

The electoral college rules have usually operated to produce Presidents who have attracted the support of a majority or a plurality in the popular vote, a comfortable majority in the electoral college and a majority of the States. No President has received fewer popular votes than his major party rival since Republican Presidents Hayes and Harrison found themselves in such a position in 1876 and 1888. Both John Kennedy and Jimmy Carter won fewer States than their Republican rivals. Eleven Presidents since 1860 (five since 1896: Wilson (twice), Truman, Kennedy and Nixon in 1968) have failed to win 50 per cent of the popular vote. Only twice has the election been decided in the House of Representatives—and not since 1824. In 1876 Congress had to set up an electoral commission to determine which candidate was to receive the electoral votes of South Carolina, Florida and Louisiana. The Commission divided on party political lines and victory went to the Republican candidate, Hayes, who trailed the Democratic candidate, Tilden, by 3 per cent in the popular vote. The unit rule usually exaggerates the winning candidate's margin in the electoral college. Only one successful candidate since 1896, Wilson in 1916, has won less than 55 per cent of the electoral votes. Five candidates have won less than 60 per cent: Wilson in 1912, Truman, Kennedy, Nixon in 1968 and Carter in 1976.

Elections can be close in another sense. In 1960 Kennedy won five States by margins of less than 1 per cent of the popular vote. If he had lost these States, he would have lost the election. Wilson in 1916 would have lost if a few voters in California had behaved differently. In 1948, Truman's lead over Dewey of two million popular votes would not have saved him if 29,294 voters had behaved differently in California, Illinois and Ohio. In contrast, Nixon was a fairly comfortable winner in most of the States he carried in 1968, despite winning only 0·7 per cent more of the popular vote than Humphrey.

The popular vote share of the winning candidate is dependent upon two factors: the division of the popular vote between the two major parties and the vote-catching appeal of minor parties. Nixon's 43·4 per cent of the popular vote in 1968 was the lowest winning share since Wilson won 41·9 per cent in 1912. But both were comfortable winners in the States and in the electoral college. In 1912 the Republican vote was divided between two candidates, the official candidate, Taft, and the Progressive candidate, Roosevelt. As a result, Wilson's mere plurality in the popular vote gained him forty of the forty-eight States and 82 per cent of the electoral college.

The extent of the winning candidate's margin in the popular vote is said to be important politically in that it determines the President's capability of effective action. Recent Presidents like Kennedy after 1960 and Nixon after 1968 have been inhibited, it is said, by their narrow margin of victory. But this margin is symptomatic only; much more important is the composition of the Congress. Both Kennedy and Nixon failed to carry many of their party's candidates into Congress on their coat-tails. Hence both experienced difficulty in dealing with Congress, where they were owed few favours in return for electoral assistance.

Close results, as in 1916 and 1948, and plurality Presidents have contributed to demands for the direct election of the President without the intermediate stage of the electoral college. Such a reform would not remove the possibility of plurality Presidents, who appear whenever a third candidate (or candidates) attract significant proportions of the popular vote (the size of the proportion required depends upon the division of the major-party vote). In September 1969 the House of Representatives passed by 339 votes to 70 a resolution recommending a constitutional amendment which would abolish the electoral college and introduce direct popular election of the President. The winner would have to receive at least 40 per cent of the vote; otherwise there would be a run-off between the first two candidates. However, no further action was taken.

Of the fourteen men who were elected to the Presidency from 1896 to 1976, nine were born in and ten were elected from Northeastern and North-Central States; four (Wilson, Eisenhower, Johnson and Carter) were born in but only two (Johnson and Carter) were elected from Southern States; one (Truman) was born in and elected from a Border State and one (Nixon) was born in a Pacific State but elected from New York. If Truman and Johnson, who succeeded to the Presidency on the deaths of Roosevelt and Kennedy, are omitted from the list, then the preference for candidates from the Northeastern and North-Central States is even more pronounced. The sample is not only biased geographically in favour of the north and eastern parts of the United States, it is also biased strongly in favour of the largest States. Four of the fourteen Presidents were elected from New York and three from Ohio. Indeed every Republican President from 1860 through 1924, except Roosevelt and Coolidge, who first became President on the death of an incumbent, came from one of three States—Ohio, Indiana and Illinois.

The most important political consequence of the electoral college system is the huge encouragement it offers to the two-party system. The location of the major executive powers in a one-man office, the Presidency, and the unit rule act against coalitions between parties behind one presidential candidate. Instead, coalitions within parties are encouraged. In addition the unit rule makes it difficult for minor parties to win electoral votes unless they can carry at least one State. This ensures that minor parties which do win electoral votes are firmly entrenched in a particular region. And this in turn limits the national appeal of minor parties. The experience of third-party candidates in the twentieth century emphasizes the regional appeal of those winning electoral college votes.

Table 4.1:

Votes for third-party candidates

Year	Candidate	Party	Share of popular vote	No. of electoral votes
1912	Roosevelt	Progressive	27·4	88
1912	Taft	Republican	23·1	8
1924	La Follette	Progressive	16·6	13
1948	Thurmond	States' Rights	2·4	39
1948	Wallace	Progressive	2·4	0
1960	Byrd	None	0·6	15
1968	Wallace	American Independent	13·5	46

President Taft, who has been described as the real minor party candidate in 1912, won 23·2 per cent of the popular vote, yet he could carry only two small States, Vermont and Utah. In contrast Roosevelt won 27·4 per cent of the popular vote and 16·5 per cent of electoral college votes. Thurmond, leading the 'Dixiecrat' break-away from the Democratic party, won five Southern States in 1948 and hence won many more electoral votes than either Taft or La Follette, who were far ahead of Thurmond in the popular vote. The regional base of Thurmond's performance is emphasized by Henry Wallace's failure as a left-wing break-away candidate from the Democrats to win any electoral votes, despite winning as many popular votes as Thurmond. In 1968 George Wallace won 6·6 per cent of the popular vote outside the South, but he won only one more State than Thurmond in 1948.

The effects of the unit rule are particularly important in a country as varied as the United States in social and political culture, in economic structure and in geographic conditions. The rule militates against the 'take-off' of a third party towards major-party status, either as a third major party or as the second major party, replacing one of the two established major parties.

Yet it must be emphasized that other features of the American constitutional system reduce the incentive to create new political parties on the part of sectional majorities who are dissatisfied with the activities of the national government. The separation of President and Congress, the ability of many State and local parties to control the behaviour of national legislators, and the legal and political powers of the States within a federal system all operate to diminish the temptation to break away from a major party. Conversely, the extreme costs resulting from splits in a major party, demonstrated in 1912, encourage the tendency to paper over the cracks while the party concentrates on attempting to win the Presidency.

Contemporary developments in the South have so far illustrated the strength of the two-party system. Southern whites, assailed by Federal civil rights legislation and the resulting increase in political participation on the part of blacks, can choose between fighting to maintain control of the Democratic party in the Southern States (thereby controlling State governments and national legislators), joining or voting for the Republican party, and attempting to create a permanent but sectional third party running candidates in some or all State and national elections. The more extreme believers in white supremacy, located mainly in the 'black belts' with the highest proportional black population, 'bolted' the Democratic party in 1948 and in 1968 to support a third-party candidate, viz., Thurmond in 1948 and Wallace in 1968. Yet this revolt was confined to presidential elections. Thurmond was elected as Democratic Senator for South Carolina in 1954 and Wallace was elected as Democratic Governor of Alabama in 1970. Apart from support for Wallace in 1968, Southern dissatisfaction with civil rights developments has led to increased support for the Republican party in presidential and in congressional elections so that a two-party South has begun to emerge.

Access to the ballot

The electoral performance of minor parties is further hindered by

State laws which make it difficult for them to get on to the ballot. American ballots consist mainly of party lists; any minor party has to satisfy certain requirements before its candidates can appear on the ballot. In particular, petitions signed by a specified number of qualified voters, signifying their support for the party, have to be submitted by a specific date. In Illinois a minor party presidential candidate used to have to present a petition with 25,000 signatures including 200 signatures from at least fifty of the 102 counties in the State. In New York the petition must have 12,000 signatures, including fifty from every county. In Alabama and Pennsylvania such petitions have to be submitted by March of the presidential election year; in Kentucky and West Virginia by April. Both types of requirement have prevented minor party candidates from getting on to the presidential ballot. In 1948, Henry Wallace and Thurmond were omitted in Oklahoma because their petitions were not submitted by the required date. Also in 1948, Wallace could not get on to the ballot in Illinois because he could not get the required 200 signatures in each of fifty counties.

The Supreme Court has modified the effects of such State regulations. The Progressive Party sued the Governor of Illinois in 1948 but the Court ruled, in MacDougal v. Green, that the relevant statutes were valid. But in 1968, in Moore v. Ogilvie, the Court reversed this decision after the presidential election had taken place. The Court's decision was in line with its reasoning in apportionment cases. Hypothetically, 87 per cent of the Illinois population, located in the forty-nine most populous counties, might have been unable to place a candidate on the presidential ballot. Such a situation, the Court reasoned, offended too strongly the principle of 'one man, one vote'.

The Court rendered a more important and more effective decision as a result of Ohio's rejection of George Wallace's attempt to get on to the presidential ballot in that State. Wallace had submitted a petition with the required number of signatures, but not by the required date in February 1968. Ohio's laws were particularly severe on minor parties; one commentator has suggested that the two-party system was effectively imposed by statute. In Williams v. Rhodes, the Court ordered Wallace's name to be placed on the presidential ballot because Ohio law restricted the right of citizens to cast their votes effectively. Wallace subsequently won 11·8 per cent of the popular vote in the State. In 1976, Eugene McCarthy was unable to get on to the ballot in New York State because some of the signatures on the required petition were held by the courts to be invalid, leaving him with insufficient signatures.

C: THE CONGRESSIONAL AND STATE ELECTORAL SYSTEMS

The 435 members of the House of Representatives are elected every two years from single-member districts, with victory going to the candidate receiving the most votes. This type of system normally punishes minor parties. The two major parties dominate House elections, winning over 99 per cent of the total of 16,061 seats from 1896 to 1970. Minor parties managed to win only 135 seats, and have not won any since 1952.

Though each State is represented by two Senators, elections are staggered so that one-third of the Senate is elected every two years. Each State functions as a State-wide, single-member constituency twice in six years for the purpose of elections to the Senate. Senators have been directly elected since the adoption in 1913 of the Seventeenth Amendment. Minor parties seldom hold more than one Senate seat. The Senate has tended to be more liberal than the House because, as urbanization increases, urban voters constitute a majority in most States, even in small States.

The House electoral system has been subjected to a radical change in one area: the construction of the basic unit, which is the congressional district. The allocation of House seats among the States is based on population as reported every ten years in the national census. All States are guaranteed at least one House district. Six States, Alaska, Delaware, Nevada, North Dakota, Vermont and Wyoming are so sparsely populated, or so small, that they merit only one State-wide congressional district. Apart from these States, the number of House seats per State is as closely related to population as is possible, given that State boundaries impose limitations in the way of absolute equality in the size of congressional districts.

The drawing of district boundaries, in terms of shape and population, for both the House of Representatives and the fifty State legislatures (all of which are bicameral in form, except in Nebraska) has traditionally been controlled by the States. Many State legislatures have in the past refused to redistrict in response to shifts in population within the State. As a result wide variations in the population of legislative districts appeared. As the dominant population shift was from rural to urban and suburban areas, districts which had been constructed when a large percentage of Americans lived in a rural society gave much greater representation to rural voters than their numbers warranted. In 1900, 60·3 per cent of the population lived in rural areas; in 1970 the number had dropped to 28 per cent. Examples of malapportionment, i.e. of districts varying greatly in population size, were legion. California redistricted in 1961; after this the largest congressional district had a population of 588,933 and the smallest a population of 301,872. In 1930 the largest New York district contained 776,425 persons, the smallest only 90,671. In Texas in 1962, the Representative for the largest congressional district, which included the city of Dallas, had 952,000 constituents; the Representative for the smallest district had 216,000 constituents. At State level, small minorities of the population could elect legislative majorities; for example in Arizona 12·8 per cent of the population could elect a majority in the upper house, while in Connecticut 12 per cent of the population could elect a majority in the lower house. In California one State Senator represented 6 million people; another represented 14,000.

This situation was perpetuated because it worked to the advantage of existing legislative majorities who were in no hurry to legislate away either their power or their tenure. The States were in control of most aspects of State and national electoral systems because the Constitution permitted it and because Congress made no attempt to change the situation. Indeed many States applied criteria other than population to the construction of State legislative districts. In 1964, only seventeen upper houses and twenty lower houses were, according to the State Constitutions, supposed to be based on population. And in several of these States the legislature ignored a constitutional obligation to redistrict in response to changes in population distribution made evident by census results. Attempts to change the situation on the part of citizens who felt that they were not granted fair representation failed ultimately because the courts adhered to the belief that such intensely political questions were not justiciable.

A more blatant cause of unequal representation resulted from the 'gerrymander', i.e. from the peculiar shaping of a legislative district to include as many supporters of the dominant political party and as few of the rival party as possible. Alternatively a gerrymander might concentrate many voters of the opposition party in one or two districts in order to permit the dominant party to win many more districts elsewhere. The term was derived from the actions in 1812 of Massachussets Governor Elbridge Gerry, who sanctioned the construction of a constituency in the shape of a salamander. 'Saddle-bags', 'snakes' or 'shoestrings', and 'frying-pans' are terms devised to describe the shapes of gerrymandered districts. Both major political parties have indulged in this practice.

Some effects of malapportionment and gerrymandering are difficult to specify. Though rural areas have been over-represented and urban and suburban areas have been under-represented, studies of policy differences between fairly apportioned and malapportioned States have not proved that such differences have been either significant or attributable to differences in apportionment. But some students of American government have claimed that malapportionment contributed to divided party control of some State institutions, to the under-assessment of farm property, to the distribution of education and welfare funds to the disadvantage of the cities, and to failure to deal with the social problems of the central city.

Malapportionment, the 'silent gerrymander', has been brought to an end as a result of a radical new stance by the Supreme Court. But it is not yet clear whether other forms of discriminatory districting will also disappear, partly because it is extremely difficult to define gerrymandering except in the case of districts of unequal population size.

In 1962, in its decision in Baker *v.* Carr, the Supreme Court entered the 'political thicket' of apportionment by claiming that the courts had jurisdiction in this field. In so doing the Supreme Court occasioned a revolution in apportionment by departing from Justice Frankfurter's opinion, explaining the verdict of the Court in the 1946 case of Colegrove *v.* Green, that the Court ought to exercise self-restraint and that citizens must seek the redress of grievances from State legislatures. Baker, a citizen of Shelby County, Tennessee, sued Carr, the Tennessee Secretary of State, on the grounds that he was unfairly represented in the lower house of the Tennessee legislature. Shelby County, which includes the city of Memphis, had a voting population of 313,435 in 1959 and elected seven representatives; Moore County possessed 2,340 voters and one representative. This was repeated elsewhere in the State, so that less than 30 per cent of the State's population could elect majorities in both houses of the legislature.

Baker's suit, which was first introduced in July 1959 in the Nashville Division of the United States District Court of Tennessee, where it was rejected, eventually came before the Supreme Court in April 1961. The lower courts had refused to claim jurisdiction despite admissions that Baker was under-represented, that the 'evil was a serious one which should be corrected without further delay' and that the Tennessee legislature was violating the State Constitution in not redistricting every ten years. By a 6–2 vote the Supreme Court claimed jurisdiction, with Justice Frankfurter, writing his last signed opinion, in dissent, but did not rule directly on the detailed merits of the case. Instead the case was returned to the lower court for a decision on the principles to be applied to the now required redistricting. The Supreme Court based its decision on the Fourteenth Amendment, which guaranteed to all citizens 'equal protection of the laws'. Severe under-representation was categorized as a loss of such protection.

Baker *v.* Carr opened the door to a number of judicial decisions which have had a profound effect upon the electoral system. In March 1963, in Gray *v.* Sanders, the Supreme Court held that Georgia's unit rule system in State-wide primary elections, comparable to the electoral college, was unconstitutional because it led to huge disparities in the value of a citizen's vote. The system, which was used in primaries nominating candidates for Governor and for U.S. Senator, divided the State into a number of units each of which were assigned votes as in the electoral college. The winning candidate in each unit won all the votes of the unit; votes were not distributed among the units in proportion to population. The system had permitted rural voters to dominate Georgia's politics for fifty years. As a result of this decision, Georgia, Maryland and Mississippi changed from unit vote primaries to popular vote primaries. Justice Douglas stated that the Court was acting in order to realize the principle of 'one man, one vote'. The Court did not say how this was to be achieved, but it did reject the Federal analogy: it refused to permit a State electoral system to survive simply because it was comparable to the Federal electoral college.

The Court emphasized its adherence to the numerical equality of individual votes by requiring, in Wesberry v. Sanders (February, 1964), that congressional districts were to be as near equal in population as practicable. Later, in Kirkpatrick v. Dreisler (1969), the Court ruled that no numerical or population variance within a State between congressional districts would be considered negligible. The results of these decisions were soon reflected in the redistricting of House seats. In elections to the 88th Congress in 1962 the size of districts ranged from 664,000 to 198,000 in Arizona, from 952,000 to 216,000 in Texas and from 803,000 to 177,000 in Michigan. By the time of elections to the ninety-first Congress in 1968 these variations had been reduced. In Arizona the districts ranged from 456,529 to 405,217; in Texas, from 451,173 to 387,794 and in Michigan, from 417,026 to 403,469.

The Court's decisions were much more controversial when they applied to State legislatures. In June 1964 the Court announced its decisions in six cases headed by Reynolds v. Sims. The Court demanded that State legislative districts in both houses of a bicameral legislature be based on population and that districts be as near equal in population size as possible. Further, in a case applying to Colorado, the Court ruled that not even a popular preference, expressed in a referendum, for a standard other than population for constructing legislative districts can justify the use of such a standard. Again the Federal analogy was rejected, because constituencies of the upper house within a State did not possess the qualities of sovereignty of States within the nation.

The creation of legislative districts of equal population size has not put an end to claims of discriminatory districting. A number of cases involving alleged social or political gerrymandering (e.g. against blacks) have been brought to the courts. One potential by-product of the newly established requirement that States redistrict in response to population changes is that the opportunities for gerrymandering have been increased. So far the courts have tended to accept jurisdiction in cases alleging racial gerrymandering, but not in cases alleging political gerrymandering. And the Courts have rejected some allegations of racial gerrymandering because of the difficulty in proving that there was racial intent alone. It has been claimed that accusations of racial gerrymandering are more likely to be substantiated by the courts when they emanate from Southern States.

The critical political reactions to the Supreme Court's decisions have not proved effective. Attempts to pass Federal legislation and constitutional amendments limiting the freedom of the Court failed. Redistricting became a particularly important task in 1970 for two reasons. Firstly, the Supreme Court decisions meant that redistricting to create congressional districts of equal population size would have to be carried out by the States very soon after the 1970 census. It was possible to delay up to 1970 on the grounds that the census would require redistricting as some States gained and others lost House seats. Given the need to redistrict after 1970 and before the 1972 elections, the results of the 1970 State elections became critical because redistricting would inevitably have partisan political effects. If one party controlled the Governor and the State legislature then it could benefit from redistricting. If it controlled the Governor or one legislative branch then it would at least have an influence in the politics of redistricting. Secondly, the 1970 census did change the distribution of House seats among the States—changes which affected the parties unevenly. Generally it was felt that the Democrats would suffer more than the Republicans. But the Democratic position was helped by the party's improved showing in the 1970 State elections, when it enjoyed a net gain of 11 Governors and eight legislative houses (4 lower and 4 upper).

D: THE SUFFRAGE

Voting turnout in presidential and congressional elections appears low in comparison with turnout in other nations: 63 per cent of civilians of voting age voted in the 1964 presidential elections and 58·7 per cent voted in the House elections; only 46·3 per cent voted in the 1966 mid-term House elections. In 1972 the presidential turnout dropped to 55·7 per cent and the congressional turnout to 51 per cent. There is considerable variation in turnout among the States; in 1964 only 33·7 per cent and 36·2 per cent voted for the presidential candidates in Mississippi and Alabama, whereas 79·2 per cent and 77·5 per cent voted in Utah and Idaho. By 1972 the presidential turnout had risen to 44 per cent in Alabama and 46 per cent in Mississippi, while the highest turnout was 70·8 per cent in South Dakota, McGovern's home State, which he failed to carry.

One reason for the comparatively low turnout even in presidential elections has lain in the fact that many Americans of voting age have been legally and extra-legally deprived of the right to vote. Many citizens failed to acquire the necessary qualifications required by the States. That such qualifications vary from State to State is one reason for differences in turnout among the States. A number of developments in the 1960s—Federal legislation, one constitutional amendment and some Supreme Court decisions—resulted in the extension of the suffrage.

The Constitution does not grant the right to vote to specific types of individual but it does, in stipulating a republican form of government, require that some Americans be permitted to vote in every State. In provisions relating to the election of the House and, in the Seventeenth Amendment, to the Senate, the Constitution lays down that voters have the same qualifications as 'electors of the most numerous branch of the State legislature'. This requirement was included because the lower house in the

State legislatures, i.e. 'the most numerous branch', had a wider suffrage than the upper house.

The lack of positive guidance in the Constitution as to the qualification of voters has left a good deal of discretion to the individual States. However, several constitutional amendments have been adopted in order to prevent States discriminating against particular sets of citizens. The Supreme Court has interpreted the Fourteenth Amendment as prohibiting racial discrimination by States legislating for the qualifications of voters. The Fifteenth Amendment prohibits the denial of the right to vote on grounds of race, colour or 'previous condition of servitude'. The Nineteenth Amendment extends the prohibition to sex.

The South managed to deny the suffrage to many blacks despite such amendments. One device was the poll tax, which needed to be paid only by those wishing to be registered to vote. Many poor people, black and white, neglected to pay it, and there were social pressures against blacks attempting to pay it. However, by 1964, when the Twenty-fourth Amendment prohibiting the denial of the right to vote in national elections, including primaries, 'by reason of failure to pay any poll tax or other tax' was adopted, only the five States of Alabama, Arkansas, Mississippi, Texas and Virginia continued to use this device. In 1966 the Supreme Court prohibited the use of the poll tax as a voter qualification in all elections.

Other devices used in the South to prevent blacks from registering and voting have been invalidated as a result of Federal legislation, which has also brought about considerable uniformity in State suffrage requirements. Residence requirements demanding that individuals reside in their election district for a certain period of time before qualifying for registration served to disqualify about 5 to 7 per cent of the population of voting age. Mississippi had the most restrictive laws, requiring a residence of two years in the State and one year in the election district. Idaho had the least restrictive requirements of six months' residence in the State and thirty days in the county. Such residence requirements, particularly effective in a highly mobile society, applied to both interstate and intrastate movements.

However, the States themselves relaxed the requirements; by 1968, thirty States had special rules permitting new residents to vote in presidential elections even if they did not satisfy the State residence requirements for voting in State elections. Nine States had rules permitting old residents to vote if they had not qualified to vote in their new State. As a result the number of citizens disqualified from voting due to change of residence fell from 8 million in 1960 to 4·8 million in 1968. Finally, when the 1965 Voting Rights Act was extended in 1970, common residence requirements were established, enabling any individual to vote in presidential elections as long as he had resided in the State for thirty days and was not open to disqualification on other grounds.

Citizens could be denied the right to vote on account of illiteracy (twenty States excluded citizens who were illiterate in English but literate in another language), mental incapacity, incarceration and classification as a pauper. Mississippi and South Carolina made no provision at all for civilian absentee voting. Some Southern States actively required a demonstration of an understanding of the Federal and State constitutions before registering voters. Since States administered election regulations, these could be applied so as to discriminate against blacks.

In 1960 there were 107,597,000 Americans of voting age. It has been estimated that 14·85 million were excluded from voting on legal grounds, while another 8·6 million were unable to vote because of illness, absence from legal residence or intimidation. Accordingly the turnout in the 1960 election might be claimed to be closer to 80 per cent than to the official figure of 64 per cent of those who might be expected to vote.

The 1965 Voting Rights Act was primarily intended to reduce the ability of Southern States to prevent blacks from registering and voting. The Act granted the Justice Department the right to supervise voting procedures and to suspend literacy and similar voting requirements in States or counties in which less than 50 per cent of the population of voting age were either registered for or voted in the 1964 presidential election. The Act was thus automatically applied in the five Deep South States, in Virginia and in thirty-nine counties of North Carolina. It contributed to the registration of nearly one million more blacks in the South between 1964 and 1968. The change in black registration was most spectacular in Mississippi where only 6·7 per cent of blacks were registered in 1964; by 1968 the proportion had increased to 59·4 per cent.

The political effects of this and other changes in the South are emerging gradually. In election districts where blacks are in a majority they may be able to capture the Democratic party machine and to nominate black candidates, a process which was given a further impetus by the apportionment revolution of the 1960s. However, registration of poor whites in the South has also increased, and this section of the Southern voting population may be turning conservative—a tendency which will not benefit the Democratic party, which could win only one Southern State, Texas, in 1968. The Voting Rights Act is one of several factors which, in increasing Southern white resentment at the policy decisions of the Democratic party and in loosening white control of Democratic party organizations, is contributing to the birth of a two-party system in the South.

The number of black elected officials has increased significantly; before 1965 there were fewer than one hundred in the South but by 1975 there were 1,652 in the South and 3,503 in the nation. But the political behaviour of whites has also been affected, partly because discriminatory electoral laws disenfranchised poor whites as well as blacks. One motivation behind the origin of such legislation was to prevent a populist alliance between poor whites and blacks. In Georgia, from 1960 to 1968, registration of whites increased from 56·8 per cent to 84·8 per cent while registration of blacks increased from 29·4 per cent to 56·1 per cent; half a million more whites registered compared to 164,000 more blacks. The increase in registration has contributed to the increased turnout in the Southern States. However, the feared populist alliance has not materialized because poor whites are the most racially conservative and hence opposed to an alliance with blacks for economic ends.

No black was elected to Congress from the South between 1898 and 1970. In 1972 two black Representatives were elected: Andrew Young, from Georgia's fifth district situated in Atlanta, and Barbara Jordan, from the eighteenth district in Texas situated in Houston. In 1974 Harold Ford won the eighth district of Tennessee located in Memphis. All three, though elected from districts where about 40 per cent of the population were black, benefited from redistricting occasioned by reapportionment.

The black caucus in the House of Representatives has increased from three in 1955 to sixteen following the 1974 mid-term elections. Blacks have been elected mainly from districts where 40 per cent or more of the voting population is black. In 1971–2, when no blacks yet represented Southern districts, ten of the twelve black Representatives were returned by districts where at least 45 per cent of the voting population was black. There were thirteen such districts at the time of the 1970 elections. Only one was in the South: Mississippi's second district, which did not return a black. The districts represented by blacks are overwhelmingly urban in character. Cities with black representation are New York (two), Los Angeles (two), Chicago (two), Detroit (two), Philadelphia, St. Louis, Cleveland, Atlanta, Baltimore, Houston, Berkeley (California) and Memphis (Tennessee).

The increase in black representation has not been extended to the Senate, where there has been only one black Senator since 1881: Senator Edward Brooke of Massachussets (Republican), who was first elected in 1966 and re-elected in 1972. Only 3 per cent of the population of Massachussets is black. No State has a black population of 40 per cent or over. Mississippi has the highest black population—36·8 per cent in 1970. Maryland has the highest black population outside the South—17·8 per cent in 1920.

The Voting Rights Act was extended for another five years in 1970. In addition to applying the provisions of the Act to certain Northern areas, notably Manhattan, Brooklyn, and the Bronx, a number of important national electoral regulations were established. Literacy tests as a qualification for voting were suspended in all elections throughout the United States. The minimum voting age was lowered to eighteen. It had been twenty-one in all States except Georgia and Kentucky (eighteen), Alaska (nineteen) and Hawaii (twenty). But this change may lead to a reduction in percentage turnout, because younger voters have been much less willing to vote than older voters.

President Nixon signed the bill despite his belief that the attempt to lower the voting age for all elections was unconstitutional. He stated that the measure, which he supported, should have been enacted by constitutional amendment. This step was taken when the Twenty-sixth Amendment lowering the voting age in all elections to eighteen was ratified on 30 June 1971.

Another consequence of the extended Voting Rights Act was the imposition of an obligation on the States to make registration and voting facilities available to potential voters living outside the State. The high proportion of eighteen- to twenty-year-olds at college meant that such facilities had to be provided if a low turnout was to be avoided. In 1972 11·2 million American eighteen- to twenty-year-olds were eligible to register and to vote, joining the 13·9 million twenty-one- to twenty-five-year-olds who had not been old enough to vote in 1968. It was estimated that 65 per cent of the 25 million new voters would register and that 42 per cent would vote. The potential behaviour of the new voters was the subject of much speculation, giving the Democrats some grounds for optimism when other indications of how the electorate would behave in 1972 were not favourable. In the event 48 per cent of the eighteen-to-twenty age group and 50·7 per cent of the twenty-one to twenty-four age group reported that they voted in 1972 in a sample survey conducted by the U.S. Bureau of the Census.* Reported turnout for the whole sample was 63 per cent compared to an actual turnout of 55·7 per cent.

The Voting Rights Act was extended for another seven years in August 1975. Literacy tests were banned permanently and the basic protection of voting rights legislation was extended to certain language minorities, notably Spanish-speaking Americans and Indians.

E: CAMPAIGN FINANCING

Responsibility for legislative measures regulating the financing of election campaigns is shared between Federal and State governments. American legislation in this area has been much more

* Statistical Abstract of the United States 1973, Bureau of the Census, Table 612.

ambitious and complex than similar legislation elsewhere. But few real restraints, as opposed to inconvenience, were imposed on contributors or on candidates until the 1970s. It remains to be seen whether major reform legislation enacted in 1972 and 1974 leads to much stricter control over campaign financing.

Federal legislation prohibits contributions to Federal election campaigns by either corporations or labour unions, requires the disclosure of itemized receipts and expenditures by candidates and their campaign committees, imposes limits on contributions by individuals and on expenditure by and on behalf of candidates, and prohibits the soliciting of civil servants for campaign contributions. The States also impose various restrictions on contributions and expenditure and require disclosure of income and spending of candidates, though there is considerable variation from State to State.

There have been periodic attempts to control the financing of election campaigns, notably around the turn of the century, in the 1920s and the 1940s. Attempts to regulate the amount and the sources of campaign contributions include the 1907 Tillman Act prohibiting corporations from contributing to campaign funds for Federal elections and the 1947 Taft-Hartley Act prohibiting Federal campaign contributions by labour unions, which had started to make substantial contributions to the Democratic party in 1936. In 1940 amendments to the 1939 Hatch Act imposed a limitation of $5,000 p.a. on contributions by any individual to parties and candidates.

These restrictions were evaded in various ways. Corporations and unions performed political activities such as advertising or registration drives, which have distinctly partisan aims and effects, or they channelled funds to individuals on the understanding that these were passed on to the candidates. Despite the Hatch Act, an individual was able to make $5,000 contributions to any number of campaign committees set up on behalf of particular candidates. Individuals could also make contributions via family members. The effect of such legislation has been to complicate the administration of party campaigns by encouraging a proliferation of committees. It may also have reduced slightly the amount of contributions actually forthcoming.

The most futile attempts to control campaign financing have placed ceilings on expenditures by candidates and their supporting committees. The 1925 Federal Corrupt Practices Act imposed ceilings of between $2,500 and $5,000 and between $10,000 and $25,000 on campaign expenditure by House and Senate candidates (the amount depending on the party's vote at the preceding election). But such limitations have been interpreted as applying to personal expenditure by candidates—their committees may spend much more (it has been estimated that the cheapest Senate campaign will cost at least $70,000). Federal and State legislation has attempted to limit committee spending. The Hatch Act imposed a limit of $3 million on campaign committees operating in at least two States; this condition merely stimulated further the proliferation of committees, each spending up to $3 million.

Congress and the States have attempted to ensure that at least the sources of campaign funds and their eventual destination are known by requiring that candidates produce itemized accounts (receipts and expenditures). The 1925 Corrupt Practices Act requiring such disclosures by candidates and their campaign committees was easily evaded because it did not apply to primary campaigns or to committees operating in one State only. It was not unusual for candidates to report no personal expenditure.

Demands for reform of campaign financing were revived in the 1960s and 1970s in response to huge rises in the costs of campaigning due to inflation, the increasing use of television as a campaign medium, and the use of polling organizations by candidates attempting to organize their campaigns in such a way as to meet the apparent views and wishes of the electorate. Estimates of the rising costs of campaigning are reported in Table 4.2.

Television absorbed 20 per cent of the $300 million spent by all candidates at all levels of government in 1968, compared to 12·5 per cent of $200 million spent in 1964. The amount spent at the national level on the presidential general election campaign has been increasing faster than total campaign expenditures especially in 1968 (when Wallace spent $7 million) and in 1972 when the Republicans spent more than twice as much as the Democrats.

Table 4.2:
estimates of campaign expenditure, 1952–72
($ million)

	1952	1956	1960	1964	1968	1972
Total costs—all levels	140	155	175	200	300	400
National spending on presidential campaign	11·6	14·0	21·4	26·6	48·1	82
Republican	6·6	7·8	10·1	16·0	25·4	55
Democratic	5	5·1	9·8	8·8	11·6	27
Radio and television	3·5	4·7	3	11·1	20·4	10·5

Source: H. B. Asher, *Presidential Elections and American Politics* (The Dorsey Press, 1976), pp. 205–222.

Reform attempts were also stimulated by the ease with which the apparent aims of campaign regulations were evaded, by accusations against several members of Congress of illegal and personal use of political funds, and by increasing evidence that personal wealth was becoming more helpful in promoting successful candidacies, especially in primary elections. In 1970 eleven of fifteen senatorial candidates in the seven largest States were millionaires. President Nixon vetoed the Campaign Broadcast Reform Bill in 1970 on the grounds that reform of campaign regulations should be tackled comprehensively and not piecemeal. The Democrats charged that the Republicans opposed the Bill, which would have limited campaign spending on television, because the Republicans were able to spend much more due to a sounder financial position.

The Nixon administration was influenced by the demand for reform into taking more active steps than previous administrations in the enforcement of existing legislation. From 1907 to 1968 only three business firms were prosecuted for violation of the 1907 Tillman Act. In contrast fourteen firms were prosecuted in 1969 for violation of similar provisions in the 1925 Federal Corrupt Practices Act.

Reformers won a major victory with the passage of the Federal Election Campaign Act, signed by President Nixon in February 1972. The major provisions of the Act imposed a spending limit of 10c per eligible voter on both presidential and congressional candidates as regards expenditure on television, radio, newspaper and billboard advertising, as a result of which the amount spent on broadcasting in 1972 was just under one-half of 1968 expenditures. The Act also limited the amount a candidate and his family could contribute to $50,000 in presidential elections, $35,000 in Senate elections and $25,000 in House elections. Most significant in the short term was an attempt to tighten up the reporting by candidates of the sources of campaign contributions and the destination of expenditures.

The legislation was due to become effective on 7 April 1972. Contributions, including cash, flowed into the Nixon campaign to avoid the new reporting requirements, making it easier for funds to be diverted to the 'plumbers' unit which burgled Democratic National Committee headquarters in the Watergate Hotel and to the 'dirty tricks' campaign to blacken the reputation of several candidates for the Democratic nomination. Subsequently, the reporting requirements sanctioned investigations into Republican financing in 1972 and into the behaviour of the Campaign to Re-Elect the President (CREEP), thus contributing to Nixon's downfall.

The Watergate scandal weakened opposition to further reforms. President Ford signed the Federal Election Campaign Amendment Act in October 1974. The amendments imposed severe limits on spending. Presidential candidates were not to exceed $10 million each in primary campaigns or $20 million in the general election. The limits imposed on spending in House and Senate general elections were to be $70,000 and $150,000 (or 12c per eligible voter) in each constituency. The amendments also imposed a total limit of $25,000 per annum on any one individual's contributions to federal election campaigns. The major reform introduced public financing of presidential, but not congressional, elections. Presidential candidates who accepted public funding would not be permitted to accept private contributions. The 1974 legislation also provided for the establishment of an independent elections commission which was given the power to seek civil injunctions against anyone violating laws dealing with campaign contributions and expenditure.

The constitutionality of the 1974 campaign finance legislation was challenged by both liberals and conservatives, including Eugene McCarthy (formerly Democratic Senator from Minnesota) and James L. Buckley (Conservative Senator from New York, 1971–76). In January 1976 the Supreme Court ruled that the method of selecting the members of the independent commission as laid down in the 1974 Act was unconstitutional because officers of Congress (the Speaker of the House and the President pro tempore of the Senate) were granted appointment powers. The Supreme Court also ruled that the expenditure ceilings violated the First Amendment's defence of freedom of political expression.

In May 1976 President Ford signed the Federal Election Campaign Act Amendment of 1976, which provided for presidential appointment and Senate confirmation of a six-member Federal Elections Commission.

FOR FURTHER READING:

H. E. Alexander, *Money in Politics* (Public Affairs Press, 1972).

H. B. Asher, *Presidential Elections and American Politics* (The Corsey Press, 1976).

R. G. Dixon, *Democratic Representation: Reapportionment in Law and Politics* (O.U.P. New York, 1968).

D. D. Dunn, *Financing Presidential Campaigns* (The Brookings Institution, 1972).

W. S. Sayre and Judith H. Parris, *Voting for President: The Electoral College and the American Political System* (The Brookings Institution, 1970).

5: Elections and Voting

A: ELECTORAL POLITICS
IN HISTORICAL PERSPECTIVE

From a comparative perspective the history of the American party system has been remarkable for the persistence of a strong two-party framework since the 1796 presidential contest between Adams and Jefferson, and for the durability of the Democratic and Republican parties. Another distinctive feature of the system has been the recurring tendency of the electorate to sustain a predominant or majority party monopolizing victory in Federal elections for periods lasting up to twenty years.

Two-party politics

Prior to the formation of the Republican party in 1854 and the confirmation of its major-party status when Lincoln won the Presidency in 1860, there had been a succession of major parties. A rudimentary two-party system comprising the Federalists led by Alexander Hamilton and the Democratic-Republicans led by Thomas Jefferson developed during Washington's two terms in office. The Federalists did not win a national election after 1798 and the party petered out as a viable political force following the 1816 elections, leaving the more popularly based Democratic-Republicans as the sole major party during the 'Era of Good Feelings' associated with Monroe's presidency. But the Democratic-Republican congressional caucus failed to agree on a presidential candidate for the 1824 election and the resulting competition between Adams, Jackson, Crawford and Clay stimulated the development of new party formations. Andrew Jackson of Tennessee won the most popular votes, but no candidate achieved a majority in the electoral college. The House of Representatives elected John Quincy Adams of Massachusetts.

The followers of Jackson gained control of Congress in 1826 and 'Old Hickory', as he was known, was elected to the Presidency in 1828. In so doing the Jacksonians created what came to be the Democratic party. Adams, who had been frustrated in his attempts to pursue an active Federal policy aimed at developing trade, industry and transportation, and Henry Clay of Kentucky, who succeeded Adams as Jackson's opponent in 1832, were National Republicans. The fluidity of party politics at this time is emphasized by the facts that Adams had been a Federalist and then, along with Clay and Jackson, a leading Democratic-Republican.

By 1836 anti-Jackson forces had formed the Whig party. From 1836 until 1852 the presidential popular vote was more evenly divided between the parties in the nation as a whole and in the several regions than in any other period in American political history. The Whigs won the Presidency with Harrison in 1840. By then two-party politics had been extended throughout the nation. The post-1824 period also witnessed the establishment of such modern features of party activity as an extensive grassroots organization decentralized in the States, the State and national nominating conventions which replaced the congressional caucus in the presidential selection process, and the widespread acceptance of the conventional rules which operate the formal provisions of the electoral college.

In the 1850s, the strains imposed on the parties by issues such as immigration, slavery and the slave or free status of areas of westward expansion destroyed the Whigs. The Republican party emerged in 1854 from the realignment in voting behaviour stimulated by these issues, which by their effect on the Whigs increased the influence of Southern interests in the Democratic party and finally led to the Civil War. The Democratic party managed to survive as a major party in the North during the period of Civil War and Reconstruction, a status eventually confirmed by a Democratic victory in the 1874 House elections, following a widespread economic depression in 1873, and by the extremely close and disputed presidential election of 1876. The Democrats and Republicans thereafter dominated the two-party system.

The continuity in American party politics represented by the survival of the Democratic and Republican parties should not disguise the occasionally significant but temporary intervention of minor parties, or the changes which have taken place in the policies of the major parties and in their sources of popular support. The People's (Populist) party threatened to bring about radical changes in the party system in the early 1890s, either through establishing itself as a viable agrarian party in several Western and Southern states, thereby complicating the workings of the electoral college, or through displacing the Democratic party as the second major party. These extreme possibilities of the Populist challenge were averted by the electoral success of the Republican party in the 1896 election. But the Populist intervention intensified the sectional conflicts which had been a recurring feature of the party system since 1800, and enabled the Republican party to dominate elections until 1930.

A new pattern of party competition emerged in the early 1930s when the parties changed positions on the issues of States' rights and the role of the Federal government. Sectionalism outside the South declined as a nationalization of electoral competition occurred, a process which was continued after World War II.

The long-term strength of the two-party framework is emphasized by the failure of minor parties to win electoral college votes in twenty-two of the thirty presidential elections since 1860. The combined major party popular vote has exceeded 90 per cent in all but five elections. Third parties have made no impact on congressional elections in the twentieth century. But break-away movements from one of the major parties determined the result of one presidential election when the supporters of ex-President Theodore Roosevelt allowed Wilson to win in 1912. And the break-away Democrats who formed George Wallace's American Independent Party in 1968 raised the possibility of a presidential election being decided in the House of Representatives for the first time since 1824.

Patterns of electoral competition

The historical sequence of national election results reveals distinct electoral phases, each characterized by particular voting alignments and specific issues. Superficially it appears that one party has dominated elections for lengthy periods of up to seventy years. The Jacksonian Democrats and their successors won six presidential elections out of the eight from 1828 through 1856 and controlled the House and the Senate following twelve of the fourteen elections from 1826 through 1852. From 1860 to 1930 the Republicans won fourteen of eighteen presidential elections and enjoyed a majority in the Senate after thirty and in the House after twenty-five of the thirty-six congressional elections. The Democrats won the Presidency in eight of the twelve elections and the Senate and the House after twenty-one of the twenty-three congressional elections between 1932 and 1976. A more detailed examination of electoral trends reveals two recurring patterns in the state of competition between the major parties: over-all predominance of one party and divided control of the elective institutions.

The defining characteristic of the first condition, one-party predominance, is the virtual monopolization of victory in national elections by one of the major parties for a period of up to two decades. The Federalists and the Democratic-Republicans enjoyed this degree of success—the Federalists up to 1798 (excluding the 1792 House election) and the Democratic-Republicans from 1800. The Jacksonian Democrats monopolized victory from 1826 until the Whigs first won the Presidency in 1840. The Republican party has monopolized electoral victory in three distinct periods since 1860: from 1860 to 1872, 1894 to 1908 and 1918 to 1930. The Democrats succeeded as the majority party in 1932 and dominated elections until defeated in the 1946 congressional elections—the party's only defeat between 1932 and Eisenhower's first victory in 1952.

One result of the electorate's periodic allegiance to a predominant or majority party despite the biennial opportunities to change election outcomes has been the relative infrequency of divided party control of Federal institutions at any given time. The parties have shared control for only thirty-six of the 116 years from 1861 to 1976 (fourteen out of forty-two years since 1933). It has been the norm for one party to win the two or three institutions (Presidency, Senate, House) at stake in any given election year. This has happened in forty-eight of the fifty-nine election years since 1860. In particular, Congress has not been divided between the parties since 1916, though such a division was a fairly common occurrence before the Senate was directly elected. Divided control of the executive and the legislature following the presidential party's loss of the House in mid-term elections was invariably followed by loss of the Presidency two years later from 1882 until Truman's unexpected victory in 1948. On only three occasions from 1860 to 1948 did divided control occur in a presidential election year: in 1876, 1884 and 1916. But a Republican President has confronted a Democratic Congress following three of the six presidential elections since 1956.

The second electoral pattern, that of divided control, is distinguished by fluctuations in the identity of the winning party in presidential elections while one party usually wins the Congress. This pattern may be based either on great stability in voting behaviour with small swings producing the fluctuating pattern (1836–48 and 1876–92) or on volatile voting behaviour (1952–76). The Whigs and Democrats were so evenly balanced from 1836 to 1852 that the Presidency changed hands at every election; the winner's margin never exceeded 7 per cent of the popular vote and both parties won at least 30 per cent of the electoral college vote in each region. No region was consistently dominated by one party, though the Middle-Atlantic States were all won by the Whigs in 1840 and 1848 and by the Democrats in 1852. However, the Democrats maintained control of Congress except in 1840 and 1842.

The second period of close competition lasted from 1874 until the presidential election of 1892. The Republicans won three presidential elections (1876, 1880 and 1888) and the Democrats two (1884 and 1892). The losing Democratic candidates won more popular votes than their victorious Republican rivals in 1876 and 1888. The Presidency changed hands in four successive elections between 1884 and 1896, while the popular vote margin between the parties was extremely small—not exceeding 3 per cent until 1896. Only in 1892 did the winning candidate receive more than 60 per cent of the electoral college votes. Congress was frequently divided between the parties, with the Democrats winning the directly elected House and the Republicans winning the indirectly elected Senate. Stability in voting behaviour was emphasized by the relatively small number of States changing allegiance from election to election—an average of six States per election from 1876 to 1892, compared to eight States from 1840 to 1852 and twenty-one States from 1952 to 1968. Two-thirds of the States voting in every election from 1876 to 1892 voted for the same party, compared to one-half from 1840 to 1852 and one State only, Arizona, from 1952 to 1968.

Close competition from 1874 to 1892 was based on the sectional sources of support for the major parties. The Democrats won every Southern and Border State from 1880 to 1892, as well as three States which were then part of the political border— Delaware, Maryland and New Jersey. The Republicans were almost as dominant in New England, the North-Central and Western regions, where only California, Connecticut and Indiana voted more than once for the Democrats; Pennsylvania, the second largest State in the electoral college, was also solidly Republican. In such circumstances the behaviour of a few key States was critical in deciding election outcomes. New York was particularly important, voting once only for the losing candidate —in 1876—as it changed its allegiance at every election.

The third period of frequent change in the identity of the winning party in presidential elections began in 1952. The Republicans have won four presidential elections and the Democrats three. The Presidency has changed hands at every second election, but the Democrats have controlled Congress apart from the eighty-third Congress in 1953–4.

Historically, the two basic types of electoral pattern have produced the five party systems labelled and summarized in Table 5.1. They do not embrace every presidential election. The election of 1824 marked the end of the congressional caucus as the principal element in the nomination process and broke up the fragile unity of the one major party. The elections of 1852 and 1856 were comfortable Democratic victories at a time when the party system and the nation were on the verge of the collapse. The elections of 1912 and 1916 constituted a short-lived Democratic success brought about by Theodore Roosevelt's decision to run as a Progressive against his party's nominee, William Howard Taft, and maintained by the outbreak of the First World War in Europe, which delayed the Republican recovery in presidential elections until 1920.

The key questions raised by the cyclical pattern concern the bases of the voting alignments supporting the distinct electoral phases and the causes of change from one phase to its successor. The social diversity of the American political system and the variety of divisive issues have given rise to rival yet complementary interpretations of electoral politics: one an economic determinist interpretation stressing socio-economic forces and the other an ethno-cultural interpretation emphasizing religious and ethnic cleavages.

Explanations of electoral alignments

Socio-economic interpretations of American electoral history assert the superiority of class and economic distinctions over ethnic and religious divisions as the decisive sources of party support. Jefferson, Jackson and their heirs in the Democratic party are presumed to have relied consistently at the polls on less well-to-do, low-status elements in society. The richer, high-status groups are estimated to have voted predominantly for Federalists, Whigs and Republicans. The priority assigned to socio-economic classes and interests is encouraged by the frequent coincidence of class, religious and ethnic characteristics. Most Irish immigrants after 1820 were Catholic and working-class. Irish Catholic support for the Democratic party before and after the Civil War is attributed to socio-economic factors, in particular the Democratic image, diligently sought after, as the representative of working-class interests. Economic issues are allocated a primary place in explanations of electoral trends: e.g. tariffs, the Bank of the United States in the 1830s, 'sound money' in the

Table 5.1:

Five American party systems 1789–1974*

Party system	Time scale	Parties	Electoral Phases	
First 'The Experimental System'	1792–1824	Federalist Democratic-Republican	(a) 1792–98 (b) 1800–16 (c) 1816–24	Federalist superiority Democratic-Republican monopoly One-party system
Second 'The Democratizing System'	1824–1852	Democrats National Republicans/ Whigs	(a) 1824–28 (b) 1828–38 (c) 1840–52	Formative stage Jacksonian monopoly Control divided between Democrats and Whigs
Transitional	1854–1858	Disintegration of Whigs; formation of Republican Party		
Third 'The Civil War System'	1860–1894	Republicans Democrats	(a) 1860–72 (b) 1874–94	Republican monopoly Divided control
Fourth 'The Industrialist System'	1896–1930	Republicans Democrats	(a) 1896–1908 (b) 1910–18 (c) 1920–30	Republican monopoly Divided control Republican monopoly
Fifth 'The New Deal System'	1930–	Democrats Republicans	(a) 1932–50 (b) 1952–76	Democratic predominance Divided control

* The labels attached to the five party systems are derived from W. D. Burnham, 'Party Systems and the Political Process', in W. N. Chambers and W. D. Burnham, *The American Party Systems* (Oxford University Press, 1967).

1896 campaign, and the economic role of the Federal government since 1932.

In contrast, the ethno-cultural school of electoral politics, which has blossomed again since the early 1960s, emphasizes the relative superiority of social and cultural cleavages based on ethnic and religious identities as influences upon voting behaviour. Religious cleavages embrace intra-Protestant divisions as well as Protestant-Catholic conflict. Ethno-cultural interpretations also identify cultural issues such as abolition of slavery, temperance and prohibition, Sunday observance and language education as decisive when changes in alignment occurred in the 1850s and 1890s.

The rival interpretations are not mutually exclusive. Socio-economic and ethno-cultural cleavages have both influenced voting behaviour and party allegiances. The electoral consequences of immigration patterns and economic trends, particularly depressions, clearly demonstrate the need for both interpretations. It is the relative weight to be assigned to socio-economic and ethno-cultural factors as influences on the social composition of electoral parties and on the pattern of salient issues in successive party systems which has become a matter of controversy among historians and political scientists. The debate about the primary sources of earlier party systems and realignments has assumed particular relevance at a time when many observers detect several parallels between the volatile electoral politics of the post-Truman era and the political circumstances preceding major realignments in the past.

The first and second party systems, from 1792 to 1824 and from 1824 to 1852, developed and disintegrated at a time when the United States was preponderantly rural, Protestant and British in origin, though immigration after 1820 diversified the religious and ethnic structure. In the first system, the Federalist party, élitist in style and attitude, represented in particular the mercantilist interests of New England and asserted the legitimacy of an active Federal role to promote economic development. The Democratic-Republicans, more popular in style, attitude and organization, were strongly supported in the South and by most farmers throughout the Union, though some planters and farmers producing cash crops preferred the Federalists.

Sectionalism, based on personal and economic factors, was a pronounced feature of voting patterns in the key elections of 1800 and 1828, which introduced the periods of Jeffersonian and Jacksonian predominance. Jefferson (Virginia) was supreme in the South as was Jackson (Tennessee), who also swept the Western States (Illinois, Indiana, Ohio, Missouri) which had entered the Union after 1800. Both were identifiable and clearly identified as Southerners. John Adams and his nephew, John Q. Adams, the defeated incumbents, both of Massachussets, were as clearly associated with New England. A leading historian of the second party system has pointed to the sectional appeals implicit in the presidential candidates as the decisive force behind the comprehensive, competitive two-party system which developed when Jackson was no longer a candidate.*

Southern support for Jackson as candidate was monolithic. But the President's choice of the New Yorker, Martin Van Buren, to succeed him as Democratic candidate, and some of Van Buren's actions in office, which offended Southern interests, introduced two-party politics to the South in 1836. Van Buren lost Georgia and Tennessee, where Jackson had won nearly 100 per cent of the vote in 1832. A severe economic depression in 1837 and the Whig's choice of a general as candidate, Harrison, led to the failure of Van Buren's bid for re-election in 1840.

One investigation of voting patterns in the second party system locates areas of Democratic strength in remoter, low-income, upland counties throughout the United States. The Whigs attracted majority support in more accessible, high-income counties where land was of higher quality.† However, ethno-cultural influences were also active in the strong support for Jackson among the Protestant Scotch-Irish who tended to inhabit frontier territory.

The contemporary challenge to socio-economic interpretations originated with the publication of Lee Benson's 'The Concept of Jacksonian Democracy' in 1961.‡ Benson concentrated on New

* R. P. McCormick, *The Second American Party System* (The University of North Carolina Press, 1966).

† W. D. Burnham, *Presidential Ballots 1836–1892* (The Johns Hopkins Press, 1955).

‡ Lee Benson, *The Concept of Jacksonian Democracy* (Princeton U.P., 1961).

York State politics from 1816 to 1844, paying particular attention to the 1844 presidential election. His main conclusion asserted that 'the Jacksonians' strongest support came from relatively high-status socio-economic groups in the eastern counties, and relatively low-status ETHNO-CULTURAL AND RELIGIOUS GROUPS [his emphasis] in all sections of New York.'* Benson attributed the main influence upon voting behaviour to 'intense ethno-cultural and religious antagonisms' or to 'localistic factors which explain diverse voting patterns in similar social environments'. The Whigs were open to persuasion on the issue of political rights for blacks and received overwhelming support in return. Irish Catholics were strongly Democratic in response to the hostility expressed towards them by native Protestant groups. Immigrants were almost exclusive in their party allegiance. The 'new' British were predominantly Whig supporters, hoping thereby to achieve speedy acceptance as worthy American citizens. Irish and German immigrants were strongly Democratic as a means of defence against anti-Catholicism. Established groups tended to divide more evenly between the parties because their party allegiance varied from State to State.

Immigration had major political consequences and provides the foundations of the ethno-cultural approach to party politics. Five million immigrants entered the United States from 1820 to 1859. Almost 70 per cent came from Ireland and Germany. Immigration provided one source of instability throughout the second party system, as anti-Catholic groups formed a series of third parties which took support from the Whigs, e.g., the Anti-Masons and the American or Know-Nothing party. Immigration increased enormously during the early 1850s, leading to the formation of the Know-Nothing party, which won 22 per cent of the popular vote in the 1856 presidential election.

The strains on the second party system originating in religious and ethnic cleavages coincided with another major conflict— economic, cultural and sectional in character—that over slavery, which provoked abolitionist sentiments among the more evangelical Protestant groups in the North and revived North-South sectionalism in the form of conflict over the balance between

* *Ibid.*, pp. 331–332.

slave and non-slave States as the United States developed west-
wards. The annexation of Texas during Polk's administration
raised the slavery issue and prompted the appearance of anti-
slavery parties, the Liberty and Free Soil parties.

The Whigs, and therefore the second party system, could not
survive the sharp increase in religious and sectional conflict in the
early 1850s. The principal political event sparking off a period of
intense conflict culminating in realignment around the Republican and Democratic parties was the Kansas-Nebraska Act of
January 1854. This legislation, a deal between Democratic
Senator Douglas of Illinois and Southern Democrats, revived the
North-South conflict over the status of slavery in newly settled
Territories. The prospect of an unanticipated increase in the number of slave States strengthened abolitionist forces in the North
who had objected to slavery on moral grounds. The abolition
question revived North-South conflicts and eliminated Southern
Whigs.

The Whigs were already under pressure as a consequence of
nativist, Protestant protests against Catholic immigration, which
had increased dramatically after 1850. The Whigs, already identified as the more Protestant of the two major parties, could not
prevent Protestant support going to the 'Know-Nothing' party,
which was more overtly anti-Catholic. The Whigs gave way to
the Republican party, formed in 1854, which was able to unite
opponents of slavery, the South and Catholicism.

The links between religion and electoral politics are varied and
complex. The allegiance of conflicting religious groups to rival
political parties can be explained in three ways. Religious groups
may regard one another as negative reference groups, so that
their members vote against parties which they believe are supported by rival religious groups. There may be a conflict in life-
styles associated with religious groups, for example, temperance
and prohibition (evangelical Protestants) as opposed to liberal
licensing attitudes (Catholics and German Lutherans). Or there
may be a conflict of religious beliefs which influence voting
patterns, as when evangelical or pietistic Protestants became
strong Republican supporters when the Civil War party system
emerged while non-evangelical Protestants and (ritualistic)

Catholics tended to support the Democrats. The Republican party favoured an active moral role on the part of Federal and State governments to ensure compliance with evangelical views on prohibition and Sunday observance. The Democratic party opposed interference with the liberty to drink beer on Sundays, thus acquiring the reputation of protecting minority group interests.

Ethno-cultural interpretations of electoral politics emphasize the religious basis of party competition between 1860 and 1892. Many Protestants, particularly evangelical sects, who had supported Jefferson and Jackson, crossed over to the Republican party. Democratic strength in rural Protestant areas of the North was virtually eliminated. However, Catholic support for the Democratic party remained extremely high and non-evangelical Protestants, particularly German Lutherans, remained in the Democratic camp. The ethno-cultural view is summed up in the claim that 'Democratic partisan loyalties were not rooted in economic class distinctions but in religious value systems.'[*]

Nonetheless, economic conditions remain indispensable to explanations of individual election results and the critical realignments of 1896 and 1932. Acute economic downturns preceded Van Buren's defeat in 1840, the 1874 Democratic success in elections to the House of Representatives, and the Republican landslides of 1894 and 1896. The realignment of 1896 was based on intense economic and ethno-cultural forces, which reinforced long-standing sectional divisions. Economic depression resulted in a Republican landslide in 1894 before Bryan, the evangelical Protestant and Populist leader, was nominated as the Democratic candidate in 1896. Although Bryan mounted a campaign based on appeals to agrarian and working-class groups, he failed because he was identified as a sectional candidate and as a religious fundamentalist whose moral views clashed with those of strong Democratic supporters in the Catholic and non-evangelical Protestant communities. The religious aspect brought the Democrats some new support from Protestants who had supported pro-

[*] P. Kleppner, *The Cross of Culture: A Social Analysis of Midwestern Politics* (The Free Press, 1970).

hibitionist parties; but it freed some working-class Catholics to support the Republican party, which appealed successfully to most Northern economic interests against Southern and Western agrarian and mining interests. 'Free silver' did not appeal to the Northern working class as a cure for economic depression.

The sectional conflicts decided the election. The Republican candidate, McKinley, won 48 per cent of the electoral college when he carried the sixteen States in the Northeast and the Great Lakes, including the four largest States, New York, Pennsylvania, Illinois and Ohio, which together accounted for a quarter of the electoral college. Bryan swept the seventeen States of the South and the Mountain region, but this sectional support brought him less than 30 per cent of the electoral college.

The sectional divisions in the 1896 realignment were intensified by subsequent political developments. Favourable economic conditions maintained Republican electoral strength in the North. The Democrats created a one-party system in the South based on the reinforcement of Civil War loyalties following the clash of economic interests explicit in the 1896 campaign. The Republicans were almost as strong in the North. Democratic candidates were able to win only sixteen of the 202 contests for States outside the South in the six Republican victories between 1896 and 1928.

The Republican era was interrupted by Woodrow Wilson's two terms in office. Wilson won in 1912 because Theodore Roosevelt's decision to run as a Progressive presented the electorate with two rival Republican candidates who together won 50·5 per cent of the popular vote but only 18 per cent of the electoral college.

The Republican monopoly of victory in Federal elections was resumed in 1920. Republican candidates averaged 62·6 per cent of the popular vote in the three presidential elections from 1920 to 1928. The votes of several ethnic groups disaffected by American intervention in the First World War, particularly Germans and Irish Catholics, swelled the Republican majority established in the realignment of 1896. So pervasive was Republican superiority outside the South that Democratic presidential candidates could win only three non-Southern States, Oklahoma in 1924 and Massachussets and Rhode Island in 1928.

The Republican era was brought to a close by the great economic depression of the 1930s. The Wall Street crash, which began in October 1929, provoked immediate electoral repercussions. Republican congressional majorities were reduced in November 1930 from 104 to two in the House and from seventeen to one in the Senate. In 1932 the Democrats swept to comfortable election victories. The New Deal policies of President Roosevelt confirmed the Democrats as the new majority party whose strength lay in an electoral coalition between the staunchly Democratic South and blue-collar workers in the cities of the more industrialized States of the Northeast. The Republican party won only one national election in the two decades after 1932, the mid-term congressional elections of 1946. Harry Truman, who succeeded to the Presidency following Roosevelt's death in 1945, was widely expected to lose in 1948. However, Truman won in the closest presidential contest since 1916.

The Democrats' loss of both Presidency and Congress in 1952 ushered in a new electoral phase in which four Republican victories in seven presidential elections up to 1976 contrast strongly with unbroken Democratic control of Congress from 1954. During this period, rapid changes in election issues and a wide variety of major party candidates have distracted the American electorate from the New Deal alignment without prompting a stable realignment in the sources of support for the parties.

Election results 1952–1976

Eisenhower's 1952 victory was largely the consequence of discontent with the Democratic administration's record in office, particularly in foreign affairs, where Truman had accepted widespread commitment to contain rather than eliminate the perceived threat of communist expansion, and stalemate rather than victory in the Korean War. Personality was also important in 1952. Eisenhower's army career and war record brought him much greater personal support than the orthodox political career of the Democratic candidate, Adlai Stevenson, Governor of Illinois. This personal factor was critical in 1956 when the force of foreign policy as an electoral issue declined. But Eisenhower's personal popularity, which enabled him to win landslide victories over Stevenson and allowed the Republicans to win very narrow victories in the 1952 elections to the House and the Senate, could not prevent the Democrats from regaining control of Congress in 1954. In 1956, control of Presidency and Congress was divided between the parties for the first time in a presidential election year since 1916.

In 1960 the religious issue created by Kennedy's Catholicism had a marked impact upon voting behaviour as Catholics gave the Democratic candidate their strongest support in the post-1932 period, higher even than the support given to Johnson in the 1964 Democratic landslide. One estimate puts the effect nationally of the religious issue as a loss of 2·2 per cent in the popular vote for Kennedy, the net result of a 16·5 per cent loss in the South and 1·6 per cent gain elsewhere. Another source estimates that Kennedy enjoyed a net gain of twenty-two electoral college votes because Catholic votes brought him Northeastern States that he would otherwise have lost (including New York and Pennsylvania) to offset the loss of States (including California) that he would have won but for the religious issue. The narrowness of Kennedy's popular vote victory over Nixon and the fact that he ran behind congressional Democrats in many districts made it difficult for the new President to live up to his campaign promise to get the country moving again.

In 1964 the Republicans nominated a conservative, ideological candidate, Senator Goldwater, the so-called minority candidate of the minority party. Untypically, foreign policy issues worked strongly to the advantage of the Democratic party because the prospect of Goldwater as Commander-in-Chief was frightening to many Americans. Lyndon Johnson, the first Southerner to be nominated by the Democrats in the twentieth century, attracted the highest ever Democratic popular vote, 61·1 per cent. The Democrats also won their highest share of House and Senate seats since 1936.

In 1968 the Democratic party was demoralized by the anti-war primary challenges of Eugene McCarthy and Robert Kennedy and by President Johnson's decision not to stand for re-election. Intra-party conflict thereafter assumed violent proportions at the notorious August convention in Chicago where Johnson's Vice-President, Hubert Humphrey, was nominated. The major issues in 1968 were the Vietnam war and the so-called 'social issue', an amalgam of concern about the apparent consequences of the activities of the civil rights movement and rising social unrest. Racial unrest prompted a former Governor of Alabama, George Wallace, to run as an independent candidate. Wallace won Southern electoral college votes which might otherwise have gone to Nixon, who was running as Republican candidate for the second time. Nixon won a very narrow victory in the popular vote and, as in 1956, a Republican presidential victory failed to dislodge the Democratic majority in Congress.

In 1972 it was the turn of the Democrats to break the rule that middle-of-the-road candidates must be nominated to maximize chances of winning by nominating Senator George McGovern from the left wing of the party. McGovern was in effect the minority candidate of the majority party. Incumbent President Nixon won the third highest victory in the electoral college and the highest ever Republican popular vote. Yet the Republican landslide in the presidential context was accompanied by very modest gains in the House and a loss of two seats in the Senate, so that the Democrats easily retained control of Congress.

The resignation of President Nixon and an increase in the number of presidential primaries led in 1976 to a contest between an incumbent but non-elected Republican President and the first Democratic candidate from the Deep South since the Civil War. The former Democratic Governor of Georgia, Jimmy Carter, won by the narrowest margin in the electoral college since 1916. But the congressional Democrats held on to the massive gains achieved in the mid-term 'Watergate' elections of 1974.

The sequence of national election results since 1952 has led to intense speculation among politicians and political scientists concerning the likelihood of another significant realignment in the state of party competition, based on changes in the sources of support for the major parties. The theme of realignment requires a detailed analysis of contemporary voting behaviour.

B: TRENDS IN CONTEMPORARY ELECTORAL POLITICS

There have been three distinctive trends in American electoral politics since 1952: volatility in presidential elections, especially in the South; marked divergences between presidential and congressional elections; and limited realignment in the sources of support for the major parties, which retain strong regional characteristics in spite of the decline of sectionalism which commenced in 1932.

Presidential elections*

In historical perspective, the post-1952 phase in American electoral history has been unique in the volatility of the voting public's reaction to the freqent changes in the decisive issues and personalities from one campaign to another. Following the run of five Democratic victories from 1932 to 1948, neither party won more than two successive elections between 1952 and 1976. Presidential elections since 1952 can be divided into two categories: the landslide elections of 1952, 1956, 1964 and 1972, and the close elections of 1960, 1968 and 1976. Incumbent Presidents Eisenhower, Johnson and Nixon easily won second terms in 1956, 1964 and 1972 respectively, but their parties' candidates were all narrowly defeated at the following elections.

Third-party candidates made a considerable impact in 1968 and 1976. In 1968 there was widespread concern that the breakaway former Governor of Alabama, George Wallace, might win sufficient electoral college votes to throw the election into the House of Representatives. Wallace won 13·9 per cent of the vote nationally, the highest poll by a third-party candidate since La Follette attracted 17·2 per cent in 1924. Wallace won 34 per cent of the popular vote and forty-six electoral college votes in the South. In 1976 Eugene McCarthy, running as an Independent in twenty-nine States, won a mere 1 per cent of the vote nationally.

* See Table 5.2 for a list of presidential and congressional election results since 1932.

But McCarthy is credited with reducing Carter's victory in the electoral college by attracting sufficient votes in Illinois, Oklahoma and Oregon to enable Ford to win their electoral votes. McCarthy's impact in 1976 was out of all proportion to his support because the contest between Carter and Ford was extremely close in many States. Nevertheless, McCarthy's vote was much less than predicted by the polling organizations, whose findings encouraged the belief that McCarthy's appeal to Democratic voters could allow Ford to win.

There have been wide fluctuations, illustrated in Table 5·2, in the winning candidate's margin of victory in the popular vote, ranging from 0·2 per cent in 1960 (Kennedy), 0·7 per cent in 1968 (Nixon) and 2·3 per cent in 1976 (Carter) to 15·4 per cent in 1956 (Eisenhower), 22·6 per cent in 1964 (Johnson) and 23·3 per cent in 1972 (Nixon). In 1964 Democratic President Johnson won the highest ever popular vote for a presidential candidate, 61·1 per cent. Eight years later, Republican President Nixon won the third highest popular vote, 60·7 per cent, and the third highest share of electoral college votes (Monroe lost only one electoral vote in 1820; Roosevelt lost eight in 1936; Nixon lost seventeen in 1972).

Volatility is also evident in the upsurge in ticket splitting since 1962. Ticket splitting is the practice of voters casting their votes for candidates of more than one party when filling the many offices at stake on any one election day. In 1968 the voters of Arkansas supported the candidacies of George Wallace for President (American Independent Party, 38·9 per cent of the popular vote), Winthrop Rockefeller for Governor (Republican, 52·4 per cent) and William J. Fulbright for Senator (Democrat, 59·1 per cent). Ticket splitting has been particularly pronounced between presidential and congressional elections. In 1972 Nixon won 60·8 per cent of the presidential vote, while the Republican party could win only 46·4 per cent in elections to the House of Representatives. Nixon carried 337 congressional districts, of which only 192 elected a Republican Representative. In 1976 New Jersey went Republican in the presidential election but Democratic House candidates won eleven of the fifteen congressional districts. Split outcomes in the electorate's choice of Governors and Senators, both with Statewide constituencies, elected on the same day, rose from 27 per cent of all such elections in the 1950s to 44 per cent of all such elections from 1964 to 1970.

Volatility has not reversed the nationalization of electoral politics which accompanied the rise of the Democratic party to majority status in the 1930s. The 1932 realignment destroyed the highly sectionalized conflict, rural South and West opposing industrial North, on which Republican predominance was based from 1896. The South remained a Democratic section in presidential elections until the Dixiecrat revolt in 1948. But two-party politics was extended in the North, based on a moderate class cleavage reflecting differences in attitudes regarding the appropriate role for the Federal government in directing the economy and alleviating the ills of economic depression. The four successive victories of Franklin Roosevelt ensured the erosion of sectionalism outside the South, though the Republican party won a majority of Northern (the term henceforth used in this chapter to refer to other than Southern and Border) House seats from 1938 until the Democratic landslide in the 1958 congressional elections.

The nationalization of electoral politics has been extended since 1952. The variation across the States in the distribution of the popular vote between the major parties in presidential elections has declined. In 1976, twenty-seven States divided their votes between Carter and Ford within the range 47 per cent to 53 per cent. The most volatile swings against Goldwater in 1964 and McGovern in 1972 demonstrated that almost every State can be persuaded to desert its longer-term tendency to support one or other of the major parties. Arizona was alone in supporting the same party, the Republicans, in all seven presidential elections between 1952 and 1976. Only Massachusetts, after voting for Eisenhower in 1952 and 1956, has supported the five Democratic candidates from 1960 to 1976. The District of Columbia, where over 70 per cent of the population is black, has supported Democratic candidates since its admission to the electoral college in 1964.

The rise of the Democratic party to majority status in the 1930s meant that sectionalism was slower to decline in the South, the

Table 5.2:

Results of Federal elections 1932–1980

Year	Presidency					House of Representatives					Senate*		
	Turnout (%)	Electoral college (No.) D	R	Popular votes (%) D	R	Turnout (%)	Popular votes (%) D	R	Seats (%) D	R	Seats (No.) D	R	Other
1932	52·4	472	59	57·4	39·7	49·7	54·5	41·4	71·9	26·9	59	36	1
1934						41·4	53·9	42·0	74	23·6	69	25	2
1936	56·9	523	8	60·8	36·5	53·5	55·8	39·6	76·5	20·5	75	17	4
1938						44	48·6	47·0	60·2	38·9	69	23	4
1940	58·9	449	82	54·7	44·8	55·4	51·3	45·6	61·3	37·2	66	28	2
1942						32·5	46·1	50·6	51·3	48·0	57	38	1
1944	56·0	432	99	53·4	45·9	52·7	50·6	47·2	55·9	43·7	53	38	1
1946						37·1	44·2	53·5	43·2	56·6	45	51	–
1948	51·1	303	189	49·5	45·1	48·1	51·9	45·5	60·5	39·3	54	42	–
1950						41·1	49·0	49·0	53·8	45·7	48	47	–
1952	61·6	89	442	44·4	55·1	57·6	49·2	49·3	48·9	50·8	47	48	–
1954						41·7	52·1	47·1	53·3	46·7	48	47	–

Year												
1956 / 1958	59·3	74	457	42	57·4	55·9 / 43	50·7 / 56·1	48·7 / 43·5	53·8 / 64·7	46·2 / 35·9	49 / 66	47 / 34	— / —
1960 / 1962	62·8	303	219	49·7	49·5	58·5 / 45·4	54·7 / 52·5	44·8 / 47·2	60·2 / 59·3	39·8 / 40·5	64 / 68	36 / 32	— / —
1964 / 1966	61·9	486	52	61·1	38·5	57·8 / 45·4	57·2 / 50·9	42·3 / 48·8	67·8 / 57	32·2 / 42·9	67 / 64	33 / 36	— / —
1968 / 1970	60·9	191	301	42·7	43·4	55·1 / 43·5	50 / 53·4	48·2 / 45·1	55·9 / 58·6	44·1 / 41·4	58 / 55	42 / 45	— / —
1972 / 1974	55·5	17	521	37·5	60·7	51·0 / 36·2	51·7 / 57·6	46·4 / 40·6	59·9 / 66·9	44·1 / 33·1	57 / 62	43 / 38	— / —
1976	54·4	297	241	50·1	48·0	n.a.	n.a.	n.a.	67·1	32·8	62	38	—
1976 / 1978	54·3	297	241	50·1	48·0	49·6 / 35·2	56·3 / 53·5	42·0 / 45·0	67·1 / 63·4	32·9 / 36·6	62 / 59	38 / 41	— / —
1980	52	49	489	41	51	not available			55·9	44·1	47	53	—

Sources: Annual Statistical Abstract of the United States (Bureau of the Census); press reports of 1980 results.

* The distribution of popular votes between the parties in elections to the Senate is not given because the staggered elections mean that the composition of the electorate changes radically every two years.

traditionally Democratic section, than elsewhere. The basis of Southern sectionalism lay in the racial situation, in the determination of whites to dominate politics and society. The eleven Southern States became typed as the 'Solid South' as a result of allocating all their electoral college votes to Democratic presidential candidates from 1880 to 1944, with the sole exceptions of Tennessee in 1920 and four Outer South States in 1928 when the Democrats nominated a Roman Catholic candidate, Al Smith of New York. The unanimous support of the Solid South enabled Grover Cleveland (1884 and 1892) and Woodrow Wilson (1916) to win the Presidency despite pronounced Republican superiority outside the South and Border States.

Several changes in voting behaviour since 1948 indicate that sectionalism in the South has been reduced to the five States of the Deep South, where the black population is the highest in the nation, ranging, in 1970, from 26 per cent in Georgia to 37 per cent in Mississippi. The Solid South was broken in 1948 when the Deep South States other than Georgia supported the Dixiecrat challenge of Strom Thurmond, who broke away from the Democratic party in protest against the tentative desegregationist moves of the Roosevelt and Truman administrations. (Thurmond was to return to the Democratic ranks as Senator for South Carolina in 1954 and 1960, but he successfully ran for re-election as a Republican in 1966 and 1974). Truman ran behind Dewey in the Northern States, but his sweep of the Outer South and the Border States ensured his election. The South was not to play such a decisive role again in the election of a Democratic President until 1976.

Since 1948 the Deep South States have continued to demonstrate strongly sectional characteristics by voting together in presidential elections in distinctive ways. Stevenson received more than half his electoral college votes in the Deep South in 1952 and 1956 (Louisiana voted for Eisenhower in 1956), when the region reverted to the traditional method of protecting white supremacy by voting Democratic in Federal and State elections. In 1960 Southern unease with growing Federal intervention in the race relations field led to electoral college support for Senator Byrd in Alabama and Mississippi. In 1964 and 1968, the Deep South was almost alone in supporting Goldwater and Wallace respectively, though South Carolina opted for Nixon in 1968.

Whites in the Deep South voted for the candidates who appeared most likely to resist or slow down the desegregation process, which was gathering pace in the 1960s with the passage of the 1964 Civil Rights Act and the 1965 Voting Rights Act. Republican candidates have enjoyed few electoral victories in the Deep South despite winning a higher share of the popular vote since 1952. South Carolina was the only State in the Deep South to elect either a Republican Governor or a Republican Senator between 1952 and 1976. In 1974 the Republican party held only 7 per cent of seats in the lower houses of State Legislatures in the Deep South.

The Outer, or Rim, South is no longer part of a Southern section in presidential elections. With the exception of Arkansas in 1968, the Outer South States did not support Thurmond, Goldwater or Wallace. Rather, several Outer South States have opted strongly for presidential Republicanism. Virginia has supported every Republican candidate since 1952 except Goldwater; Florida and Tennessee were loyal to Eisenhower (twice) and Nixon (three times) but rejected Goldwater and Ford. Texas also supported Eisenhower in 1952 and 1956, but Kennedy's choice of Lyndon Johnson as vice-presidential candidate in 1960 brought Texas, the fourth largest unit in the electoral college, back into the Democratic camp. Although Johnson did not stand for re-election in 1968, his influence kept Texas loyal to Humphrey when the five other States in the Outer South went to Nixon. Texas was the only State in the Outer South not to elect at least one Republican Governor and Arkansas the only State not to elect a Republican Senator between 1952 and 1976. In 1974 the Republican party was still electorally weak at State level in the Outer South, winning only 17 per cent of seats in the lower houses of State Legislatures.

The faster growth of Republican support in the Outer South compared to the Deep South is the consequence of differences in reactions to changing race relations. Racial issues have had less electoral impact in the Outer South, where the black population is smaller, ranging in 1970 from 12·5 per cent in Texas to 22.2 per cent in North Carolina. Republican support in the Outer South has been most pronounced among the white, urban middle class, particularly in areas of industrial development.

In 1968, George Wallace demonstrated the electoral potential of the racial issue nationally when he won Democratic primaries in Maryland and Michigan and attracted 8 per cent of the popular vote outside the South in the presidential election. Wallace's success in 1968, and the improvement in the Republican position in the South encouraged the party's electoral strategists under Nixon to attempt to build a permanent source of electoral college votes for Republican candidates there. To this end Nixon followed a 'Southern strategy', which commenced with the selection of Spiro Agnew as vice-presidential candidate in 1968 and the nominations in 1969 and 1970 of two Southerners, Haynesworth and Carsewell, to the Supreme Court. The Southern strategy was held to be responsible for the resignation of several liberal officials from the Justice Department in protest against the Nixon administration's reluctance to proceed with desegregation measures, such as 'busing'.

The entire South was solid in 1972 for the first time since 1944. Nixon's sweep of the South, where he won some of his highest popular vote margins, made the likelihood of the Democrats regaining the South appear rather remote. But the 1976 Democratic primaries led to the nomination of a former Governor of the Deep Southern State of Georgia, whose subsequent victory over Ford was heavily dependent upon the South, where he carried every State except Virginia. Unlike Kennedy in 1960, Carter won fewer electoral college votes than his Republican opponent outside the South. The choice of a Southerner as presidential candidate was the vital factor in the Democratic victory in 1976. No other feature of the campaign can explain the return to the Democratic camp of the three Outer South States (Tennessee, Florida and Virginia) which had voted Republican in 1952, 1956, 1960, 1968 and 1972.

Carter also benefited from two other features of the 1976 campaign. There was no repeat of the Wallace intervention of 1968 because Wallace, who competed unsuccessfully in the Democratic primaries, was a spent force—confined to a wheelchair as a consequence of an assassination attempt during the 1972 campaign. Moreover, the racial issue was not as influential as in 1968 and 1972 because its character was changing: black militancy was on the decline; economic opportunities for middle-class blacks were improving; and the 'social issue' about the pace of integration, which helped Nixon in 1968, was less influential in 1976, giving way to concern about economic trends such as unemployment and inflation. Nevertheless, Gallup data indicate that a narrow majority among white voters preferred Ford to Carter in 1976. But the Democrats received partial compensation in the near-unanimous support of black voters, which enabled Carter to win several States which would otherwise have gone to Ford, including Mississippi, where Carter's winning margin was less than 2 per cent of the popular vote.

Despite the decline of sectionalism outside the Deep South and the volatile reactions of the electorate in 1964 and 1972, there have been considerable elements of stability in the sources of support for the major parties in presidential elections. Variations in demographic conditions and in related political attitudes give a distinctive regional flavour to the stable electoral alignment evident in the closely contested elections of 1960, 1968 and 1976, when twenty-eight States and the District of Columbia, more than half the electoral college, supported the same party each time. Twenty-two States, including the Southern States other than Texas (Democratic) and Virginia (Republican), changed allegiance at least once.

These regional sources of support for the major parties in 1960, 1968 and 1976 are illustrated in Table 5.3. The nineteen States with a consistent preference for presidential Republicanism are located mainly among the sparsely populated, fairly rural, small-town States in the Farm Belt, Mountain and Pacific regions, where Carter could carry only Hawaii and Minnesota in 1976. The Republican stronghold, which Johnson alone among Democratic candidates since 1952 has been able to break, occupies 27 per cent of the electoral college in the 1970s. Only California and Indiana have more than ten electoral college votes. New Hampshire and Vermont are all that remain of the old Republican section in New England; Oklahoma and Virginia are the only two among the Southern and Border States.

In contrast, Democratic strength in presidential elections lies heavily in the Northeast and in some of the larger, more industrialized States. Only nine States supported Kennedy, Humphrey and Carter, but, along with the District of Columbia, which has supported the Democratic candidate in every election since 1964, they occupy 27·5 per cent of the electoral college. Five of the strongly Democratic States (Maryland, Massachusetts, New York, Pennsylvania and Rhode Island) are located in the Northeast, a region which provided Democratic candidates with 43·8, 58·6 and 33·3 per cent of their electoral votes in 1960, 1968 and 1976. Hawaii, Minnesota, Texas and West Virginia also voted Democratic in the three closely fought elections.

Table 5.3:

Party shares (%) of electoral college votes by region in 1960, 1968 and 1976

Region	Votes in electoral college (%) in 1970s	1960 D	1960 R	1968 D	1968 R	1976 D	1976 R	1960, 1968 and 1976 combined D	1960, 1968 and 1976 combined R
Northeast	25·1	91·7	8·3	80·5	19·5	73·3	26·7	82·1	17·9
Midwest	17·8	48·5	51·5	21·4	78·6	37·5	62·5	35·7	64·3
Farm Belt	6·9	25·6	74·4	25·7	74·3	27	73	26·1	73·9
Mountain	6·5	21·7	78·3	0	100	0	100	7	93
Pacific	12·6	5·7	94·3	21	79	6	94	11	89·1
Border	6·5	53·8	43·6	19·5	80·5	77·2	22·8	50·5	49·5
Outer South	15·6	58·2	41·8	30·8	61·7	85·7	14·3	58·6	38·9
Deep South	8·6	71	0	0	17	100	0	56·8	5·6

With the more loyal States evenly divided between the two major parties, the winning candidates in 1960, 1968 and 1976 owed their success to changes of allegiance among the remaining twenty-two States. In 1960, Kennedy's overwhelming strength in the Northeast, where he lost only the very small States of Maine, New Hampshire and Vermont, was sufficient to offset Nixon's superiority elsewhere outside the South and Border, giving Kennedy 54 per cent of Northern electoral votes. Kennedy also won a majority of Southern and Border electoral votes. In 1968 Nixon led Humphrey in every region except the Northeast. The Democrats' net loss, relative to 1960, of three Northern States, including Illinois and New Jersey, allowed Nixon to win 58 per cent of Northern electoral votes. The Democrats lost the South, Texas apart, because of the impact of the racial issue. The Wallace intervention took electoral college votes away from Nixon rather than Humphrey. In 1976, Carter was slightly less successful than Humphrey in the North where the Democratic loss, relative to 1968, of Connecticut, Maine, Michigan, and Washington was not quite offset by gains in Delaware, Ohio and Wisconsin. But thirteen of the fifteen Southern and Border States voted for Carter and secured his election.

Thus the outstanding feature of presidential elections since 1952 has been the electorate's volatile reactions to the frequent changes in campaign issues and candidates. Eisenhower's victories were the result of discontent with the Truman administration's record in foreign affairs and the personal appeal of the soldier candidate. The landslides of 1964 and 1972 were characterized by the choice of minority candidates, who were seen by voters as ideological, by the party which was out of office. The winners of the close elections benefited from the impact of short-term issues which gave them a majority of electoral votes among the States given to changing their allegiance—Kennedy's overwhelming appeal in the Northeast and in the Catholic community in 1960, the impact of the Vietnam war and the racial issue along with the Democrats' near-annihilation in the South in 1968, and Carter's inherent appeal as a Southerner in the South in 1976.

Congressional elections

The behaviour of the American electorate has been less volatile in congressional than in presidential elections. Despite biennial elections and primary elections the lowest percentage of incumbent Representatives re-elected to the House in recent years was 86·9 per cent in 1964. The relative stability of the electorate's response to parties, candidates and issues presented in congressional elections is emphasized by Democratic victories in every congressional election since 1932 except 1946 and 1952. But there has been a limited realignment in the regional sources of support for the congressional parties which, by reducing the number of Southern Democrats in the House, has had significant effects upon congressional politics. (See Section B, Chapter 8 below.)

Roosevelt's presidential victories in 1932 and 1936 were accompanied by Democratic landslides in congressional elections. In 1936 the Democrats won over three-quarters of House seats, including a majority in every region except the Farm Belt and New England. But by 1940 the Democratic share of House seats had fallen to just over 60 per cent, and a majority of Republican Representatives were returned from New England, the Middle-Atlantic States, and Midwest and the Farm Belt.

Between 1938 and 1956, the Democrats had to rely for their control of House committees and procedure upon huge majorities in the Southern and Border delegations to offset smaller but none the less comfortable Republican majorities elsewhere. In 1950 the sparsely populated Mountain States were the only region outside the South and Border to return a majority of Democratic Representatives to the House. The Republican share of Northern seats varied from 87 per cent in the Farm Belt, where only Minnesota returned Democratic Representatives, to 55·6 per cent in the Middle-Atlantic States.

The 1958 mid-term elections brought an end to the pronounced Republican superiority in Northern congressional disstricts and mark the beginning of a limited realignment, illustrated in Table 5·4, in the regional sources of support for the congressional parties. Northern Democrats have on balance enjoyed an increase in influence in the House as a consequence of two distinct developments. Firstly, the Solid Democratic South, which remained intact throughout the 1930s and 1940s, has since been undermined as the number of Republican Representatives elected from the South rose from two in 1950 to thirty-six in 1972, falling back to twenty-seven in 1974 and 1976. Secondly, since 1958 the Democratic party has been winning a higher proportion of its New Deal constituency in the more heavily industrialized and urbanized States.

Between 1958 and 1976, Democrats won a majority of Northern House seats in five of the ten elections, usually on the basis of landslide victories: against economic recession in 1958, against Goldwater in 1964, and against the Republican party's unavoidable links with the Watergate scandal in 1974. In 1976, the Democrats held on to the gains of 1974, so that the new Democratic President inherited a Congress with an unusually large Democratic majority. Nevertheless, in elections such as 1960, 1962, 1966, 1968 and 1972 the Democrats remained dependent for control of Congress on winning the bulk of Southern and Border districts, despite the gradual emergence of a two-party South since 1952. Changes in the relative weight of the Northern and Southern elements of the Democratic party are clearly indicated in Table 5·4 by a comparison of 1958 and 1974. The proportion of Southern Representatives in the Democratic party in the House has fallen from over 40 per cent in the 1946–1956 period (from almost 55 per cent in the Republican landslide year of 1946) to around 30 per cent since 1964 (falling to 27·8 per cent in the Democratic landslide year of 1974).

Table 5.4:

Regional composition of House Democratic majorities in mid-term elections 1942–74

Region	1942	1946	1950	1954	1958	1962	1966	1970	1974
South	+101	+101	+101	+92	+92	+84	+60	+52	+54
Border	+10	0	+22	+21	+23	+16	+12	+18	+21
North	−102	−159	−87	−84	+15	−17	−11	+5	+72
U.S.A.	+9	−58	+36	+29	+130	+83	+61	+75	+147

The Republican party has been partly compensated for the deterioration in its position in the North by making inroads into the Solid Democratic South. The Republicans have made the more substantial gains in the expanding Outer South, where the number of Republican-held districts increased from two in 1950 to twenty-five in 1972. Gains were made in every election from 1966 until 1972, when Tennessee and Virginia elected more Republicans than Democrats. The Republicans lost six seats in 1974. In the Deep South the Republicans did not win any seats until 1964. But Goldwater's deliberate appeal to the South on the racial question led to seven Republican gains, breaking a long-lasting Democratic monopoly, which were increased in 1972 when the Republicans, strongest in Alabama and Mississippi, held at least one district in every State in the Deep South. In 1974 the Republicans lost their single seat in Georgia, so that 1972 marks the high point of the Republican advance in the South, when the party held 32·5 per cent of Southern congressional seats compared to 25 per cent in 1976.

The return of a Democratic President in 1976 put the seal on a strong upturn in Democratic electoral fortunes which began in 1974. The Democrats entered 1977 in control of thirty-seven governorships and thirty-six State legislatures. The Republicans held only twelve governorships and controlled both legislative houses in only five States.

C: THE DETERMINANTS OF VOTING BEHAVIOUR

The central concept in explanations of American voting behaviour is partisanship or party identification. Survey evidence indicates that two-thirds of the electorate have consistently acknowledged an identification with one or other of the two major parties. Feelings of partisanship, however they are acquired, are considered to constitute the principal influence upon the voting decision when individuals choose between rival party candidates at election time. However, partisanship is not the only influence; salient issues, perceptions of party policy, the personalities of candidates, and views on governmental performance in relation to dominant campaign issues are also present. The distribution of partisanship in the electorate as a whole does not predetermine election outcomes because not all voters are partisan, because turnout rates vary, and because even strong partisans, not to mention weaker brethren, may be tempted away from the preferred party by passing issues and candidates.

The social bases of partisanship and the impact of issues and candidate personality upon voters are analysed below, following a description of trends in partisanship. The post-1952 distribution of partisanship in the American electorate as a whole, based on the findings of the University of Michigan's Survey Research Centre, is detailed in Table 5.5.

Table 5.5:
Distribution of partisanship 1952–1972

Identification	1952	—54	—56	—58	—60	—62	—64	—66	—68	—70	—72
Democrats	47	47	44	47	46	46	51	45	45	43	40
Republicans	27	27	29	29	27	28	24	25	24	25	23
Independents	22	22	24	19	23	22	23	28	29	31	35

The pattern of party identification highlights three distinctive features in the electorate's collective attitude to the major parties. First, the Democrats have consistently enjoyed the support of the larger 'party in the electorate'. The margin of superiority of Democratic over Republican partisans has varied between 15 per cent in 1956 and 27 per cent in 1964. Approximately 45 per cent of the electorate has been offering some degree of psychological commitment to the Democrats compared to the 25 per cent claiming Republican identification. The majority status accorded the Democratic party is based upon its firm lead in party identification and on its electoral record since 1932. The strength of Democratic party identification is attributed to the change in public attitudes towards the parties initially stimulated by the failure of the Hoover administration to alleviate the distress associated with economic depression commencing in 1929, and maintained by Roosevelt's New Deal policies which identified the Democrats as the party of Federal action to promote social and economic welfare. Partisans are divided into strong and weak categories. The proportion of strong partisans, whose defection

F

rate at the polls is usually low, has not exceeded 40 per cent in the post-1952 period.

The second feature of party identification is the presence of a sizeable body of Independents whose voting decisions can be critical in deciding election outcomes. The Independents make it necessary for even the majority party to appeal beyond the ranks of its own partisans in order to win. The conventional wisdom that the parties ought to adopt middle-of-the-road candidates rather than representatives of the Democratic left or the Republican right—sound advice in the light of the experiences of Senators Goldwater and McGovern—is supported by the presence of large numbers of Independents. Independents have been the least interested in politics rather than the most dispassionate judges of policy distinctions between the parties.

The third feature concerns change in the distribution of party identification. The absence of major change in party identification attracted the attention of commentators in the 1950s and 1960s. Eisenhower's victories were accordingly analysed as merely temporary aberrations from the norm of Democratic control of both Presidency and Congress. Minor changes in the distribution of party identification did occur. Basic Republican strength in the electorate attained its peak during Eisenhower's presidency, whereas Democratic partisanship was highest in 1964. But changes in partisanship have become much more pronounced since 1966. The proportion of Independents has risen from 23 per cent in 1964 to 35 per cent in 1972. Both major parties have experienced a decline in partisan commitment relative to earlier peaks. Even in 1972, the year of the anti-McGovern landslide, Republican partisanship fell 2 per cent while Democratic partisanship dropped 3 per cent.

The nationwide distribution of partisanship described in Table 5.5 disguises the major differences between South and Non-South and between whites and blacks, which are illustrated in Table 5.6. The emphatic Democratic superiority in the nation as a whole relied heavily on a huge advantage in the South and on a comfortable lead among Catholics to overcome a Republican advantage among Northern white Protestants. The decline in Southern white identification with the Democratic party, which was particularly evident in 1960 in reaction to Kennedy's Catholicism, and which then became even more pronounced in 1968 and 1972 in response to the racial issue, has been offset by declining Republican identification among Northern white Protestants. The Democratic lead in partisanship has also benefited from the increase in black registration and voting and a marked increase in Democratic identification from 1964 onwards. The decline of 6 per cent in Democratic superiority between 1964 and 1968 is the net result of a 9 per cent decline among whites (90·6 per cent of the voting age population in 1968) and a 16 per cent gain among blacks (9·4 per cent of the voting age population). Democratic identification has declined dramatically in the South, falling from 56 per cent in 1964 to 26 per cent in 1968 in the twenty-one to twenty-eight-year-old Southern white category. But there has been no parallel move towards Republican identification, which has remained low.

Table 5.6:

Democratic lead in partisanship by region, race and religion 1952–1972

Group	1952	1956	1960	1964	1968	1972
U.S.A.	21	15	16	27	21	17
Whites	18	13	14	23	14	12
Blacks	39	31	28	67	83	59
White/Protestant/South	68	64	40	49	37	29
White/Protestant/North	—12	—16	—19	+ 1	— 8	— 6
Catholics	36	30	32	35	30	32

Sources: Survey Research Centre election studies reported in N. H. Nie, S. Verba and J. R. Petrocik, *The Changing American Voter* (Harvard U.P., 1976).

Philip Converse calculated on the basis of elections between 1952 and 1960 that a 'normal' Democratic vote of 54 per cent could be anticipated on the basis of the distribution of partisanship in various sections of the electorate.* The Democratic share

* P. E. Converse, 'The Concept of a Normal Vote' in A. Campbell *et al*, *Elections and the Political Order* (J. Wiley, 1966).

of the popular vote in House elections varied between 49·2 per cent in 1952 and 57·2 per cent in 1964, averaging 52·6 per cent in twenty years since 1952. The Democratic share of the presidential vote has been considerably lower than 54 per cent, with the single exception of 1964, as the sequence of campaign issues and candidates, including Wallace in 1968, attracted a larger defection rate among Democratic than Republican identifiers and a larger Republican share of Independents.

The behaviour of weak partisans and Independents, roughly 60 per cent of the national electorate, determines election outcomes. In 1948 partisan defection was low, although highest among weak Republican partisans, as Truman gained his largely unexpected triumph in a low turnout election decided by the underlying distribution of partisanship. Independents, whose turnout was low at 54 per cent, had a slight preference for Truman (54 per cent) over Dewey (45 per cent). In 1952 and 1956 Eisenhower received the votes of more than one-third of the weak Democratic partisans and two-thirds of the Independents who voted. In 1960 the Democratic advantage in partisanship was sufficient to elect Kennedy despite a higher defection rate among Democratic partisans and the smaller share (46 per cent) of Independents.

Earlier periods of one-party predominance electorally are now assumed to have rested upon a comparable distribution of partisanship favouring one of the two major parties, and presidential elections are classified in relation to the distribution of partisanship. Elections won in accordance with the pattern of party identification are defined as maintaining elections, since partisanship as the major influence on voting behaviour secures victory for the majority party. Elections won by the minority party are classified as deviating elections; here the net impact of campaign issues and candidates is sufficiently strong to turn many voters away from their commitment to the majority party without destroying that commitment.

Realigning or critical elections occur when the distribution of partisanship changes to a new but relatively stable equilibrium, producing a new majority party in the process. The elections of 1860, 1896 and 1932 are generally cited as examples of realigning elections, though the changes in voting behaviour characterizing the realignment may take place over two or three elections and are contingent upon continuity in or reinforcement of the political conditions underlying the realignment.

Not so much attention has been paid to the nature of alignments during periods when no majority party was apparent in election outcomes. Statistical information about party identification is available for the New Deal party system alone, particularly since 1952, so that there is considerable controversy regarding partisanship in earlier party systems. The Whig victories in 1840 and 1848 and the Democratic victories in 1884 and 1892 have been treated either as deviating elections lost by the majority Jacksonian and Republican parties or as evidence of approximate equality in partisanship. Both periods were notable for stable rather than volatile voting patterns. Both gave way to the dominance of a majority party when events such as the Kansas-Nebraska Act or the depression of the 1890s coincided with other tensions, notably ethno-cultural conflicts and sectional antagonisms, to stimulate the major or critical realignments of 1860 and 1896.

The bases of partisanship

Studies of British electoral behaviour emphasize the stability of a high level of class support for the two major parties and the phenomenon of working-class conservatism as the most significant qualification of dominant class norms in voting behaviour. In contrast American studies emphasize a volatile electorate and diverse sources of support for the major parties. Class is a significant factor in the determination of American voting patterns, though the influence of class is neither as extensive nor as stable as in Britain. The principal social forces qualifying the influence of class are religion and race. The major contrast in the political behaviour of American social classes lies in the considerable middle-class support for the Democratic party.

The Survey Research Centre's data on party identification shows that class defined by occupation (manual workers or blue-collar workers as opposed to non-manual workers or white-collar workers) is positively related to support for the major parties. There is a consistent tendency for the proportion of Democratic identifiers to be greater within manual sections of the electorate than within comparable non-manual sections: for example blue-collar Catholics are more heavily Democratic than white-collar Catholics, while Protestant manuals are more Democratic than Protestant non-manuals.

But the links between class and party identification are strongly qualified by religion. The Survey Research Centre found the following proportions of Democratic identifiers, excluding the South, in 1964 and 1968.

Table 5.7:

Democratic identifiers among religious groups in 1964 and 1968

	Catholics		Protestants	
	1964	1968	1964	1968
Manual	58	55	41	37
Non-manual	48	42	30	25

In 1964 and 1968 the proportion of Democratic identifiers was higher among middle-class (non-manual workers) Catholics than among working-class (manual workers) Protestants. Evidence collected by Gallup and by the Survey Research Centre indicates that middle-class Catholics have been consistently more Democratic than working-class Protestants both in party identification and in voting behaviour since 1932. Frequently a majority of middle-class Catholics have voted for Democratic presidential candidates, as in 1936–1948, 1960 and 1964. From 1932 to 1968 the only occasion when Democratic electoral support was higher among working-class Protestants than middle-class Catholics occurred in 1952, when only 35 per cent of the latter voted for Adlai Stevenson. The strength of Democratic identification among Catholics is most evident, other than in 1960, in deviating elections such as 1952 and 1956 when the Democratic candidate retained majority support among working-class Catholics (63 per cent and 60 per cent) but not among working-class Protestants (43 per cent and 44 per cent). Only middle-class Catholics earning over $15,000 p.a. indicated higher Republican than Democratic identification in 1964.

Religion has been a better indicator than class of the partisan leanings of middle-class Catholics. The influence of the ethnocultural forces which initiated strong Catholic support for the Democratic party in the nineteenth century has clearly persisted, even though Catholic support for Democratic presidential candidates has varied in accordance with the political forces producing the general volatility of the electorate. In 1964 middle-class white Protestants earning less than $10,000 were evenly distributed between the major parties. Only the wealthier middle-class Protestants earning over $10,000 were strongly Republican in partisanship.

The distributions of party identification by religion, occupation and race all contribute to the superior strength of the Democratic party in the electorate. Although there are more Protestants than Catholics, Protestants are much more evenly split between the two major parties, while Catholics are preponderantly Democratic. The description of the social characteristics of partisans by Flannigan indicated a Republican lead in 1964 and 1968 in only three categories, all Northern Protestants: white-collar workers, farmers and the retired.* Pomper found only one socio-economic group at the national level where Republican identifiers outnumbered Democratic in the 1960s, which was professional workers, though even they showed a narrow Democratic lead in 1964.†

Black Americans have become overwhelmingly Democratic in partisanship. Blacks constitute 11 per cent of the American population. The Democratic party identification of blacks shot up in the 1960s, the civil rights decade, from 44 per cent in 1960 to 74 per cent in 1964 and 85 per cent in 1968. Blacks, who were Republican supporters following the Civil War, were attracted to the Democratic party in the 1930s by Roosevelt's economic wel-

* Flannigan, *Political Behaviour of the American Electorate*, 2nd ed., (Allyn and Bacon, Boston, 1972), pp. 51–56.
† G. Pomper, *The Performance of American Government* (The Free Press, New York, 1972), pp. 68–69.

fare policies. Though blacks show up as more Democratic than whites in Survey Research Centre data for 1952 and 1956, the differences were relatively small. In 1959 19 per cent of blacks identified with the Republican party. However, the explicit Goldwater appeal for Southern white votes—he voted against the 1964 Civil Rights Act—and the increasing identification of the Democrats as the liberal and interventionist party in the civil rights arena completed the shift of blacks to Democratic partisanship.

The increase in black voter registration facilitated by the Civil Rights and Voting Rights Acts, the increase in Democratic identification, and an increase in black turnout has increased the contribution of blacks to the Democratic voting coalition from 7 per cent in 1960 to 19 per cent in 1968, when the Wallace intervention and Nixon's victory reduced white support for Humphrey. In 1972, despite McGovern's demoralizing campaign performance, 87 per cent of blacks supported the Democratic candidate when other traditionally Democratic voting groups such as Catholics, union families and manual workers were supporting Nixon by clear if limited majorities.

American Jews divide between strong Democratic partisanship and Independence, showing very little identification with the Republican party. This is partly due to the Democrats' image as the party more likely to protect minorities. It is also accounted for by long-standing left-wing sympathies in the Jewish community, which gave the Socialist Party considerable support in the years from 1910 to 1920, and by the decisions of Democratic Presidents Roosevelt and Truman to enter the Second World War against Germany in 1941 and to recognize and aid the new State of Israel in 1948. Ambiguities in McGovern's attitude to the Middle East conflict in 1972 led to fears that the Republican party would capture the Jewish vote, which could be critical in New York City and New York State in any closely contested election. In the event the Republican vote among Jews rose from 16 per cent in 1968 to over 30 per cent in 1972.

Although most social groups indicate a clear preference for one of the parties, few identify as strongly as do blacks and Jews. Both parties possess a heterogeneous social base, especially the Democrats. In 1968 Protestants (32 per cent) and Catholics (29 per cent), white-collar (23 per cent) and blue-collar (22 per cent) workers contributed almost equally to the set of 'strong' Democrats. In contrast 'strong' Republicans were much more heavily Protestant (73 per cent) than Catholic (13 per cent), while white-collar workers (41 per cent) outnumbered blue-collar workers (20 per cent) by two to one.

The allegiance of several sections in the electorate has been changing. Increasing support from the black community has given the Democrats partial compensation for the decline in partisanship among whites, particularly in the South. One other group which appears to be moving closer to the Democrats is the suburban whites, previously thought of as primarily Republican. In 1960 44 per cent of white suburbanites identified as Republicans; by 1970 only 26 per cent identified themselves as Republicans, compared to 39 per cent Democrats and 35 per cent Independents. The rise in Independents illustrated in Table 5.5 is most pronounced among younger voters and in the South. The proportion of Democratic identifiers among thirty to thirty-nine-year-olds fell 16 per cent in the 1960s. The proportion of Independents among white Protestant Southerners rose from 18 per cent in 1960 to 38 per cent in 1970, while the proportion of Democratic partisans fell from 61 per cent to 41 per cent.

The electoral impact of partisanship and the changing pattern of issues and candidates upon the voting behaviour of demographic groups is illustrated in Table 5.8. The dominant party preferences of various groups defined by occupation, race and religion are clear. However, the volatile reactions of such groups are also evident. Manual workers were more Democratic than white-collar workers in every election. A majority of manual workers supported and a majority of white-collar workers opposed the Democratic candidate in five of the seven elections between 1952 and 1976 (counting the major party vote only in 1968). But Eisenhower attracted 50 per cent of manual votes in 1956 while Nixon won 57 per cent in 1972. Johnson won a majority of professional and white-collar workers in 1964. The Democratic dependence on strong Catholic support to offset superior Republican strength among Protestants is evident in every election except 1964. But a majority of Catholics preferred Nixon to McGovern

Table 5.8:

Voting by social groups in presidential elections since 1956

Group	1956 Stev. %	Ike %	1960 J.F.K. %	Nixon %	1964 L.B.J. %	Gold. %	1968 H.H.H. %	Nixon %	Wallace %	1972 McG. %	Nixon %	1976 Carter %	Ford %
U.S.A.	42·2	57·8	50·1	49·9	61·3	38·7	43·0	43·4	13·6	38	62	51	49
Men	45	55	52	48	60	40	41	43	16	37	63	52	48
Women	39	61	49	51	62	38	45	43	12	38	62	52	48
White	41	59	49	51	59	41	38	47	15	32	68	48	52
Non-white	61	39	68	32	94	6	85	12	3	87	13	83	17
College	31	69	39	61	52	48	37	54	9	37	63	43	57
High school	42	58	52	48	62	38	42	43	15	34	66	54	46
Grade school	50	50	55	45	66	34	52	33	15	49	51	59	41
Prof. and Business	32	68	42	58	54	46	34	56	10	31	69	43	57
White collar	37	63	48	52	57	43	41	47	12	36	64	51	49
Manual	50	50	60	40	71	29	50	35	15	43	57	59	41
Under 30 years	43	57	54	46	64	36	47	38	15	48	52	56	44
30–49 years	45	55	54	46	63	37	44	41	15	33	67	52	48
50 years and older	39	61	46	54	59	41	41	47	12	36	64	48	52
Protestants	37	63	38	62	55	45	35	49	16	30	70	46	54
Catholics	51	49	78	22	76	24	59	33	8	48	52	55	45
Republicans	4	96	5	95	20	80	9	86	5	5	95	11	89
Democrats	85	15	84	16	87	13	74	12	14	67	33	80	20
Independents	30	70	43	57	56	44	31	44	25	31	69	48	52
Members of labour union families	57	43	65	35	73	27	56	29	15	46	54	62	36

Based on Gallup Poll survey data, 1956–72. The 1976 data is based on a CBS News survey reported in the *New York Times*, 4th November 1976.

in 1972. The loyalty of partisan Democrats and Republicans has usually been high. The highest Republican defection rate (20 per cent) occurred in 1964, whereas McGovern lost the support of one-third of Democratic partisans in 1972.

The changes in partisanship during the period of electoral volatility in presidential elections have given no clear indication of the outlines of any potential realignment of the parties in the electorate. But it is evident that partisanship has not functioned as effectively as a determinant of voting behaviour in presidential elections as in congressional elections, or as in the unbroken sequence of Democratic victories from 1932 to 1948. The explanation of electoral volatility lies in the emphatic changes in the political issues and in the impact of presidential candidates since 1952.

Issue voting

Short-term electoral forces confined to one or two presidential campaigns have strongly influenced the voting behaviour of independents and weak partisans in favour of the minority Republican party. Public attitudes towards the performance of the incumbent or outgoing President, towards rival party policies on dominant campaign issues and towards the major party candidates have severely qualified the influence of partisanship, so as to produce the volatility apparent in presidential elections since 1952. Partisanship has exercised more influence upon voting behaviour in congressional elections because, as indicated by the lower turnout, the congressional electorate includes a higher proportion of partisans.

The explanation of the volatile pattern of election results lies principally in the changing sequence of campaign issues reflecting conflicts inherent in American society. Political scientists commonly distinguish between two types of election issue which influence voting behaviour independently of partisanship, policy or position issues and value or valence issues. Policy or position issues are characterized by clear differences in the alternative policies offered by the parties as solutions to particular problems. The major parties have differed on the merits of 'busing' as a means of terminating racial discrimination in education, on the merits of withdrawal of American troops as an appropriate solution required by the failure to pacify South Vietnam, and on the merits of an active Federal role including deficit spending if necessary in order to reduce unemployment, to provide Medicare facilities or to initiate environmental programmes to alleviate the consequences of pollution.

The significance of a position issue for electoral politics depends upon the parties offering relatively unambiguous policies, upon the electorate's evaluation of the urgency of the problem underlying the rival policies and upon the ability of voters to recognize differences between the parties. Many studies of the role of position issues in electoral politics have suggested that voters are largely unaware of policy differences between parties on issues regarded as important by politicians and the media. The Eightieth Congress (1947–48) was notable for the Taft-Hartley Act passed over a Truman veto by the Republican congressional majority produced by the 1946 elections. The Act prohibited the closed shop and granted the Attorney General injunction powers to delay strikes judged to constitute a danger to national health or safety. The Taft-Hartley Act was accordingly repugnant to trade unions. Truman emphasized the shortcomings of the Act in the 1948 campaign, as well as a second issue on which the parties were divided: government sponsorship of public housing. Yet one-third of the electorate in Elmira, New York could place correctly only one of the candidates' positions (Truman and Dewey) on one of the two issues.*

The electorate's marked lack of awareness of party differences on position issues has led to emphasis being placed on a second category of campaign issue. Value or valence issues are characterized by near-unanimous agreement on the desirability of achieving such goals as prosperity, peace and victory and of avoiding depression, defeat in war and military stalemate.† Frequently election results are decided by the apparent consequences of the incumbent administration's actions (e.g., depression in the early

* B. Berelson, P. Lazarsfeld and W. McPhee, *Voting* (University of Chicago Press, 1954), pp. 227–230.

† See D. Butler and D. Stokes, *Political Change in Britain* (Macmillan, 1969), pp. 173–192.

1930s, failure to win in Vietnam in 1968) or upon the contrasting images of the parties in respect of general goals based upon the electorate's past experiences of the parties in office; the Democrats are regarded as the party of prosperity and the party of war.

The relative electoral significance of policy issues compared to verdicts on the consequences of governmental action or inaction, i.e. valence issues, may be difficult to determine. A large measure of agreement on a general objective, such as racial desegregation, may be accompanied by conflict regarding the alleged consequences of policies designed to achieve that objective, in this case race riots, decline in property values and decline in education standards interpreted as the consequences of civil rights progress.

Position issues and valence issues have in the past combined to spark off a major realignment in the sources and the extent of support for the major parties. The Democratic party won convincingly in 1932 because a large section of the electorate blamed the Hoover administration for failing to maintain prosperity. But the succession of Democratic victories can also be attributed to the electorate's perception that Democratic New Deal policies would protect individuals from the consequences of economic depression more effectively than Republican policies. The combination of the outbreak of the depression during a Republican administration and Roosevelt's New Deal measures led to the replacement of the post-1896 alignment based on sectionalism by a qualified class-based cleavage in the 1930s. Democratic party identification was particularly heavy among young voters and previous non-voters, whose behaviour sustained the Democrats' majority status when Republican partisans who defected from 1932 to 1936 returned to supporting Republican congressional candidates from 1938 and presidential candidates from 1940. The Democrats acquired the image of the party of prosperity, whereas the Republicans were typed as the party of hard times.

Though defecting partisans may be tempted away temporarily from the chosen party by transient political issues, their sense of party identification is largely based upon perceptions of party differences in relation to key issues. Such perceptions are acquired either directly through experience or inherited through the family, which remains a major agent of political socialization. In the 1850s moral misgivings about slavery coincided with economic conflicts over the status of new States (slave versus non-slave) to elevate the newly formed Republican party to a position of dominance outside the South. Religion persisted as a major element in electoral politics by functioning as a signpost to immigrants and new voters regarding the appropriate party to support. Conflicting religious values stimulated unambiguous policy differences between the parties in such areas as prohibition, Sunday observance and language.

Major realignments occur when an issue or set of related issues dominates a particular campaign and subsequently establishes a new and stable pattern of party identification. The volatility of the electorate since 1952 has suggested to some observers the disintegration of the New Deal alignment and the majority Democratic coalition. It remains to be seen whether a key issue comparable to slavery in the 1850s or the appropriate role for the Federal government in the 1930s will emerge to provide the basis for stable voting patterns and a successful majority party.

The marked contrast in voting behaviour between the New Deal–Fair Deal era until the end of the Truman presidency and the post-1952 volatility is the product of a largely autonomous and changing pattern of campaign issues. The divisions in partisanship developed during the 1930s continued to dominate voting behaviour until 1952. Truman's victory in 1948 was based upon the Democratic lead in partisanship, the predominance of economic issues usually favourable to the Democrats, and the explicit class appeals in the campaign, which attracted a 75 per cent working-class vote for Truman and the highest degree of class voting in the post-1932 period. The campaign was fully consistent with the Democrats' majority status based upon party identification.

The deviating elections which Eisenhower won in 1952 and 1956 demonstrate the decisive influence which perceptions of rival candidates can exert on election outcomes, particularly when the more salient issues are not those on which the prevailing pattern of partisanship is based. The 1952 Republican victory was based on widespread concern that charges of corruption in the Democratic administration held substance, on Eisenhower's unique non-partisan appeal as a candidate and on the rise in importance of foreign policy issues. Alternative policy proposals were not central to the outcome. Rather, evaluations of governmental performance were uppermost as voters signified discontent with evidence of corruption in the administration and with stalemate in Korea. By 1956 Eisenhower's personal popularity became critical when foreign policy issues carried less impact. Party identification was more influential in congressional elections, where the Democratic vote held up sufficiently in 1956 to confirm the Democratic Congress which had been returned in the 1954 mid-term elections.

The 1960 presidential election was dominated by reactions to Kennedy's Catholicism. Protestants and Catholics disagreed about the propriety of a Roman Catholic President. Consequently partisan defections were more evenly divided between the major parties than in 1952 and 1956. The 'normal' Democratic majority was apparent in congressional voting behaviour, since more Democratic Representatives were returned than in the 1952–1956 elections. But Kennedy ran behind many Democratic congressional candidates, because the religious issue reduced the Democratic presidential vote in what was otherwise a typical maintaining election.

Ideological or explicit position issues are believed to have had little impact on elections in the 1950s. Rather party identification dictated the behaviour of strong partisans while opinions relating to governmental performance or to candidates influenced defecting partisans and independents so as to produce two deviating elections and a narrow victory for the majority party in 1960. Survey Research Centre data has been analysed to show that voters were slow to recognize major policy differences between the parties in the 1950s. But such data also indicates a growing and largely accurate awareness from 1964 of policy differences between the parties.* The preferences of partisans on policy issues such as aid to education, medical care, school integration, job guarantees and fair employment have conformed increasingly to their own party's stance. The Democratic party was increasingly identified as the liberal party favouring Federal action to achieve goals relating to these issues.

* G. Pomper, 'From Confusion to Clarity: Issues and American Votes, 1956–1968', *APSR*, Vol. LXVI, June, 1972.

In 1964 Senator Goldwater's explicit ideological appeal—offering 'a choice, not an echo'—had a major impact upon voting behaviour, partly because of intra-party dissension which provoked liberal Republicans, who had supported Lodge, Rockefeller and Scranton for the nomination, to vote in large numbers for Johnson. Any advantage accruing to Goldwater from his conservative States' rights position on the racial issue was more than offset, outside the Deep South, by the adverse consequences of his conservatism on social welfare matters and the atypical image of the Democrats as the party most likely to keep the United States out of war. Though the Democrats benefited from Goldwater's somewhat 'trigger-happy' image, the electorate was more concerned about domestic economic and welfare issues. Adverse references to Goldwater as a candidate were based mainly on his policy positions. The 1964 result was consistent with the finding that Republican supporters are much less conservative than Republican activists, a condition which emphasizes the advantages of a middle-ground rather than a clearly right-wing presidential candidate.

The passing of the Civil Rights Act in the summer of 1964 and Goldwater's conservative stance on civil rights issues contributed to a dramatic increase in black support for the Democratic candidate from 68 per cent in 1960 to 94 per cent in 1964. The low salience of the civil rights issue in 1964 for whites outside the Deep South is indicated by Goldwater's poor showing in the Outer South and Border States, where most whites were opposed to desegregation measures.

By 1968 'civil rights' attitudes had developed into a major influence upon voting. Analysis of the 1968 election, which secured the presidency for Richard Nixon, is complicated by the intervention of George Wallace, a clear issue candidate presenting unambiguous policy positions. Two clear position issues have been identified in the 1968 campaign: Vietnam (withdrawal, status quo, escalation) and civil rights (push on with or slow down desegregation measures such as 'busing' and open housing). Views on governmental performance were also evident in public discontent with developments in the Vietnam war and with an increase in violence in the streets, both in general and arising particularly from 'peace' demonstrations against the war and racial disturbances. The Survey Research study of the 1968 election revealed insignificant changes in the distribution of partisanship and in public attitudes towards policy options regarding Vietnam and racial discrimination. It was rather the intensification of social and external problems during the Johnson administration that led to Humphrey's defeat. The failure to win in Vietnam, the mounting human and financial cost of the war, and the breakdown in 'law and order' in the United States were interpreted as evidence of failure.

There is controversy among American political scientists about the significance of issues in 1968. In 1972 a series of articles in the *American Political Science Review* presented opposing views. One analysis of Survey Research Centre data found that Humphrey's vote was much lower than expected on the basis of a normal vote calculation among voters who regarded Johnson as a poor or very poor President, among those in favour of escalation in Vietnam (who outnumbered those in favour of withdrawal by two to one), among those who favoured the use of force to maintain law and order as a priority over correcting the problems of poverty and unemployment, and among those believing that civil rights leaders were pushing too fast.* This suggests that policy preferences as well as discontent with administration achievements influenced voting behaviour. However, causal relationships between specific policy preferences and voting were not established. Another study based on survey evidence relating to Vietnam denied that policy preferences influenced voting because the electorate could not decide where Nixon and Humphrey stood in relation to specific policy proposals.†

However, the electorate was not responsible for the failure to differentiate between the major party candidates on policy criteria. Rather the candidates were ambiguous, deliberately so, in their treatment of the Vietnam problem as a campaign issue. But even when a candidate took a clear stand, those voting for him because of the issue involved did not necessarily do so because

* R. N. Boyd, 'Popular Control of Public Policy: A Normal Vote Analysis of the 1968 Election', *American Political Science Review*, Vol. LXVI, June 1972.

† B. Page and R. Brady, 'Policy Voting and the Electoral Process', *American Political Science Review*, Vol. LXVI, June 1972.

they agreed with him. The Survey Research Centre found that the New Hampshire primary supporters of Senator Eugene McCarthy, fighting for the Democratic nomination as an anti-war candidate, were protesting against failure in Vietnam rather than supporting McCarthy's position.

Wallace's policy positions were clearly stated and clearly perceived. His policy proposals attracted votes from like-minded individuals, favouring segregation, tough measures against those threatening law and order, and a stronger stand in Vietnam. The Wallace intervention did not cost Humphrey the election because Wallace supporters preferred Nixon to Humphrey. It appears that Wallace attracted votes because of the policies he stood for, whereas Humphrey lost votes because of his close identification with the failures of the Johnson administration.

The 1972 election was dominated by the electorate's hostile reaction to the Democratic presidential candidate, who attracted the smallest share of the vote, 37·5 per cent, of all Democratic candidates since 1928. Several factors contributed to this result. McGovern, like Goldwater, split his own party. He represented minority elements, in particular the young and the blacks, and projected the image of an ideological candidate from his party's left wing. The effects on organizational support for him were severe, because the union movement declined to endorse McGovern, and though many individual union branches and union members worked for him the concerted union organization and finance which improved Humphrey's position considerably during the final weeks of the 1968 campaign were withheld. In addition, McGovern's campaign was the victim of ill luck and ineptitude. In particular the bizarre circumstances surrounding the withdrawal of the vice-presidential candidate, Senator Tom Eagleton of Missouri, who was discovered to have received hospital treatment for a nervous condition, emphasized the shortcomings of the McGovern campaign.

The debate about 'issue voting' has been continued by the authors of *The Changing American Voter*, who have analysed Survey Research Centre data from 1952 to 1972.* Their major con-

* N. H. Nie, S. Verba and J. R. Petrocik, *The Changing American Voter* (Harvard University Press, Cambridge, 1976).

clusion posits a significant change in influences upon voting behaviour, beginning with the 1964 election. Up to 1960 'pure party
voting predominates',* i.e., partisanship was the most effective
determinant of voting behaviour, although enough weak Democratic partisans and Independents joined Republican identifiers
to return Eisenhower to the White House in 1952 and 1956. But
since 1964 'a high level of issue consistency' on the part of many
voters has rivalled partisanship as an influence upon individual
voting decisions.† The electorate can be divided into liberals and
conservatives with respect to a wide range of issues. In the case of
liberal Republicans and conservative Democrats, partisanship
and issue orientation clashes. Electoral outcomes still depend
upon the dominant issues in each campaign. Conservative
Democrats voted strongly for Nixon in 1972.

The explanation of the volatility of the presidential electorate
since 1952 lies principally in the fact that the economic issues on
which the Democratic lead in partisanship was created in the
1930s have not been the most influential electoral issues since
1952. Rather foreign policy problems implicit in American's
world role, domestic unrest over civil rights developments and
crime in the streets, and the ideology or religion of individual
candidates have intervened to reduce the influence of partisanship. The pattern of salient campaign issues is largely autonomous
because government cannot fully control the social consequences
of individual policies nor predict electoral reaction. Democratic
defeats in 1952 and 1968 were due in large measure to the
electorate's hostile reaction upon learning that the implications of
America's world role involved costly containment rather than
speedy, conclusive victory. The difficulties inherent in attempting
to defeat an incumbent President have contributed to the emphatic right-wing or left-wing presidential candidates selected by
the party not in control of the White House. The Republican
party in 1964 and the Democratic party in 1972 were both
temporarily controlled by militant activists whose views, unusually, prevailed in the candidate selection process.

* Ibid., p. 306.   † Ibid., p. 349.

FOR FURTHER READING:

A. Campbell, P. E. Converse, W. E. Miller, and D. E. Stokes, *The American Voter* (J. Wiley, New York, 1960).

W. N. Chambers and W. D. Burnham, eds., *The American Party Systems*, 2nd ed. (Oxford University Press, New York, 1975).

W. H. Flannigan and N. H. Zingale, *Political Behaviour of the American Electorate*, 3rd ed. (Allyn and Bacon, Boston, 1975).

N. H. Nie, S. Verba and J. R. Petrocik, *The Changing American Voter* (Harvard University Press, Cambridge, 1976).

R. G. Niemi and H. F. Weisberg, eds., *Controversies in American Voting Behaviour* (W. H. Freeman, San Francisco, 1976).

6: Political Parties

The American party system has since the mid-sixties been at the heart of arguments about the adequacy of government in the United States. Political developments since 1948 have revitalized the long-standing debate about the links between the constitutional and social bases of American politics, the definitive features of the party system and the attributes and outcomes of the governmental process. Prominent among such developments have been: the pronounced volatility of the electorate in national and State elections; the nomination of minority, ideological candidates by the Republicans in 1964 and the Democrats in 1972; the loss of control of the Democratic presidential nomination process suffered by Roosevelt's coalition of labour leaders, State and city bosses, congressional Democrats and Southern Democrats; and the increase in political violence and mass protest which accompanied the civil rights movement and the attempt to secure the withdrawal of American forces from Vietnam. Consequently, there has been considerable speculation about the potential for change in the structure of the major parties and the functions of party in the political system.

American political scientists have reacted in various ways to the developments enumerated above. There is a marked contrast between those who feel that there is no safe alternative to the limited but vital activities and functions performed by parties throughout much of American political history, and those who believe in the urgent need for, or even in the possible emergence of, responsible parties to deal with the perceived crisis. Others have discerned a gradual decline in the significance of party in the political system. The cry for responsible parties has been taken up most forcefully by J. M. Burns, who defines the party system as 'a four-party system that compels government by consensus and coalition rather than a two-party system that allows the winning party to govern and the losers to oppose'.* The idea of responsible parties is viewed critically by those historians and political scientists who, in stressing that the parties are the product of a particular American environment, adhere to the belief that party characteristics, whatever the implications for government, are still the necessary 'price of union' in a dangerously heterogeneous society. Indeed a leading contemporary exponent of this view considers that 'any serious attempt to reform the parties toward policy responsibility would do violence to history and to modern political institutions.'†

A: THE NATURE OF THE PARTY SYSTEM

The party system possesses four outstanding features. Firstly, the national and State parties are very decentralized. Secondly, there is a preoccupation with electioneering and the recruitment of party candidates at the expense of policy making. The relative unimportance of policy formulation as a national party function is most apparent in the inability of the majority party in Congress to wrest the initiative in policy making from Presidents of the minority party. Thirdly, American parties are non-ideological. Although the United States is a major industrial nation, there is no major socialist or labour party. Fourthly, owing to the decentralized, electioneering and non-ideological character of the parties, the policy decisions of government are determined much less by intra-party politics than in many other liberal democracies. In other words, despite the domination of electoral politics by the Democratic and Republican parties, they may be classified as non-governing parties.

There is much less of a recognizable party hierarchy than there is in Britain. The President often appears to be largely unbound

* J. M. Burns, *The Deadlock of Democracy* (Prentice-Hall, Englewood Cliffs, N.J., 1963), p. 7.
† T. Lowi, 'Party, Policy and Constitution in America' in W. N. Chambers and W. D. Burnham (eds.), *The American Party Systems* (Oxford University Press, New York, 1967), p. 241.

by party considerations when making appointments to his own political staff and to leading governmental offices. President Nixon was thus able to deny himself the advice of professional party politicians, an unhappy choice which contributed to the Watergate crisis and his own eventual withdrawal from political life.

Three distinct forces have contributed to these definitive features of the party system: the Constitution; a relatively low level of class consciousness and a general hostility towards collectivist principles; and social heterogeneity. The separated national institutions remove the necessity present in parliamentary systems for a majority in the legislature to support the political executive. Rejection of the President's policy proposals does not result in his resignation, and consequently party loyalty is weaker than in parliamentary systems.

The electoral system, particularly the biennial elections to the House of Representatives and the device of primary elections, encourages a preoccupation with electioneering which, given the President's security of tenure, ensures that voting in Congress is aimed at gaining and maintaining support for individual Congressmen at the polls. The federal system requires that parties are organized on a State and local basis, and thus sub-national centres of power are created which rival the national party organs.

Social conditions reinforce the institutional pressures making for decentralization. The two-party system may appear to be an unlikely institution in such a heterogeneous society. But many of the diverse social forces in the United States have found sufficient protection in the decentralized party system to perpetuate the two-party form. Decentralization can be regarded as the price paid for the two-party system, in that if there are to be but two parties then these must be decentralized in structure. The relative weakness of class divisions throughout American history helps to explain the absence of a disciplined left-wing working-class party which would have had a major centralizing impact upon party structure generally.

The consequences of two decentralized, non-ideological, non-governing parties have been aptly summarized in R. E. Neustadt's remark: 'what the Constitution separates, our parties do not combine.'* American parties do not conform to the responsible party model encountered in many parliamentary systems, in which an oligarchic structure embracing all levels of party organization and a high degree of legislative party cohesion are encouraged by the need to support or to replace a government drawn from one or more parties. Rather the potential for stalemate between President and Congress implicit in independent tenures, in the presidential veto and in the requirement of a two-thirds majority to override it, is strengthened by the inability of either of the major parties to act cohesively in Congress. Consequently in modern times a Democratic President such as Kennedy has failed to dominate a Democratic Congress, while in turn the Democratic majority in Congress has been unable to assert itself against Republican Presidents Nixon and Ford. Congress is not organized to rival, let alone replace, the President as the major source of legislation. A major congressional reform of budgetary procedure which became operational in 1976 is intended merely to enable Congress to consider the presidential budget in a more comprehensive and more organized manner; the initiative remains with the President.

Nevertheless, loose party organization prevents a complete stalemate between President and Congress when control is divided between the parties. And the parties are still the principal device whereby elections are organized and made meaningful for the voters.

Party organization and membership

Decentralization and lack of discipline are the most significant structural characteristics of the parties. National party institutions do not exercise strict control over State parties; nor do State parties always work enthusiastically for the presidential candidate, and they seldom control local organizations in counties and cities. Executive parties centred on the President and State Governors cannot rely upon strong support from their party colleagues in the legislatures. Legislative outcomes in Congress and State Houses

* R. E. Neustadt, *Presidential Power* (Wiley, 1960), p. 33.

are frequently determined by voting across party lines because the
formal party leaders cannot impose strict discipline upon their
nominal followers. However, within the counties and cities the
party organizations may be hierarchically controlled.

There are four sorts of party elements in national politics.
First, there is one informal executive or presidential party working
at the behest of the incumbent President. Second, there are two
congressional parties, each with a formal, elected leadership, that
make some attempt at developing cohesion on organizational and
policy matters, though the business of Congress itself is heavily
decentralized to committees and their chairmen because the
parties are weak. Third, there are two National Committees,
whose functions are mainly of a service kind, though the Democratic National Committee has been a major battleground in the
attempt to reform the Democratic party since 1967–8. Fourth,
two national conventions are held every four years to nominate a
presidential candidate and construct a campaign programme, i.e.,
a statement of agreed party policy. The organization of the parties
at national level is a matter for the parties themselves. Party
organization at State and local levels is laid down in varying
detail in State legislation.

The parties as national institutions are frequently described as
loose federations or confederations of State and local parties.
Decentralization begins with the individual participant in party
affairs because there is no provision for card-carrying, subscribing
membership nationally or in the States. In States with closed
primaries, intending voters are required to declare a preference
for the party in whose primary they wish to participate, either
when registering to vote in elections or when turning up to vote in
the primary. Such a declaration provides a formal definition of
party membership, although registration is a State, not a party,
procedure. In States with open primaries any voter can participate in a party's primary, but only in one primary in any given
election.

Primaries are now almost universal in the nomination of party
candidates to national and State public office. There is no
national primary in the presidential nomination process, though
convention delegates chosen by the primary method are on the

increase. Office holders in State party organizations may be chosen in primaries. Party primaries make it possible for 'anti-organization' or reform candidates to win the right to contest elections to public office at State and national levels at the expense of the nominees of the regular party organization or incumbent office holders. In 1974 Senator W. J. Fulbright, Chairman of the powerful Senate Foreign Relations Committee, was defeated in an Arkansas primary. The primary system accentuates decentralization by weakening the control over the nomination process of party organizations, compared with methods in which local party committees select the candidate.

Because of the absence of an enrolled mass membership, American parties have been classified as 'cadre' parties in which office holders and their supporters carry out party functions without either the stimulus or the constraints imposed by mass membership. The low level of concern with policy formulation is partly attributable to this aspect of party structure, though the absence of a demand for mass membership is also a symptom of the absence of profound ideological or programmatic differences between the major parties. Democratic party reformers have attempted to introduce provisions for individual membership on a mass basis in the hope that more centralized disciplined parties would evolve.

The States specify organizational structures to which the parties must adhere, though there are many variations. The most prominent levels of party organization are usually the precinct or ward, the county, and the State. But party committees may be required in the many electoral constituencies, such as congressional and State legislative districts. The main function of each layer of party organization in the States is to organize the party's electoral effort at that level. Policy making is left to the 'party in office', consisting of party members elected to executive and legislative office.

The smallest party unit is the precinct, which is the basic electoral district, complete with its designated polling station and election officials, though it is not a local government constituency. Precincts vary in size from 200 to 2,000 voters. Precinct party officials—precinct captains or committeemen—may be elected in primary elections or at a precinct convention or caucus attended by local party activists. The ward is the smallest public constituency in towns and cities with mayor-council and council-manager forms of government. Ward committees and party committees in townships, villages and parishes in rural areas are often required, though many party committees are moribund, even at election time. In some States, such as Illinois, ward committeemen elected by primary appoint precinct captains. The principal function of the precinct and ward party officials is to develop and nurse loyal party voters, and ensure that they turn out on election day. Precinct captains were the 'troops' in the notorious urban machines which survived on patronage, i.e. the powers of local government to dispense jobs and contracts to deserving individuals, in return for commitments to vote, finance or work for the party organization.

Precinct and ward committeemen may collectively form the county committee, the next layer of party organization. Or members of the county committee may be elected in party primaries. There are over 100,000 precincts and 3,000 counties. The county committees select the county chairmen, who are frequently powerful party figures. Mayor Daley of Chicago was the chairman of the Cook County Democratic committee.

The State committee forms the top level of State party organization. The composition of State committees varies considerably. Frequently State committeemen are chosen by the county committees. Or they may be elected by party voters in primaries or at county conventions attended by activists. The State party chairman is nominally elected by the State committee, but effectively the choice lies with the party's candidate for Governor.

The two National Committees constitute the top layer of the formal party organization. Both are federal in composition. The National Chairmen are chosen by the presidential candidates, though the defeated party's national committee frequently deposes his choice as chairman, as when the appointees of Goldwater in 1964 and McGovern in 1972 left office shortly after the November elections. The major functions of the National Committee include fund raising and campaign management, though President Nixon relegated the Republican National Committee to a minor campaign role in 1968 and in 1972. One of the main problems facing the national chairmen is co-ordinating their campaign activities with those undertaken by rival organizations such as the congressional campaign committees.

The National Committees may on occasion play a major role in internal party politics. The Democratic National Committee and its Chairmen have been at the centre of the battle for control over the presidential nomination process, a conflict which has concentrated on nomination procedures rather than policy. In general, the National Committees are less significant as national party institutions than the congressional parties to be described in Chapter 8, Section B, below.

The role of ideology

Ideology, like class, is not without significance in the American political system. Ideology does divide both rival politicians and the electorate, but to a much lesser extent than in most European countries. The two major parties have been distinguishable in the twentieth century, particularly since the New Deal, with respect to the use of governmental powers to protect the interests of rival socio-economic groups. But they are less distinctive in this way than the two major British parties. American trade unions and the Democratic party have not subscribed to the collectivist sentiments enshrined in Clause IV of the Labour Party constitution: there has been no significant attachment in the United States to socialism or to state intervention as means of accomplishing radical changes in socio-economic relationships. Many commentators emphasize the unifying influence of an ideological consensus in the United States which includes 'a commitment to democracy, to the Constitution, and to the key social and economic institutions of American life: privately owned business firms, universal free public education, separation of church and state, religious toleration and the like'.*

The weakness of any collectivist impulse has been of fundamental importance to the American party system because it has

* Robert A. Dahl, *Democracy in the United States: Promise and Performance*, 3rd ed. (Rand McNally, 1976), p. 295.

contributed to the absence of a socialist or labour party and therefore to the decentralized and non-programmatic or non-ideological
aspects of the major parties. European experience suggests that
socialist and labour parties develop integrated, hierarchical structures and high legislative cohesion based on mass membership
organization and on distinctive ideological or programmatic
aims. The more traditional, right-wing parties representing
business and propertied classes have been forced in self-defence to
acquire similar organization and comprehensive policy programmes. The major American parties, encouraged in their
decentralized structure by constitutional provisions and by a
highly diversified society, have not had to contend with the
challenge of a major socialist or labour party. Before explaining
the absence of such a challenge it is necessary to describe briefly
the links between organized labour and the Democratic party.

A majority of manual workers usually support the Democratic
presidential candidate; and the more industrialized, urbanized,
blue-collar constituencies return Democratic candidates to Congress. The AFL-CIO leadership has normally endorsed Democratic candidates since the New Deal, though McGovern was not
endorsed in 1972. Organized labour contributes a major part of
the finance and effort expended by the Democratic party in
election campaigns. Thus organized labour is part of the Democratic electoral coalition. Nevertheless the Democratic party is
not classified as a labour party because trade unions are not
directly affiliated to the party.

A socialist party, defined by the commitment of its members to
a particular ideology, may depend upon the electoral support of
organized labour without including unions directly in party structure. Conversely a labour party, to which unions are affiliated,
need not be socialist in ideology. Both types of party tend to be
centralized and disciplined. Neither exists in the United States.

The absence of major socialist or labour parties has been
attributed to the lack of a feudal tradition, the grant of universal
male suffrage in a pre-industrial society still predominantly
agrarian in character, immigration as a source of ethno-cultural
cleavages rivalling socio-economic divisions as the bases of party
politics, and the relative abundance of the American economy at

various critical stages in party development. These factors are believed to have contributed to a low level of class consciousness, especially among the working class, and to organized labour's reluctance to participate in politics directly through the medium of a dependent political party. Instead, it assumes an active pressure group role and follows an aggressive business unionism in relations with employers.

The explanation of the absence of a centralized left-wing party is essentially developmental in character. The party system developed in a unique combination of environmental and constitutional conditions. American society produced the first modern political parties on the basis of a relatively widespread suffrage prior to the establishment of industrial mass production. The party system which emerged from the Civil War was based as much on sectional and religious antagonisms as on socio-economic conflicts. Rapid industrialization and urbanization in the half century after the Civil War did not stimulate the growth of a major socialist or labour party at a time when such parties were transforming European politics. The most common explanations of this major difference between the United States and Europe (including Britain) emphasize the relative lack of class consciousness in American political culture.

Several environmental conditions reduced the political significance of social class. Pre-industrial America was characterized, because of its colonial and revolutionary origins, by the absence of the feudal tradition which in Europe made a hierarchical society seem part of a natural order. Consequently there was less stratification along class lines in the United States than in nineteenth-century Europe. The implications for the developing party system of a less stratified society were heightened by an even more critical political condition: the American working class, unlike its European counterpart, did not experience the powerful stimulus to class consciousness inevitable in the struggle to secure the right to vote. Rather members of the American working class received the vote on becoming of age or on stepping off the boat. In addition class divisions were rivalled by ethnic, religious and regional cleavages as the instrumental bases of party politics.

Another environmental condition explaining the differences in party development in Europe and the United States was the superior wealth of the New World. The social conditions of the growing urban working class at the turn of the century in the United States were hardly characterized by universal abundance, but conditions were not so miserable as in Europe, as a society embracing many immigrants was well aware.

The Republican era (1896–1930) began with an increase in working-class support for the business-oriented party on account of the economic conflict between industry and agriculture which exacerbated political antagonisms between North and South inherited from the Civil War. The industrial proletariat was 'distracted' by Bryan's agrarian stance. An attempt was made to create a major socialist party. Its presidential candidate in 1912, Eugene Debs, won 6 per cent of the vote. But that was the high point of the party's success at the polls.

Labour leaders were unsympathetic to the attempt to develop a major socialist party; they also explicitly rejected the alternative of a labour party. S. M. Lipset has argued that organized labour has accepted the dominant American value system of individualism and social egalitarianism, which is hostile to the development of class consciousness but conducive to militant collective bargaining.* The major unions were of the craft rather than the industrial type and thus, since unionization has always been less widespread in the United States than in Europe, provided a weak base upon which to construct an explicitly class-conscious political party. Labour leaders decided on a formal neutrality with respect to the major parties partly because political conditions were unfavourable; for example, until the 1930s the Democratic party, more sympathetic to the aims of organized labour, was for a long time the minority party in the regions where organized labour was strongest.

A widely shared ideological perspective has reduced the potential for party conflict over the constitutional regime and the private enterprise socio-economic system. The dominant ideology of American society has contributed along with institutional conditions (the electoral system, separation of President and Congress, primary elections) to the decentralization of party structure and

* S. M. Lipset, *The First New Nation* (Doubleday Anchor, 1967), Chapter 5.

to the absence of any significant demand for responsible parties. The landslide defeats suffered by candidates thought to be ideological in 1964 and 1972 bear witness to a marked consensus with respect to a legitimate relationship between state and society. The most influential electoral forces since 1952 have been judgements as to governmental competence in dealing with foreign policy problems such as the Korean and Vietnam wars, or domestic problems such as rising crime and the racial situation. The electorate does not seem to choose between presidential candidates on the basis of points of principle and candidates do not always make clear such differences between them. For a variety of reasons, therefore, American parties have often been characterized as Tweedledum opposed to Tweedledee.

Yet clear differences in policy outlook have distinguished and continue to distinguish the parties. During most of the nineteenth century the Democratic party defended States' rights and adopted a laissez-faire attitude towards Federal government. The Federalist-Whig-Republican parties favoured a mercantilist attitude involving an active Federal role in aid of business and industry. Hence the Republicans supported and the Democrats opposed a high external tariff.

The realignment of 1932 and the New Deal legislation enacted by the Roosevelt administration entailed a turn-round in party positions as the Democratic party pursued an active national role in support of economic and social reform. The Republican party defended States' rights in the face of Democratic interventionism and emphasized the need for balanced budgets. The Democratic party is now widely regarded as 'liberal' on socio-economic issues and favourable to organized labour and the Republican party is typed as economically 'conservative' and favourable to business. Survey findings indicate that party differences on policy issues are much more pronounced between the rival sets of party leaders than between the two parties in the electorate (there is a distinct division between Republican leaders and their more conservative followers). But it appears that the liberal-conservative divide became much more extensively perceived and acknowledged in the 1960s.

B: THE NOMINATION OF
PRESIDENTIAL CANDIDATES

The formulation of party programmes and the nomination of presidential candidates at the conventions held by the major parties every fourth year during the summer preceding the November presidential election constitute the most visible evidence that national party organizations exist and perform positive functions. Party rivalry and the loss of patronage and political power involved in failing to win the Presidency usually encourage both parties to nominate a moderate candidate capable of appealing to the electorate in the larger industrialized States while retaining the support of confirmed partisans throughout the nation. Nevertheless the national conventions have always demonstrated the federal and coalitional aspects of the two major parties. The conventions were frequently characterized up to the 1920s by prolonged bargaining and protracted balloting, which on occasion ended in the nomination of minor candidates who came to the convention with little support, e.g. Polk (1844), Pierce (1852), and Harding (1920).

The autonomy of the national convention has declined in the face of the development of the presidential primary, which can demonstrate the abilities of rival candidates to win or to lose votes, and the public opinion poll, which puts a premium on candidates being or quickly becoming well known and acceptable to the general public. Only four conventions since 1932 have required more than one ballot. Roosevelt was nominated in the fourth ballot in 1932 and Stevenson in the third in 1952. Willkie was chosen in the sixth ballot in 1940 and Dewey in the third in 1948. The ensuing opening-up of presidential nominations has been extended, by the Democrats at least, to permit the nomination of a Roman Catholic (John Kennedy in 1960) and two Southerners (Lyndon Johnson in 1964 and Jimmy Carter in 1976), though Senator Muskie admitted in 1972 that he considered the nation not yet ready to accept a black as a vice-presidential nominee, meaning that he felt that the party ticket would suffer.

G

Occasionally intra-party conflict has overcome the desire to win the Presidency or, if winning seems remote no matter who is nominated, to lose as narrowly as possible. When the Republicans nominated Taft in 1912, knowing that Roosevelt would lead a third-party challenge, and Goldwater in 1964, 'the minority candidate of the minority party', they were destroying whatever chances they had of winning. The strong primary challenge to incumbent President Johnson by Democratic Senators McCarthy and Kennedy in 1968 gave the Democratic candidate, Humphrey, a bad start, contributing to Richard Nixon's relatively narrow victory. And the nomination of a candidate from the left wing of the Democratic party contributed to the smashing Republican victory in 1972.

Reforming the nomination process 1968–1976

The presidential nomination process became the major target in the 1960s for advocates of reform of party structure and policy commitments, particularly in the Democratic party. A vigorous Democratic reform movement grew out of internal conflicts aroused by American involvement in Vietnam under a Democratic President. It started with the challenge to Lyndon Johnson in the 1968 primaries, and then in reaction to the nomination of Johnson's Vice-President, Hubert Humphrey, developed into an attempt by liberal and left-wing Democrats to create a responsible, more representative political party at all levels of party activity.

The reformers' eventual failure to bring about major changes in the structure of the Democratic party illustrates the strength of the forces, in particular the demands of the electioneering function, making for decentralized parties. The reform movement did provoke one major change of long-term significance in the nomination process: an increase in the number of States holding presidential primaries, a reform which made possible the Democratic nominations of McGovern in 1972 and Carter in 1976.

Advocates of change in party policy and party structure can follow three complementary strategies. First, they can attempt to gain control of local and State party organizations by encouraging their supporters to increase their participation in party meetings.

Secondly, they can run reform candidates in primary elections in the hope that the electorate will support such candidates. The Democratic caucus in the House of Representatives has been liberalized by the success of this strategy in 1972 and 1974. Thirdly, reformers can attempt to change national and State party rules and State legislation governing the nomination of party candidates. The three strategies were present in the attempt to reform the Democratic party, which in essence began in December 1967 when Senator Eugene McCarthy announced his intention to challenge President Johnson for the party's nomination in 1968.

The Democratic selection process was radically overhauled following the events of the Chicago Convention and the loss of the 1968 presidential election. The process of reform was commenced at the turbulent Chicago convention itself, when the unit rule whereby all members of State delegations could be bound to support the candidate favoured by a majority (the rule could be imposed by a State convention or by the delegation itself) was abolished. The rule, which was applied mainly by Southern States, became a factor in the struggle between McCarthy and Humphrey. McCarthy's supporters had hoped to use the unit rule issue as a symbol of the lack of democracy in the nomination process. But Humphrey defused this issue by agreeing to the rule's abolition. The 1968 Convention also voted to guarantee that the delegate selection process for the 1972 nomination would take place openly in 1972 itself, and not earlier, to prevent delegates from being chosen before the full list of presidential candidates was known.

In 1969 the Democratic National Committee established two Commissions (the Commission on Party Structure and Delegate Selection and the Commission on Rules) which made extensive recommendations designed to reform the nomination process. The Commission on Party Structure and Delegate Selection was chaired initially by Senator McGovern; the Commission on Rules was chaired by another leading liberal Democrat, Representative James O'Hara of Michigan. Most of their recommendations were adopted by the National Committee in February 1971.

The most vital change was derived from the 1968 convention's commitment to open selection; State parties were to permit all party members to participate in all public party meetings and, to this end, meetings were to be publicized; in addition written rules on delegate selection were to be adopted. The aim was to reduce the influence over delegate selection of professional party officials and prominent party members holding public office. The number of delegates elected or selected at congressional district level was to be increased at the expense of Statewide selection or election.

A contentious quota recommendation was contained in a vague exhortation to State parties to encourage a full representation of previously under-represented groups in State delegations to the national conventions. Quotas were implicitly established to ensure 'adequate representation' for blacks, women and American youth (defined as eighteen- to twenty-nine-year-olds). Generally, the social composition of State delegations was to parallel the social composition of each State. In 1972, the quota principle led to challenges to many delegations being brought before the Credentials Committee and subsequently before the entire convention. Mayor Daley's Chicago delegation, whose members were elected in the Illinois delegate primary but uncommitted to any candidate, was rejected because the quotas were not respected fully. Subsequently there were complaints that many other distinctive but more traditional Democratic supporters, such as ethnic and religious groups and blue-collar workers, were not given quotas.

The Commission on Rules reported in September 1971. Its recommendations that speeches at the convention be curtailed, that convention committees meet in public, and that restrictions be placed on 'favourite son' candidates were also accepted in the hope that the nomination process would be more open and less under the influence of the party professionals.

The reform of the Democratic nomination process had three major consequences for the party in 1972. First, the reforms contributed to the nomination of a radical candidate, described as a prairie populist, from an unfashionable State, who was not widely regarded as a major candidate before the primaries commenced. McGovern's radicalism was based on his anti-Vietnam

war stand, his promises to reduce drastically the United States'
forward position in international politics, and his domestic proposals regarding welfare, taxation and minimum income. His
success in winning the nomination was due partly to this radical
appeal, which brought him an enthusiastic, volunteer organization. Even more basic was his own personal success in the
primaries. McGovern came to the Miami convention with more
than 1,000 delegate votes either formally or informally committed to him by the primaries. He also did better than the other
candidates in States choosing delegates in party meetings rather
than in primaries. Many such delegates were uncommitted, but
McGovern won a majority of the committed delegates. The reform of delegate selection procedures, the strong support of
activists organized to profit from these reforms, and the results of
the 1972 primaries led first to the nomination of a minority
candidate from the party's left wing, and then to electoral
humiliation in the November presidential election.

Table 6.1:

Representation at the major party conventions in 1968 and 1972

Group	Democratic convention		Republican convention	
	1968	*1972*	*1968*	*1972*
Youth (18–29)	4%	21·4%	1%	8·7%
Blacks	5·5%	15%	1·9%	4%
Women	13%	39·9%	17%	30·1%
Senators	40	15	—	—
Representatives	85	49	—	—

Second, the composition of the 1972 convention was markedly
different from its predecessors, as can be seen in Table 6.1. The
representation of particular social categories (youth, women, non-
whites, i.e., Blacks, Chicanos, Indians) increased spectacularly
at the 1972 Democratic convention. It has been estimated that 80
per cent of delegates in Miami were attending a national convention for the first time. The Republicans also increased representa-

tion for these groups, especially the youth group, though women were represented in much greater strength in 1968 and in 1972 than the two other 'minority groups'. The changes at the Republican convention were necessitated by the Democratic reforms which appealed to the minority groups, including feminists. Republicans were also encouraged by the possibility that members of these groups might be won over to the Republican party at a time when voting behaviour was volatile.

Third, McGovern's ideological stance and the social composition of the 1972 Democratic convention were symbols of and contributions to an internal conflict which led to the withdrawal of national AFL-CIO support for the Democratic presidential candidate, to the formal or informal disassociation by several Democratic Congressional candidates of their own campaigns from the presidential campaign, and to the launching of a 'Democrats for Nixon' campaign effort spearheaded by John Connally, former Governor of Texas and Secretary of the Treasury in the first Nixon Administration. There was much speculation about the outcome of a battle for control of the Democratic party between the coalition established by Roosevelt in the 1930s and a new coalition of minority groups and hitherto disaffected sections of the community, variously described as suburban liberals, Kennedy-McCarthy remnants, students, peace people, blacks and feminists. However, organized labour's rejection of McGovern was not universal. Many union branches worked for the Democratic candidate. The main blow to the Democratic campaign came from the loss of the organizational and fund raising capacities of the Committee on Political Education.

McGovern's humiliating defeat made it essential for electoral purposes that a truce be reached between the 'old' and the 'new' Democratic coalitions. A first step was the removal of McGovern's appointee as National Committee chairwoman, Mrs. Jean Westwood. The new chairman, elected by the National Committee in December 1972, was Robert Strauss (Texas). The 1972 convention sanctioned the institution of a new Committee on Delegate Selection which became known as the Mikulski Commission after its chairwoman, a member of Baltimore City Council.

The Mikulski Commission recommended, in October 1973, a new set of delegate selection rules, applicable in primary and non-primary States, which were in the main accepted by the National Committee in March 1974, and by the unprecedented mid-term party conference held in Kansas City (Missouri) in December 1974. Recommendations included the introduction of proportional representation at all levels of delegate selection except the congressional district, the allocation of at least 75 per cent of delegates to electoral units no larger than the congressional district, the banning of open party primaries, the right of presidential candidates to approve delegate candidates identifying with them, and the right of delegates to stick to their stated preferences at the national convention.

The most controversial issue remained quotas for minority groups in State delegations to the Democratic convention. The strictly arithmetic definition of 'adequate representation' for minorities, based on the social composition of each State, which the 1972 Miami Convention in effect enforced, was not acceptable to the Mikulski Commission or to the National Committee. Instead the Commission recommended that State parties be required to make provision for 'affirmative action programmes' designed to encourage full participation on the part of all groups of Democrats. Mandatory quotas were not permitted. State parties which established satisfactory programmes would not then find their delegations challenged at the 1976 Convention. A Compliance Review Commission chaired by the former New York City Mayor, Robert Wagner, was established to pass judgement on the affirmative action programmes to be drawn up by the State parties in preparation for the 1976 nomination process.

In 1976 the more liberal Democratic candidates, Harris and Udall, failed to arouse the enthusiasm of the activists or the support of the primary voters, who had secured the nomination for George McGovern. The attempt to begin the creation of a disciplined, national party failed when the electorate rejected McGovern so decisively. However, the changes in the nomination process which were commenced in 1968 survived the electoral catastrophe suffered by its sponsors in 1972, and made a major contribution to the nomination of another outsider in 1976, Jimmy Carter, who went on to win the Presidency.

The apportionment of delegates

The key formal elements in the presidential nomination process are the formulas adopted by the parties in order to apportion convention votes among the States, and State laws governing the selection of convention delegates.

Three rival principles have been prominent in the debate on how to apportion convention votes among the States: States should be represented equally as States; they should be represented predominantly on the basis of population; they should be assigned a number of convention votes in relation to a chosen index of party strength at the polls. The first two principles have long been recognized in that both parties have linked the representation of States at the convention to the composition of the presidential electoral college. Both parties have also introduced bonus votes, rewarding States electing their respective candidates in national and State elections, in order to cope with different problems arising out of the role of the South at national conventions.

In 1912 the Republicans re-nominated President William Howard Taft against the challenge of ex-President Theodore Roosevelt, who had won most of the presidential primaries. Taft's success at the convention was due to the support given to him by delegates from non-primary States. His margin of victory was provided by the Southern delegations, represented on the same basis as all other States despite the Republican party's extremely weak position in the one-party South. Taft got Southern support because he dispensed Federal patronage to Southern Republican party officials, and because Roosevelt's progressive platform was not favoured by Southern Republicans. Roosevelt's intervention as a third-party candidate in the presidential election let Woodrow Wilson into the White House. The Republicans introduced bonus convention votes in 1916 in order to reduce the influence of the Southern States at the convention stage of the nomination process.

The Democrats, reconstructed after 1932 as an effective party in the North as well as in the South, abolished in 1936 the convention rule requiring a two-thirds majority for the nomination of presidential and vice-presidential candidates. This rule had operated to give the South a veto in the nomination process, although the Civil War had ruled out the prospect of a Southern candidate securing the nomination. The abolition of the two-thirds rule was accompanied by a promise to introduce bonus votes which would compensate the South slightly. This promise was duly carried out in 1944.

The Democrats' apportionment system is determined by the National Committee about one year prior to each convention. A major change was introduced in time for the 1972 convention which was apportioned according to two principles. Firstly, every State, and the District of Columbia, received three times its vote in the electoral college, the size of which is based mainly on population. Secondly, additional votes were distributed in proportion to the average number of popular votes (not electoral votes) in each State for the Democratic candidate in the three preceding presidential elections, a formula based on population qualified by popular support for Democratic candidates. The same rules applied in 1976. The electoral college provision determined 54 per cent of convention votes (1,614) and the bonus votes 46 per cent (1,386) in 1972.

The operation of Democratic apportionment rules is illustrated by the difference in the number of convention votes assigned to Florida and New Jersey, both of which were allocated seventeen electoral college votes following the 1970 census and therefore were guaranteed fifty-one convention votes (3 × 17) in 1972 and 1976. New Jersey, where Democratic presidential candidates in 1960, 1964 and 1968 received 4,517,852 votes, was awarded an additional fifty-eight votes at the 1972 convention. Florida received an additional thirty convention votes in 1972 on the basis of 2,374,034 popular votes for Democratic candidates in the three preceding elections.

Each Republican Convention establishes the apportionment rules to be applied to its successor. Thus the 1972 Convention determined that the following rules should apply in 1976. First, every State received six votes irrespective of population. Second, every State received three votes per congressional district, the number of districts being determined by population. Third, every State which supported the Republican presidential candidate in 1972 received four-and-a-half votes plus 60 per cent of its electoral college vote. Fourth, States were to receive additional votes for satisfying the following conditions: electing a Republican Governor, electing a Republican Senator (two votes if two Republican Senators were elected), and electing a majority of Republican Representatives to the State's House delegation in the appropriate elections preceding 1976. The District of Columbia, Puerto Rico, Guam and the Virgin Islands were given thirty convention votes between them. The Republicans increased the number of convention votes from 1,348 in 1972 to 2,259 in order to include representatives of the social groups under-represented at earlier conventions.

By and large the same States appear in the lists of the largest States in the electoral college and the two conventions. Texas fell below Ohio at the Republican convention in 1972 because Texas did not return a Republican Governor or Senator or a majority of Republican Representatives in any of the relevant elections in 1968 and 1970, though Republican Senator John Tower had been elected in 1966. But the change in Republican apportionment rules for 1976 made bonus votes heavily dependent on supporting the Republican candidate in the 1972 presidential election. Since every State except Massachussets duly did so, the bonus votes provision rewarded States in proportion to their standings in the electoral college, restoring Texas to fifth place and dropping Massachussets, the tenth State in the electoral college, to fourteenth place in 1976.

New York retained top place in the Democratic order in 1972, despite losing first place in the electoral college to California. New York cast 12,121,657 votes for the Democratic candidates in 1960, 1964 and 1968 compared to the 10,892,042 votes cast by California. California received the highest number of Democratic convention votes in 1976 because New York's vote for Nixon in 1972 reduced the difference between California and New York in popular votes for Democratic candidates. New Jersey and

Massachussets appear above Florida in the Democratic order because both gave more support to Democratic candidates. Texas came below Ohio and Michigan at the Democratic convention in 1972 and 1976, despite giving more electoral college votes to Democratic candidates in preceding elections, because of much lower turnouts and because the Wallace intervention meant that Humphrey's winning share of the Texas vote in 1968 was only 41·1 per cent, whereas he won 43 per cent of a higher turnout when losing Ohio in 1968. The Democratic apportionment system was more favourable to the ten largest states, which received 53 per cent of convention votes in 1972 compared to 43 per cent of Republican convention votes.

The selection of convention delegates

The formal rules and political customs governing the selection of State party delegates to national conventions have been more influential than delegate apportionment systems in determining the outcomes of the nomination process since the Republicans introduced bonus votes after 1912 and the Democrats abolished the two-thirds rule in 1936. There are three methods of delegate selection: direct appointment by State and local party committees; primary election by registered voters; and election by party members at State and local caucuses or conventions. State governments determine the legal boundaries of delegate selection. Their major decision is whether to require primary elections, which reduce the control of the party organizations over the nomination process. Party members holding public office and party organization officials have exercised much greater influence when the appointment and convention methods of delegate selection have been used. In 1968 the Democratic Governors of Georgia and Louisiana determined the composition of their State delegations to the Chicago convention while State party committees in Arizona, Arkansas, Maryland and Rhode Island selected the delegates. Since 1968 there has been a dramatic rise in the use made of the primary method of delegate selection.

The number of presidential primaries has increased rapidly from seventeen in 1968 to twenty-three in 1972 and to thirty in

1976. The ten largest States held primaries in 1976. In 1968, 3 per cent of the Republican national convention delegates were chosen by appointment, 41 per cent by primary and 56 per cent by convention. In the Democratic party, 13 per cent of the delegates were chosen by appointment, 41 per cent by primary and 46 per cent by convention. However, in 1976 the Republicans chose 69 per cent and the Democrats 78 per cent of national convention delegates by primary. Consequently the 'primary route' has become mandatory for most aspirants to presidential office, though some, like Senator Humphrey in 1976, might hope for a draft at the National Convention if the primaries do not produce a winner.

The popularity of the presidential primary varies considerably from region to region. In 1976 the five Midwestern States all held presidential primaries, as did four of the five Middle-Atlantic States (the exception was Delaware), seven of the ten Outer South and Border States (the exceptions were Missouri, Oklahoma and Virginia), four of the six New England States (the exceptions were Connecticut and Maine), and the District of Columbia. In contrast, only two Farm Belt States (Nebraska and South Dakota), two Pacific States (California and Oregon), two Deep South States (Alabama and Georgia), and three Mountain States (Idaho, Montana and Nevada) preferred the primary to the convention or caucus methods of choosing and committing national convention delegates.

The presidential primary was devised in order to open up the presidential nomination process to ordinary citizens on the assumption that more would participate in elections than in meetings of party activists. Primary voters either directly select national convention delegates who are usually pledged to particular presidential contenders or, by choosing between the presidential candidates themselves, they determine how convention delegates selected by other means, such as local party caucuses, are distributed among the presidential candidates. In addition to committing national convention votes to the candidates, presidential primaries may prove decisive by demonstrating the relative vote-catching appeal of rival candidates.

The first presidential primary was held in Florida in 1904.

Twenty-six States were holding presidential primaries by 1916. But the number had dropped to sixteen by 1935 and remained around that level for thirty years. Seventeen primaries were held in 1968. Then, in response to the wide-publicized criticisms of the Democratic nomination process in 1968, six States initiated or reintroduced the presidential primary in time for the 1972 campaigns: Maryland, Michigan, New Mexico, North Carolina, Rhode Island and Tennessee. Eight more States decided to hold presidential primaries in 1976: Arkansas, Kentucky, Texas, Georgia, Mississippi, Idaho, Montana, and Nevada. New Mexico was the only State to drop the primary for the 1976 nominations.

Though the details of State primary legislation vary considerably, there are two basic types of presidential primary: the preference poll and the delegate primary. In the preference poll, sometimes caricatured as the 'beauty contest', the voter states his preference for party presidential nominee from a list of rival candidates. A binding preference poll commits convention delegates, irrespective of how they are chosen, to particular presidential candidates. In an advisory preference poll, the electorate's verdict is not taken into account when convention delegates are chosen. But advisory preference polls are usually held along with delegate primaries in which voters choose between individual delegate candidates or slates of delegate candidates, whose preferences as presidential candidate are known, and who are then committed to that candidate at the national convention. Uncommitted delegate candidates are also permitted to run in most delegate primaries. Primary States may require a preference poll, or a delegate primary, or both. Some primary States use a mixture of the primary and caucus methods for selecting delegates.

The Democratic National Committee's reform of delegate selection in 1974 stimulated several changes in State laws regulating delegate selection in 1976. However, several States did not adopt all the necessary legislation because some Democratic rules clashed with traditional practices, such as Wisconsin's open primary. The reform movement was much weaker in the Republican party, and, as a result, new or amended rules of delegate selection in the States often allowed some discretion to the parties, as in choosing between an advisory and a binding preference poll.

The types of presidential primaries held by State Democratic parties in 1976 are listed in Table 6.2. Seventeen held binding preference polls (the Republicans held eighteen) compared to only three in 1960. Three of the binding preference polls were accompanied by delegate primaries in which voters were able to select the delegates who were distributed between the presidential candidates on the basis of the preference poll; the remaining fourteen Democratic parties combined a binding preference poll with the caucus or convention method of selecting delegates committed to the presidential candidates in proportion to their performance in the preference polls.

Eight Democratic parties (seven Republican parties) held advisory preference polls in conjunction with delegate primaries. Four States held delegate primaries only (although Ohio's delegate primary in effect included a preference poll in which the voters selected thirty-eight at-large delegates from slates of delegate candidates committed to several presidential candidates). One State, Vermont, held an advisory preference poll but no delegate primary. (Republican parties in Georgia and Maryland required binding preference polls, whereas the Democratic parties preferred advisory preference polls; the reverse applied in Montana.)

Democratic national rules required that 75 per cent of the delegates in each State delegation, chosen by the primary or by the caucus methods, be selected in electoral units no larger than a congressional district. Most Democratic parties took up the option to elect or to appoint up to one-quarter of the delegates on a Statewide basis, although these had to be allocated between the presidential candidates in proportion to their showing either in a Statewide preference poll or in the over-all distribution of delegates in the delegate primary.

The reformers also aimed at applying proportional representation to the distribution of delegate votes between presidential candidates at all levels of delegate selection. But, owing to objections from many State parties, proportional representation was made mandatory only for electoral units larger than the con-

Table 6.2:

Types of Democratic presidential primary 1976

	Binding Preference Poll		Advisory Preference Poll		No Preference Poll	
No delegate primary	Massachussets	104	Vermont	0		
	Florida	81				
	North Carolina	61				
	Wisconsin	68				
	Indiana	75				
	Michigan	133				
	Arkansas	26				
	Idaho	16				
	Kentucky	46				
	Nevada	11				
	California	280				
	Oregon	34				
	Montana	17				
	S. Dakota	17				
	Number of delegates	969		0		
Delegate primary	District of Columbia	17	New Hampshire	17	New York	274
	Tennessee	46	Illinois	169	Texas	130
	Rhode Island	22	Pennsylvania	178	Alabama	35
			Georgia	50	Ohio	152
			Nebraska	23		
			West Virginia	33		
			Maryland	53		
			New Jersey	108		
	Number of delegates	85	Number of delegates	631	Number of delegates	591
TOTAL		1054		631		591
% delegates won by Carter:		40·8%		40·2%		42·9%

gressional district. State parties were permitted a 'loophole' whereby all delegates elected at congressional district level or below could be allocated to the popular vote winner at that level. Twelve Democratic parties accepted the 'loophole' provision, whereas seventeen State parties (all the States with binding

preference polls) required proportional representation at all
levels.

The reformers' aim was to abolish the controversial 'winner-
take-all' primaries, in which one candidate could win all the
delegates in a State convention delegation by coming first in a
Statewide preference poll. Ironically, the last major beneficiary of
the 'winner-take-all' primary was George McGovern, who took
all of California's 271 delegates by virtue of winning 44·9 per cent
of the popular vote compared to 39·7 per cent for Hubert
Humphrey—who therefore received none of California's delegates.
A vital procedural dispute at the 1972 Democratic Convention
in Miami over the legality of California's 'winner-take-all' system was resolved on the convention floor in McGovern's favour.
In 1972 McGovern won all the delegate votes in Massachussets
(102) and Oregon (34) by coming first in the popular vote in
every congressional district. In 1976 the Republicans permitted
'winner-take-all' primaries in California and the District of
Columbia. Carter won all the delegates in only one State, his
home State of Georgia, where he won 83·4 per cent of the popular
vote.

Delegate primaries held along with advisory preference polls
are none the less decided by the electorate's views on the presidential candidates. Most States require delegate candidates to
describe themselves on the ballot as committed to named presidential candidates or as uncommitted. Presidential candidates
organize slates of committed delegate candidates in order to
maximize their strength at the convention when balloting begins.
New York did not permit delegate candidates to indicate on the
ballot a commitment to presidential candidates until 1976, when
the State legislature changed the rules of delegate selection,
leaving it to the State parties to decide whether to make such
information available to the voter. The Democrats took advantage
of the change, the Republicans did not. West Virginia did not
allow the presidential preferences of delegate candidates to be
listed on the ballot in 1976.

States requiring delegate primaries without a binding preference poll usually permit the entry on the ballot of slates of
delegate candidates which are uncommitted, or committed to a

presidential candidate who is not a serious contender, or to a presidential candidate whose consent has not been asked for or obtained. In 1976 the Illinois delegate primary enabled delegate candidates organized by Mayor Daley of Chicago and committed to a non-candidate for the Presidency—Senator Adlai E. Stevenson III—to win eighty-six of the 169 available votes. Although Carter won 48·1 per cent of the vote in the advisory preference poll he could win only fifty-nine delegates. This device is favoured by politicians like Mayor Daley of Chicago in the hope that control of such delegates will allow them a voice at the convention. Daley endorsed Carter on 9 June 1976, ensuring that Stevenson delegates would vote for Carter at the Democratic Convention.

The question of who should participate in the party primaries led to conflict between the Democratic party and the State of Wisconsin. Democratic national rules confined participation in Democratic primaries to registered Democrats. The nature of party registration varies from State to State. Fifteen of the primary States and the District of Columbia provided for party registration in advance of the presidential primaries, and so could limit voting in each party's primary to that party's registered supporters—if they so wished. Five States had completely open primaries because there was no provision at all for party registration (Alabama, Georgia, Idaho, Montana and Vermont) and therefore voters could choose either party's ballot on entering the polling booth. Eight States required intending voters to state a party preference at the polls in the expectation that partisans would choose their own party's ballot. Such primaries are classified as closed, since they are confined to each party's registered supporters, but like open primaries, are susceptible to 'crossover' voting: supporters of a rival party may give up the right to vote in their own party primary, especially when the result is a formality, to support a candidate in the rival party who represents their point of view. George Wallace, who came second in Wisconsin in 1972, winning 22 per cent of the vote compared to McGovern's 29·6 per cent and Humphrey's 20·7 per cent, is thought to have benefited from Republican 'cross-overs'; but in Michigan, where Wallace won 51 per cent of the vote, he was helped much more by the influence of the 'busing' issue on Democratic voters than by the State's open primary. States sometimes permit the voter to 'write-in' the name of any candidate not on the ballot paper. Hence the occasional influence exercised by 'write-in' campaigns, usually organized rather than spontaneous. In 1964 the two leading Republican candidates, Goldwater and Rockefeller, were both defeated by Henry Cabot Lodge on a 'write-in' vote in the New Hampshire primary which traditionally starts off the primary season.

Reformers in the Democratic party wanted to ban 'cross-over' voting. Therefore the primary States with provision for registration of party preference were expected to restrict participation in the Democratic primary to the party's registered voters (nothing could be done where party registration amounted to no more than indicating a party preference on polling day). The Democrats' aim of party purity clashed with Wisconsin's long-running tradition of the open primary. And the Wisconsin State Government, despite providing for party registration, would not pass the required legislation to enable the Democrats to restrict voting in the presidential primary to the party's own supporters. The deadlock was broken in March 1976 when the Compliance Review Commission of the Democratic National Committee accepted Wisconsin's open primary on condition that proportional representation was applied at congressional district level, where fifty-eight of Wisconsin's sixty-eight delegates were to be chosen.

No fewer than 2,276 of the 3,008 delegate votes at the 1976 Democratic Convention in New York City were distributed between the presidential candidates and uncommitted delegates (elected in delegate primaries) in accordance with the wishes of the primary electorate in twenty-nine States and the District of Columbia. The remaining 732 delegate votes were distributed on the basis of voting at party meetings in the non-primary States.

Carter won 938 convention votes in the preference polls and delegate primaries, 41·2 per cent of the available votes, on the basis of 39 per cent of the popular vote. (McGovern won almost 65 per cent of a smaller number of delegate votes from the primary States on the basis of winning 25·3 per cent of the popular vote.) Carter won seventeen primaries and came second in eight. He also won 221 committed delegates by the caucus method of delegate selection, giving him a total of 1,151 committed votes of the 1,505 required for nomination. By the time of the convention Carter had picked up the votes of many uncommitted delegates and delegates released by candidates who withdrew before the convention began.

Carter, like McGovern in 1972, was assured of victory at the convention by virtue of his popular support in the primaries. He won the largest convention vote (74·4 per cent) for a non-incumbent on the first ballot since 1908, benefiting from the increase in presidential primaries compared with 1972. Unlike McGovern, he did not have the advantage of a 'winner-take-all' victory in California, which provided McGovern with almost 18 per cent of the convention votes he needed to win and secured him the nomination. Carter attracted more convention votes than any other candidate everywhere except in the West where he was strongly challenged by Governor Edmund G. Brown of California and Senator Frank Church of Idaho.

The significance of presidential primaries

In 1952 Estes Kefauver, Senator from Tennessee, won twelve of fourteen Democratic primaries but lost the nomination to Adlai Stevenson, who did not compete in any of the primaries. In 1972 George McGovern won the Democratic nomination, following unexpected success in the primaries, even though he was not rated as a major contender before the primaries began.

The precise contribution of presidential primaries to the outcome of the nomination process is determined by the number of delegates who can be formally committed to the rival presidential candidates, the relative standing of the candidates as indicated in public opinion polls before the primaries begin, and the political circumstances in each party prior to and during the primary season from February to June. Usually it is the nomination process of the party losing the preceding presidential election which is the more open to influence on the part of the primaries, though incumbent Presidents such as Johnson in 1968 and Ford in 1976 have been strongly challenged.

Primaries may serve merely to confirm the front runner who has established himself as his party's most likely choice in the two or three years prior to the nomination process. Primaries may be more influential by proving indispensable to the success of an outsider who defeats the front runner at the polls or by effectively deciding, in the absence of a front runner, between several candidates of equal standing. Primaries may prove indecisive by not producing a clear leader. The increase since 1968 in the number of presidential primaries has almost certainly increased their significance, although it remains possible for a number of candidates to reach the convention as credible contestants if success in the primaries is fairly evenly divided between them.

Opinions vary as to the significance of primaries prior to 1976. Keech and Matthews argue that where there has been an identifiable front runner, which usually has been the case, he has won the nomination. The only exception since 1936 was Senator Muskie, who was widely believed before the primaries began in 1972 to be the likely winner of the Democratic nomination.* Studies of public opinion suggest that primaries usually confirm the front runner. A more influential role for the primaries has been suggested by Gerald Pomper, who has estimated that between 1912 and 1932 four candidates were 'substantially aided' in their fight for the nomination: Wilson (1912), Coolidge (1924), Hoover (1928) and Smith (1928); and that primaries were insignificant in 1916, 1920 and 1924.† In contrast, eight candidates benefited between 1936 and 1960: Landon (1936), Roosevelt (1940), Dewey (1944), Truman (1948) and Dewey (1948), Eisenhower (1952), Stevenson (1956) and Kennedy (1960). Since 1960 four more candidates, Goldwater (1964), Nixon (1968), McGovern (1972) and Carter (1976) have been helped on their way to their party's nomination by success on the primary trail.

Primaries are contested because they offer a potentially successful strategy to candidates who either would not win, or who cannot rely on winning, convention support by other means. In

* W. R. Keech and D. R. Matthews, *The Party's Choice* (Brookings, 1976).

† G. Pomper, *Nominating the President* (W. W. Norton and Company, 1966), p. 108.

the process the presidential office has become open, if not always attainable, to individuals who might otherwise have been rejected as presidential candidates: Roman Catholics (Smith and Kennedy), political outsiders (Carter) and politicians who were not regarded as belonging to the centre of their party (Goldwater and McGovern). Primaries not only commit some delegates; they also demonstrate the ability or the inability to attract popular votes. Even one or two primaries may produce a potential winner who is thus acceptable to party officials and party workers.

Primary success was particularly vital to John Kennedy in 1960 and George McGovern in 1972 because both were thought to possess major defects as candidates, Kennedy as a Catholic and McGovern as a radical. Kennedy's successes in Wisconsin and especially in West Virginia demonstrated that he could win the votes of Catholic and Protestant alike. As a result his well organized campaign to win the support of delegates chosen by appointment or in party conventions, who have often been controlled by State and city bosses, was also successful, except in the South which preferred Lyndon Johnson. In 1972 McGovern's victory rested upon both the reform of Democratic selection procedures, which decreased the influence of party regulars, and his success in the primaries.

Primaries have not only contributed to the nomination of a Catholic like Kennedy and an outsider like McGovern; they have also eliminated strong candidates. This was particularly true of Muskie in 1972, who failed to attract sufficient popular support to overcome the challenge of rivals representing the various sections of the Democratic party, particularly the McGovern challenge supported by the party's more liberal left wing, galvanized by the Vietnam and racial issues.

Nixon won most of the Republican primaries in 1968 and was thus able to get rid of his image as a 'loser' of popular elections. He was helped by his party's experience in 1964 which removed the conservative Reagan as a threat except in the South, by Rockefeller's inability to decide, in public at least, whether or not he was a candidate, and by his own popularity with State parties gained by his willingness to campaign for the party at the grassroots level after the 1964 humiliation. Rockefeller did not enter the primaries in 1968 because his pollsters found little popular support for the New York Governor.

Changes in delegate selection since 1968 have clearly increased the influence of voters in primary elections at the expense of the party organizations over the choice of presidential candidates. In 1972 and 1976 the Democratic party, attempting to win back the Presidency, nominated candidates who possessed disadvantages which would have made it unlikely they would win the nomination in earlier years—McGovern as a left-wing radical, and Carter as a Southerner. In 1976 the increase in the number of primaries enabled Ronald Reagan to run President Ford very close in the struggle for the Republican nomination. The Democratic primaries in 1972 led to the withdrawal of the front runner, Muskie. In 1976 the primaries established a front runner, Carter, though none had existed when the primaries began.

FOR FURTHER READING:

H. A. Bone, *American Politics and the Party System*, 4th ed. (McGraw Hill, New York, 1971).

L. D. Epstein, *Political Parties in Western Democracies* (Praeger, New York, 1967).

F. J. Sorauf, *Party Politics in America*, 2nd ed. (Little Brown, Boston, 1972).

W. R. Keech and D. R. Matthews, *The Party's Choice* (The Brookings Institution, Washington, 1976).

W. J. Keefe, *Parties, Politics and the Public Policy in America*, 2nd ed. (The Dryden Press, Hinsdale, Illinois, 1976).

7: The President

A: THE POWERS OF THE PRESIDENT*

The office of President of the United States created by the framers of the Constitution of 1787, like the stronger governorship provided for in several States in the second phase of State constitution making from 1777, was an adaptation of the English monarchy and the royal or proprietary governorship of colonial rule to the republican form of government of the independent United States. There was a single chief executive, independent of the legislature, but elected to his office for a fixed term. The powers of the President were like those exercised by or in the name of the English monarch, though made subject to additional checks and balances.

The executive roles of the President

Article II of the Constitution vests 'the executive Power' in the President. It makes him Commander-in-Chief of the armed forces. It authorizes him to 'require the Opinion, in writing, of the principal Officer in each of the executive Departments, upon any Subject relating to the Duties of their respective Offices', and to 'receive Ambassadors and other public Ministers'. It charges him to 'take Care that the Laws be faithfully executed'.

Article II provides that the President shall nominate and with the consent of the Senate appoint ambassadors and consuls, judges of the Supreme Court and all other officers of the United States, unless for inferior officers the Congress vests the appointment 'in the President alone, in the Courts of Law, or in the Heads of Departments'. It empowers the President to make

* See Table 1.1 for a list of the Presidents.

treaties, provided that two-thirds of the Senators voting on them concur. Article I of the Constitution vests the power to declare war in the Congress.

The powers of the President listed in the foregoing two paragraphs provide the basis for the roles of the President as the chief executive of the Federal Government, the chief conductor of the foreign policy of the United States and its Commander-in-Chief in military affairs and war. In performing these roles the President may exercise a discretionary independent authority, held by the Supreme Court to be implied by the general phrases of Article II and to inhere in the executive branch under the separation of powers. However, the Supreme Court has only infrequently been called upon to define the bounds of this authority or the extent to which it may be restricted by the other branches, because Presidents have usually come to practical accommodations with the Congress or the courts.

Chief executive

While the Congress may by statute impose a duty on an executive officer, including the head of a cabinet department, which cannot be set aside by presidential order and is enforcible in the courts, the President himself has no judicially enforcible responsibility with respect to the performance of his official duties. The scope of the duty of the President to take care that the laws be faithfully executed was at issue in the case of *In Re* Neagle, decided by the Supreme Court in 1890. Neagle was a deputy United States marshal assigned by presidential order to protect a Supreme Court Justice whose life had been threatened, while the Justice rode circuit in California. When the man who had made the threat attacked the Justice, Neagle shot and killed the attacker. State officers arrested Neagle, claiming that there was no statutory authority for the presidential order. The Supreme Court made it clear that the President's law enforcement duty extended beyond the express terms of statutes and treaties to include 'the rights, duties, and obligations growing out of the Constitution itself, our international relations, and all the protection implied by the nature of the government under the Constitution'.

In 1868 President Andrew Johnson was impeached for alleg-
edly violating the Tenure of Office Act of 1867, which had been
passed over his veto and which provided that the tenure of any
executive officer, including a cabinet officer, appointed with the
advice and consent of the Senate could only be terminated, except
at the end of a term specified in law, by senatorial confirmation of
a successor. In 1869 the Act was amended so as to allow also for
simple removal by the President with the consent of the Senate.
In 1887 Grover Cleveland, following his successful struggle the
previous year as Democratic President with the Republican-
controlled Senate over the Act's operation, secured its repeal.

A rider to an appropriation Act of 1876 provided that post-
masters appointed with the consent of the Senate should serve for
four years unless removed sooner by the President with senatorial
consent. In 1926, in the case of Myers v. United States, the
Supreme Court held that the restriction on their removal by the
President was unconstitutional. In the Opinion of the Court
Chief Justice Taft, a former President, declared that, while the
Congress might put restraints on the removal of officers appointed by heads of departments, the President's power to remove
presidential appointees in the executive branch could not be
qualified by statute. The Tenure of Office Act had been unconstitutional, too.

Taft's Opinion cast doubt on the validity of statutes protecting
from political removal presidentially appointed members of commissions established by law to perform regulatory functions independently of presidential direction. These independent
regulatory commissions combine executive, legislative and judicial activities. They enforce statutes and generally watch over
the activities of those engaged in their fields. They make rules
under their statutory authority which have the force of law. They
hear and decide cases involving alleged infractions of the statutes
and rules, rival claims to licences and other benefits, and other
relevant disputes.

Shortly after taking office in 1933, President Franklin Roosevelt removed a member of the Federal Trade Commission who
had been appointed by President Coolidge and re-appointed by
President Hoover, with senatorial consent and for the seven-year

term of office, not for any of the grounds for removal laid down in law—inefficiency, neglect of duty and malfeasance in office—but because 'the aims and purposes of the Administration with respect to the work of the commission can be carried out most effectively with personnel of my own selection.' In 1935, in the case of Humphrey's Executor *v.* United States, the Supreme Court upheld the statute restricting the President's power of removal. While Justice Sutherland's extravagant Opinion of the Court, which declared that the commission was a 'quasi-legislative' and 'quasi-judicial' body 'wholly disconnected from the executive department', is now a constitutional curiosity—for a time the independent regulatory commissions were referred to as a 'fourth branch' of government—the Supreme Court has continued to distinguish between an unqualified power of the President to dismiss presidential appointees when he is supervising executive activities and a restricted power to dismiss officials when they perform quasi-judicial functions provided for in legislation.

In 1792 a committee of the House of Representatives, conducting the first full congressional investigation, into a disaster that befell a general sent to shoot Indians, asked executive officers to testify and produce relevant papers and records. After consulting his cabinet, President Washington saw that the committee obtained all that it asked for. But he and his cabinet were of 'one mind' that the executive should withhold papers whose disclosure 'would injure the public'. Later he refused to give the Congress a copy of the instructions to John Jay that had guided Jay in negotiating a treaty with Great Britain in 1794.

In 1807, during the trial for treason of Aaron Burr, Vice-President from 1801 to 1805, Chief Justice Marshall (presiding while on circuit) subpoenaed President Jefferson to produce documents, excerpts from which the President indirectly supplied. Jefferson reserved the right to decide for himself whether he should appear in court. Marshall, while asserting the right of the courts to compel the President's attendance if necessary, found the papers enough. Burr was acquitted. The practical accommodation reached between Jefferson and Marshall (who were bitter enemies) left the constitutional issue between the President and the judiciary unresolved.

Indeed, the claim of Presidents to the privilege of withholding executive information from the other branches was not directly ruled upon by the Supreme Court until 1974. Despite the much greater use of the claim after 1941 to protect security files on Federal employees from congressional probing, especially in the 'McCarthyite era' from 1950 to (at least) 1954–5, the term 'executive privilege' seems not to have been officially used until 1958.* In 1974, in the case of United States *v.* Nixon, arising from President Nixon's refusal to turn over tapes and documents of his conversations with his aides and advisers to the court trying the 'Watergate case', the Supreme Court, in a unanimous decision of the eight Justices taking part, held: that there is a presumptive executive privilege to withhold confidential communications of the executive branch; that it is the province of the Supreme Court finally to determine the validity of a claim to executive privilege; and that, while President Nixon's generalized claim could not prevail over the need for disclosure of all relevant information in a criminal trial, a specific assertion of privilege against disclosure of military, diplomatic or sensitive national security secrets could be allowed. Nixon lost, precipitating his resignation from office. But the Presidency won a great deal in the *obiter dicta* (statements not necessary to decide the instant case) of Chief Justice Berger's Opinion of the Court.

Chief diplomat

In Re Neagle, Myers *v.* United States and United States *v.* Nixon are milestones in the Supreme Court's recognition of the independent authority of the President as the chief executive of the Federal Government. In foreign and military affairs a broad independent authority of the President was successfully invoked from the outset of government under the Constitution.

In representing the United States in international affairs the President uses whom he wishes to conduct negotiations: official ambassadors, personal envoys, the Secretary of State, special assistants or himself. (The Department of State was made responsible in its early years for a variety of domestic matters as

* Raoul Berger, *Executive Privilege* (Harvard U.P., 1974), p. 1.

well as foreign relations. It has subsequently been relieved of virtually all of its home department duties, but vestiges remain: Secretary of State Henry Kissinger received President Nixon's resignation.)

Although the President often seeks the support of the Congress for a major declaration of foreign policy, President Washington set the precedent for independent declarations by his Neutrality Proclamation of 1793 with respect to the war between Great Britain and France. Instead of giving aid to France, with which the United States had entered into an alliance during the War of Independence, the country was to 'pursue a conduct friendly and impartial toward the belligerent powers'. Critics of the Proclamation argued that it had infringed the power of the Congress to decide upon war or peace. In 1794 the Congress passed a Neutrality Act. In 1823 President Monroe announced the Monroe Doctrine, which warned the European powers not to interfere with states in the Western hemisphere that had declared their independence, in his annual message to the Congress.

In this century by far the most common form of international compact negotiated by the executive is not a treaty, requiring ratification by two-thirds of the Senate, but an executive agreement, which requires either no congressional action or, if legislation is needed to implement it (as by the appropriation of money), approval by simple majorities of the two Houses. Possibly treaties but not executive agreements supersede prior Acts of the Congress; otherwise the two forms seem to be of like legal effect, and no distinction can be made between their subjects. Indeed, agreements have sometimes replaced treaties that the Senate has failed to ratify. Texas was admitted to the Union in 1845 under an agreement endorsed by a joint congressional resolution (which to take effect must meet the requirements for enactment of a bill), after the Senate defeated a treaty of admission in 1844. President Theodore Roosevelt made an agreement with Santo Domingo in 1905, extending United States control over that country, after the Senate failed to ratify a treaty.

In the century from 1789 to 1889 there were roughly equal numbers of treaties and executive agreements. In the next half-century to 1939 there were almost twice as many agreements as treaties, reflecting the emergence of the United States as a world power in the Spanish-American War. President McKinley used the executive agreement to establish the terms by which the Spanish-American War was ended, formally by treaty. The United States ended its state of war with Germany and Austria-Hungary in the First World War, after the Senate's failure to ratify the Treaty of Versailles negotiated by President Wilson in 1919, in accordance with a joint congressional resolution signed by President Harding in 1921. In 1940 President Franklin Roosevelt disposed of fifty destroyers to Great Britain in return for the lease of bases in British possessions in the Western hemisphere without resort to treaty or legislation.

Between 1940 and 1970 the United States entered into 310 treaties and 5,653 executive agreements (excluding wholly secret agreements). While the great majority of executive agreements were made in pursuance of treaties ratified by the Senate or with congressional legislative support, either before or after their negotiation, in the aftermath of the Korean war of 1950–3 and again towards the end of the Vietnam war, neither of which was declared by the Congress, many members of the Congress, especially Senators, tried to put curbs on the President's capacity to commit the United States without or with little congressional involvement. Limited success was achieved in 1972 by the enactment of a bill requiring all non-secret executive agreements to be reported to the Congress within sixty days, and secret agreements to the specialist committees on foreign policy of the two Houses.

Commander-in-Chief

Article I of the Constitution empowers the Congress to raise armies, provide a navy, make rules for the government of the land and naval forces, and 'provide for calling forth the Militia to execute the Laws of the Union, suppress Insurrections and repel Invasions'. Article II makes the President 'Commander-in-Chief of the Army and Navy of the United States, and of the Militia of the several States, when called into the actual Service of the United States'. Article IV, Section 4, requires the United States to protect each State against domestic violence on application of the State's legislature or, when the legislature cannot be convened, its executive. The Supreme Court has held that the guarantees of Article IV, Section 4, give rise to 'political questions': that is to say, the decisions of the political branches of the Federal Government about them are not subject to judicial review.

From 1792 Federal legislation has provided for the President's use of military forces to enforce Federal law when enforcement by the ordinary course of judicial proceedings is obstructed. The first occasion was President Washington's call-up of militia from four States in 1794, in order to break the 'Whisky Rebellion' against the collection of a tax on distilleries. In the late nineteenth and early twentieth centuries Presidents used troops to deal with disturbances arising from labour disputes, sometimes at the request of State authorities under Article IV, although the need to enforce Federal law could also be invoked. President Cleveland sent troops to Chicago during the Pullman strike of 1894, over the protest of Governor Altgeld of Illinois, to 'remove obstructions to the United States mails'. In 1957 President Eisenhower sent contingents of the 101st Airborne Division into Little Rock, Arkansas, and 'federalized' the Arkansas National Guard, to overcome Governor Faubus's obstruction of a Federal court order requiring the desegregation of Little Rock schools. Presidents Kennedy and Johnson similarly evoked Federal authority against Southern obstruction of desegregation decrees.

The United States has engaged in hostilities against other states on many occasions, starting with a naval war with France in 1798–1800. Usually there has been little fighting, as when the Marines landed in pursuance of the Roosevelt Corollary to the Monroe Doctrine, announced by President Theodore Roosevelt in 1904 and abandoned by President Franklin Roosevelt, under which the United States intervened in Latin-American countries on behalf of 'civilized' (investing) nations.

The Congress has put the United States into 'declared' wars only five times: in 1812, 1846, 1898, 1917 and 1941. The declaration of war against Mexico in 1846 was a recognition of the hostilities provoked by President Polk's dispatch of troops to occupy disputed territory. In 1941, before the Japanese attack on Pearl Harbor, Hawaii, in December led to declared war between the United States and the Axis powers, President Roosevelt had sent troops into Greenland and Iceland and ordered the navy to 'shoot at sight' when protecting convoys, to ensure that a steady flow of munitions reached Britain: the Lend-Lease Bill authorizing financial aid had been enacted in March.

The Congress sometimes places legislative limits on the deployment of military forces abroad. When the first peacetime conscription legislation was passed in 1940, the Congress restricted the use of the troops raised to the 'Western hemisphere'. In 1941 President Roosevelt decided that Iceland was in the Western hemisphere. In 1973 the Congress passed a War Powers Act, over President Nixon's veto, barring the President from committing forces to combat for more than sixty days without specific approval by the Congress (unless the Congress is physically unable to convene). A military aide with the black box containing the coded orders enabling the President to take the irrevocable decision to unleash nuclear war stays by the President at all times.

Following the firing of the first shots of the Civil War in April 1861, President Lincoln convened the Congress to meet in special session on 4 July and meantime invoked all his constitutional and statutory powers, and more, to wage war against secession. He called upon the State governors for militia troops, ordered a naval blockade of Southern ports, enlarged the regular army and navy and authorized the enlistment of volunteers, suspended the writ of habeas corpus for persons arrested by the military in designated areas and released unappropriated funds to private persons for services relating to the mobilization of forces. Preserving the nation overrode constitutional niceties.

In 1863 in the Prize Cases, in which the validity of Lincoln's blockade was upheld, a majority of the Supreme Court agreed that the President must determine the degree of force the crisis demanded. After the war, the Court condemned the use of military courts where the ordinary courts were functioning. During the Second World War in 1944 the Supreme Court upheld the removal in 1942 of citizens of Japanese descent from the West Coast to detention camps. After the war, in 1946, the Court held invalid the substitution of military for the ordinary courts in (the then Territory of) Hawaii by executive action following the attack on Pearl Harbor.

In 1862, President Lincoln issued his Emancipation Proclamation freeing as at 1 January 1863 'all persons held as slaves within any State or designated part of a State the people whereof shall be in rebellion against the United States'. He invoked 'the power in me vested as Commander-in-Chief' and justified the Proclamation as 'a fit and necessary war measure'.

During the Second World War President Roosevelt was angered by the success with which the 'farm bloc' obstructed price control legislation in the Congress. On 7 September 1942, he sent a message to the Congress giving it until 1 October to act: 'Inaction on your part by that date will leave me with an inescapable responsibility to the people of this country to see to it that the war effort is no longer imperiled by threat of economic chaos. In the event that the Congress should fail to act, and act adequately, I shall accept the responsibility, and I will act.' The threat was effective.

In 1952, during the Korean war, which like the Civil War was undeclared, President Truman put the private steel industry under government control to stop a labour dispute disrupting production required for the war effort. In the case of Youngstown Sheet & Tube Company *v.* Sawyer a majority of the Supreme Court for the first time struck down in wartime conditions a resort to inherent executive power. But Truman had refused to follow procedures laid down by the Taft-Hartley Labor-Management Relations Act, passed over his veto in 1947. The thinking of most of the Justices (there were one Opinion of the Court, five concurring opinions and one dissenting opinion: the Court divided six to three on the merits) left considerable scope for a President not running directly counter to legislation.

The legislative and judicial roles of the President

Article II of the Constitution provides that the President 'shall from time to time give to the Congress Information of the State of the Union, and recommend to their Consideration such Measures as he shall judge necessary and expedient'. It empowers him to call one or both Houses into special session, and to adjourn them if they disagree about the time of adjournment. The adjournment power has never been exercised.

Article I provides that every bill that shall have passed the two Houses shall, before it becomes law, be presented to the President. If he approves, he signs it. Otherwise, while the Congress is in session, he may, within ten days (Sundays excepted) after a measure has been delivered to him, return it to the House in which it originated together with his objections to it: this 'regular veto' may be overridden by two-thirds majorities of both Houses; if the President does not return the measure in the time allowed, it becomes law, whether he signs it or not. However, if the Congress adjourns before the constitutional ten days have passed, the President may then exercise a 'pocket veto' simply by not signing the measure. This veto is absolute.

The President is now often referred to as the chief legislator, as well as chief of state, chief executive, chief diplomat and commander-in-chief of the armed forces, of the United States. His proposals on behalf of the executive branch provide the basis for most of the major legislation of the Congress, though they are subject to amendment and often not adopted at all. It has been calculated that between 1948 and 1964 about seven in ten of the President's proposals relating to defence and foreign affairs were adopted, but only four in ten of those relating to domestic affairs. However, such calculations do not take into account that the President and members of his administration may put much more effort into attempting to secure congressional approval of some proposals than of others: they may not press some at all.

In trying to influence the content of legislation, whether based on his own or other proposals, the President may indicate that he will veto a measure if it contains certain provisions. He thus tries to minimize the effect of not having the power to veto an item of a bill. When a bill containing items of which he disapproves is presented to him, he must decide whether what he likes or needs in the bill outweighs his objections and whether he is in a position in relation to the Congress to veto the bill, have the veto sustained and secure a new measure more to his liking.

Compilations of the numbers of vetoes differ slightly; but from

H

1789 through 1974 Presidents vetoed fewer than one in thirty-five measures passed by the two Houses of the Congress, using (according to one reckoning) the regular veto 1,348 times and the pocket veto 996 times. Two-thirds of the vetoes were of private bills. Eighty-four (regular) vetoes were overridden by the Congress.

Especially since World War II, Presidents have sought to exercise a virtual veto over items in budgetary legislation by impounding funds appropriated by the Congress. In a number of court cases brought against President Nixon's impoundments, the executive actions were invalidated as contrary to Acts authorizing the expenditures. The Congressional Budget and Impoundment Control Act of 1974 requires the Congress to align its particular tax and spending proposals with an overall budgetary policy and the President to report recisions and deferrals of expenditure to the Congress. Recisions must be approved by the Congress within forty-five days. Deferrals may be vetoed by either of the two Houses.

The President nominates and with the consent of the Senate appoints Federal judges (see Chapter 9). Article II of the Constitution empowers him 'to grant Reprieves and Pardons for Offences against the United States, except in cases of Impeachment'. In 1974 President Ford invoked this power to grant former President Nixon a full pardon for all offences against the United States which he may have committed while President.

B: THE EXECUTIVE BRANCH

The Constitution vests the executive power in the President alone. Article I makes the Vice President the presiding officer of the Senate, with a tie-breaking vote only. He has no other constitutional function, except to succeed to the Presidency or to serve as Acting President if the President is unable to discharge the powers and duties of his office.

The Federal administration

The references in Article II to 'the principal Officer in each of the executive Departments' and 'the Heads of Departments' seem to imply that the Federal administration was to be organized as a number of executive departments under single heads acting as the chief advisers to the President in their respective fields. President Washington developed the practice of calling together the Secretaries of State, War, and the Treasury—the heads of the three original executive departments created by the Congress—and the Attorney General (the Department of Justice was not created until 1870) in order to discuss with them matters upon which he wanted their collective judgement. By 1793 they were referred to as the President's cabinet. By 1795 Washington had found it necessary for effective government that the cabinet members hold broadly similar political views.

Few permanent administrative organizations were created as agencies independent of the cabinet departments before 1913 (in which year the cabinet departments became ten in number). Most of the independent agencies—such as the Department of Agriculture, headed by a Commissioner of Agriculture from its establishment in 1862 until it was raised to cabinet status under a Secretary of Agriculture in 1889—were under single heads, too. The major exceptions were the three-member Civil Service Commission created by the Pendleton Act of 1883 and the Interstate Commerce Commission established by an Act of 1887, amended in 1889. Other regulatory commissions were created from 1913. In the First World War a number of wartime agencies were chartered as government corporations, as a means of obtaining more operating and financial flexibility than in the usual administrative organizations.

While the President usually regarded the cabinet officers as his chief advisers, he alone decided whether he followed their advice. He might rely more on personal advisers, especially if he was a President promoting the independence, or the independent initiative in policy making, of his office. For while the fact that very few presidential nominations of cabinet officers have been rejected by the Senate is largely explained by the normal willingness of the Senators to allow the President to select his own chief administrators, it also reflects presidential awareness that some nominations would not stand a chance. In obtaining legislation and money for their departments, cabinet officers seek support

Table 7.1:

The Executive Branch

(Only bodies mentioned in Section B are shown)

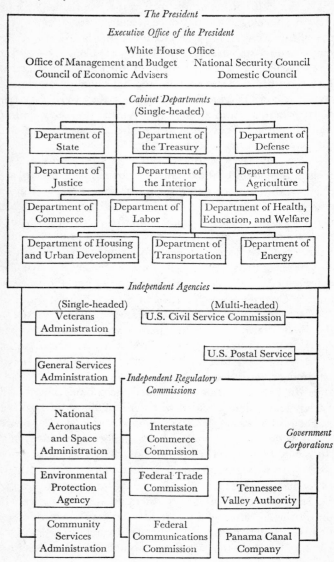

The President

Executive Office of the President

White House Office
Office of Management and Budget   National Security Council
Council of Economic Advisers   Domestic Council

Cabinet Departments
(Single-headed)

Department of State	Department of the Treasury	Department of Defense
Department of Justice	Department of the Interior	Department of Agriculture
Department of Commerce	Department of Labor	Department of Health, Education, and Welfare
Department of Housing and Urban Development	Department of Transportation	Department of Energy

Independent Agencies

(Single-headed)   (Multi-headed)

Veterans Administration   U.S. Civil Service Commission

U.S. Postal Service

General Services Administration   *Independent Regulatory Commissions*

National Aeronautics and Space Administration   Interstate Commerce Commission

Government Corporations

Environmental Protection Agency   Federal Trade Commission

Tennessee Valley Authority

Community Services Administration   Federal Communications Commission

Panama Canal Company

from, and usually respond to, both the President and the Congress. President Jackson's 'kitchen cabinet' and President Wilson's Colonel House were entirely the President's men.

When President Franklin D. Roosevelt took office in 1933, there were 591,000 civilian employees in the executive branch of the Federal Government and 244,000 members of the armed services. After four years of his New Deal, there were 878,000 civilian employees. There were more than a hundred separate major administrative organizations. The creation of new agencies, often with overlapping jurisdictions with the old and among themselves, was the chief administrative device used in initiating new programmes to rescue the country from the great depression and carry out economic and social reforms. Roosevelt was adept at using competing advisers, so as to keep himself well informed and in a position really to take many important decisions himself.

Following the report of the President's Committee on Administrative Management (the Brownlow Committee) in 1937, the Administrative Reorganization Act of 1939 gave the President authority for two years to initiate reorganization plans (from which, however, twenty-one administrative boards and commissions were specifically exempted), to take effect unless the two Houses of the Congress disapproved them by concurrent resolution within sixty days. Except for short periods there has since then been legislation enabling the President to initiate reorganizations, subject to varying conditions and restraints. Like the Brownlow Committee, two Commissions headed by former President Hoover, which reported in 1949 and 1955, advocated a much simpler hierarchy under the President of organizations engaged in executive activities. Since 1937 the overall number of major separate organizations has fallen; but new independent agencies continue to be created, because Presidents believe they launch new programmes more effectively than existing organizations (or at least secure more initial publicity) and because members of the Congress believe independent agencies are, on the whole, less subject to presidential control and therefore more subject to congressional influence than the cabinet departments.

To direct the Federal administration, the Brownlow Committee reported, 'the President needs help. . . . He should be given a small number of executive assistants who would be his direct aides in dealing with the managerial agencies and administrative departments of government. These assistants would be in addition to his present aides who deal with the public, with the Congress, and with the press. . . . They should be installed in the White House itself, directly accessible to the President.' In 1939 the first reorganization plan under the Administrative Reorganization Act established the Executive Office of the President, setting up in it a White House Office in which to locate such assistants (six of whom had been authorized by the Act) and drawing together in it agencies instrumental to central administrative management, of which by far the most important was the Bureau of the Budget, established in 1921 and placed in the Treasury Department at that time, though made directly responsible to the President from the outset.

In mid-1945, between the end of the Second World War in Europe and the surrender of Japan, there were 3,787,000 civilian employees in the executive branch of the Federal Government and 12,123,000 members of the armed services. In mid-1975 (to which time the details given in the present tense below refer) there were 2,848,000 civilian employees in the executive branch and about 2·1 million members of the armed services. (Federal office holders appointed by the President, heads of departments or courts of law, as provided for in Article II of the Constitution, are 'officers'; if appointed by others, 'employees': but for statistical purposes they are all called employees.) Of the civilian employees in mid-1975 2,000 were in the Executive Office of the President, 1,737,000 in eleven cabinet departments (referred to officially as the executive departments) and 1,109,000 in independent agencies, of which perhaps fifty to sixty are of more than very minor importance. Information about employment excludes employees of the Central Intelligence Agency, which was established under the National Security Council in 1947, and of the National Security Agency within the Department of Defense.

Executive Office of the President

The White House Office includes the immediate personal assistants to the President: assistants for advising and carrying out duties for him in fields of policy (such as national security affairs), for liaison with the heads of administrative organizations and operating bureaux in the Federal administration and for relations with the Congress, the President's party and major interest groups; the Press Secretary (for relations with all the information media); the Special Counsel to the President; and military aides.

The Office of Management and Budget (as the Bureau of the Budget has been called since 1970) prepares the annual budget proposals of the President and monitors Federal spending as an instrument of presidential oversight of the administration. It is generally responsible for improving the techniques of administrative management. On behalf of the President it 'clears' routine proposals for legislation from departments and agencies and reviews measures passed by the Congress before the President signs or vetoes them.

The assistants in the White House Office and the Director of the Office of Management and Budget are personal appointees of the President, for whom senatorial confirmation is not required. A number of bodies have been added to the Executive Office of the President because, like the Council of Economic Advisers created by the Employment Act of 1946, they advise on broad areas of policy formulation or because, like the erstwhile Office of Economic Opportunity created by the Economic Opportunity Act of 1964 to administer President Johnson's 'Poverty Program', their location in the Executive Office is thought to give them special prestige. The President's appointments of their members or heads need senatorial approval. (President Nixon downgraded the 'Poverty Program'. In 1974 the Office of Economic Opportunity was replaced by an independent agency, the Community Services Administration.)

In 1949 the Congress placed the National Security Council, which had been created by the National Security Act of 1947, in the Executive Office of the President. It is composed of the President, the Vice-President, the Secretary of State and the Secretary of Defense, together with other officers chosen by the President to attend. In 1970 President Nixon provided, in a reorganization plan, for the establishment of a Domestic Council, composed of the President, the Vice-President, the heads of the cabinet departments not in the N.S.C. and other appropriate chief officers. By then the cabinet had ceased altogether to be a source of collective advice on policy.

President Eisenhower created an Operations Co-ordinating Board to follow through the decisions reached in the National Security Council. President Kennedy abolished the Board, to protect the President's freedom to make *ad hoc* arrangements about seeking advice and implementing decisions. Under President Nixon, Dr. Henry Kissinger was, as a White House assistant, the chief adviser for foreign and national security affairs from the start, in 1969. When Kissinger also became Secretary of State in September 1973, his new appointment was regarded as enhancing not his position but possibly that of the State Department (and of the President, who was then attempting to ward off impeachment). Since White House assistants claim executive privilege to avoid their being questioned by congressional committees, the Senate obtained assurances when confirming Kissinger's cabinet appointment that he would not invoke the privilege associated with one of his offices in order to withhold information about the other. In November 1975 President Ford relieved him of his White House Assistantship.

Cabinet departments

The eleven cabinet departments* are: State; Treasury; Defense; Justice; Interior; Agriculture; Commerce; Labor; Health, Education and Welfare; Housing and Urban Development; and Transportation. By far the largest is the Department of Defense, containing the non-cabinet departments of the Army, the Navy and the Air Force. In mid-1975 it had 1,042,000 civilian employees.

The heads and assistant heads of departments are political appointees of the President requiring senatorial approval. Members of the Congress regard them as primarily the President's men. The highest operational organization in the departmental

* In August 1977 a new cabinet Department of Energy was established.

structure is the bureau (though it may, for example, be called a 'service', an 'office' or an 'administration'). Only some bureau chiefs are political appointees.

Although the administrative reorganizations of recent decades have generally strengthened the control of the heads of departments over their bureaux, the specialized standing committees and the subcommittees of the Appropriations Committees of the Congress exert countervailing pressures on the bureaux with which the committee members are especially concerned. It is to preserve this influence that the legislature refuses to give the executive a completely free hand to reorganize. The Army Corps of Engineers, whose civil works help stuff the 'pork barrel', is particularly close to the Congress. Widespread congressional support for Mr. J. Edgar Hoover, the Director of the Federal Bureau of Investigation from 1924 to 1972, buttressed by his files on the private lives of politicians, made Hoover virtually independent of his nominal superiors in the Department of Justice and the President.

Independent agencies

Next to the Defense Department, the U.S. Postal Service is the largest Federal employer, with 699,000 employees in mid-1975. Until the 1930s the Post Office employed more than half of all Federal civilian employees (except during and for a few years after the involvement of the United States in the First World War). The Postmaster General, a member of the cabinet from 1829, was the chief dispenser of party patronage jobs. With reduction of the patronage element in Federal employment to minor proportions since the Second World War, the Post Office ceased to be an important political base. As a strongly unionized, labour-intensive service in a period of relatively full employment, it became a political embarrassment. In 1971 the Postal Service commenced operations as an independent agency under an eleven-member Board of Governors, nine of whom are appointed by the President with the consent of the Senate for overlapping nine-year terms: the others are the Postmaster General (the chief executive officer) and the Deputy Postmaster General (the chief operating officer), both appointed by the Board of Governors.

The majority of the largest independent agencies are organized, like the departments, under single heads: the Veterans Administration (213,000 employees in mid-1975); the General Services Administration (39,000), which performs a variety of 'housekeeping' functions for the Federal Government; the National Aeronautics and Space Administration (26,000); and the Environmental Protection Agency (11,000). Besides the Postal Service, there were only two multi-headed agencies with more than 10,000 employees in mid-1975: the three-member Tennessee Valley Authority (28,000), incorporated by an Act of the New Deal Congress in 1933, whose dams on the Tennessee River provide flood control, electricity and recreational benefits for the region; and the Panama Canal Company (12,000). Both are wholly government-owned corporations, as are about ten other corporations in and outside the executive departments, but the independence of the Panama Canal Company is only formal. Its board of directors is appointed by the Secretary of the Army acting for the President; and its president and chief executive officer is the Governor of the Canal Zone, appointed by the President and reporting as Governor to the Secretary of the Army.

There are seven independent regulatory commissions, such as the Interstate Commerce Commission, the Federal Trade Commission and the Federal Communications Commission. Originally, independence meant primarily freedom from partisanship. The commissioners are appointed by the President with the consent of the Senate for staggered terms of office longer than his own, and must include members of more than one party. Later, independence came to mean primarily freedom from presidential supervision, as sanctioned by the Supreme Court in the Humphrey's Executor case in 1935.

The Brownlow Committee recommended that the executive and legislative functions of the commissions be lodged in departments; the first Hoover Commission, most of their executive functions only: even that was not generally acceptable to the Congress. Instead, the executive activities of each commission have been put under its chairman, who serves as chairman at the pleasure of the President. The commissions tend to fall under the influence of the interests they regulate, which cultivate close relations with them and the congressional committees concerned with legislative oversight of their activities.

Legislative and judicial agencies

There are a few agencies of the Federal Government that are not regarded as part of the executive branch at all. The General Accounting Office, which audits the receipt, expenditure and application of public funds, and the 'copyright' Library of Congress, which provides the Congressional Research Service (formerly the Legislative Reference Service) for the Congress, are legislative agencies. The Comptroller General of the United States in charge of the General Accounting Office is appointed by the President with the consent of the Senate for a term of fifteen years and may be removed only by a joint resolution of the Congress for specified causes or by conviction on impeachment. The Administrative Office of the United States Courts is a judicial agency (see Chapter 9).

Federal administrators

Federal administrators directly concerned with determining policy are known as political executives. Presidents fill the two to three hundred principal political executive positions with leading men from business, the professions (especially law) and academic life, and also with a few military men (especially immediately after the Second World War), appointive office holders and incumbent or defeated elective office holders. Republican Presidents appoint more businessmen, especially industrialists; Democrats, more professors. But all draw broadly from the élites of American society. Indeed, a fair number of those drawn into government serve several spells as political executives under Presidents of both parties. For after attracting men to Washington to start a new administration, the President comes increasingly to rely, as the first appointees leave (perhaps finding public administration not to their taste or talents; or simply wanting to resume making more money), on the 'in-and-outers' prepared to come in again.

The élites are not tightly knit together. Dwight Eisenhower had not met George Humphrey, who became his unusually influential Secretary of the Treasury, before he became President-elect. Nor had John F. Kennedy met Dean Rusk, who became his Secretary of State, or Robert McNamara, who became his unusually influential Secretary of Defense. A President-elect's talent scouts play a key role in the formation of a new administration, especially when there is a change from one party to the other. Although some politicians who helped the President secure nomination and election are rewarded, the task is to find men for the jobs, not jobs for the boys.

There are, all told, about 2,200 posts whose occupants are policy makers or closely associated with policy makers. While most of the positions are filled by 'in-and-outers', the largest single group of appointees is of career officials, many of whom do not lose career status when they agree to occupy posts in which they are expected to further the current administration's policies but who may then be moved from them to other, perhaps lower, posts without regard to normal civil service procedures.

Almost all Federal administrators are career officials. The Pendleton Act of 1883 and subsequent legislation allowed the President to extend the 'classified' merit system administered by the Civil Service Commission to posts currently held by non-civil service appointees, who were thereby 'blanketed' in the civil service. By 1901, when Theodore Roosevelt (who had been a Civil Service Commissioner from 1889 to 1895) became President, less than half the employees in the executive branch were in 'classified' posts; by 1909, when he left office, the ratio of 'classified' to other posts was almost two to one. By 1933, it was more than three to one, but it fell below two to one again during the New Deal.

After the Second World War the 'classified' system was extended to almost all posts not covered by other merit systems, such as that for the Foreign Service (whose appointments, like those of regular officers in the military services, are formally made by the President with the consent of the Senate) and the systems established by particular bureaux and agencies (for example, the F.B.I. and the T.V.A.). In 1953, after twenty years of Democratic administrations, the new Republican administration removed a few positions from the civil service; but in this as in other respects it soon became clear that the main changes that had taken place in the Federal administration were permanent. When President Nixon took office in 1969, only about 6,500 posts (including the 2,200 policy-making posts referred to above) in 3 million could be filled by political appointments.

Even in the general 'classified' service, officials are largely re-cruited for and make their careers in particular departments or other agencies. In 1968 the Civil Service Commission reported that more than half the officials in the highest administrative supervisory grade (General Schedule 15) and the so-called 'super grades' (GS-16 to GS-18, which overlap in importance the lower political-executive positions) had spent all of their govern-mental service in a single agency. The great majority had not changed agencies since attaining the lowest administrative supervisory grade (GS-13).

Career officials are thus 'agency-oriented', as are most political executives, who tend to go to the agencies where their outside experience is relevant. Furthermore, individual members of the Congress concentrate on watching the agencies of particular in-terest to them and their constituents, and work their way on and up the appropriate specialized standing committees: the ad-ministrators of the typical agency know that the oversight of a standing committee is permanent and intense while that of the President is likely to be transitory. Finally, both the agency and the committee are the permanent objects of pressures from the agency's special 'clientele' among the public and organized interest groups. Experience and circumstances lead senior Federal administrators, like the members of the Congress, to further particular policies and programmes. Only the President provides general leadership.

C: PRESIDENTIAL LEADERSHIP

The President of the United States is the public person of whom the American child is first aware. The initial image of a protective

'father figure' becomes overlaid by more complex feelings towards the holder of the office, who as chief of state represents the
nation but as chief of his party is a focal point of controversy. The
office continues to be accorded great respect.

The making of the Presidency

George Washington, the 'Father of his Country', sought with
success to make the Presidency, like a monarchy, 'respectable'
(his word). Andrew Jackson was the first 'People's President':
'the direct representative of the American people'. His political
opponents assumed the name of Whigs, against 'King Andrew'.
Abraham Lincoln (an old Whig and new Republican) was
'Father Abraham', the 'Great Emancipator' and the martyred
saviour of the Union.

In the 1890s Henry Jones Ford perceived the potential in the
nineteenth-century presidency which has been realized in the
twentieth century: 'The truth is that in the presidential office, as
it has been constituted since Jackson's time, American democracy
has revived the oldest political institution of the race, the elective
kingship.' Theodore Roosevelt, who as Vice-President succeeded
President McKinley when the latter was assassinated in 1901,
added a new dimension to the office. The youngest man to become President, and an advocate of the 'full baby carriage', he
with his wife and six children made the President's the nation's
'First Family'. Today everything about the President is news.

In his autobiography published in 1913 Roosevelt wrote that
he had acted as 'a steward of the people'. To act so, he had not
thought it necessary to 'find some specific authorization'. He
believed that it was the President's right and duty 'to do anything
that the needs of the nation demanded unless such action was
forbidden by the Constitution or by the laws'. In holding this
view of presidential power he placed himself in the 'Lincoln-
Jackson school' in contrast to his successor, Taft, whom he placed
with Buchanan, Lincoln's irresolute predecessor. While wryly
noting the associations, Taft agreed that he disagreed with
Roosevelt: 'ascribing an undefined residuum of power to the
President is an unsafe doctrine.' But in 1926, in the Myers case,

Taft as Chief Justice of the Supreme Court found in the Constitution an unspecified absolute authorization for the President to remove his appointees from the executive branch.

Woodrow Wilson wrote in 1908 that the President's 'office is anything he has the sagacity and force to make it'. For most of his own incumbency (1913–21) he was more successful in obtaining legislation he wanted from the Congress than any President since Jefferson, who had until the last year of his second term controlled the party he had created. Jefferson had worked behind the scenes. A poor speaker, he had stopped the practice of the President's delivering his annual State of the Union message to the Congress in person. Wilson restarted it. The State of the Union address has become a televised event.

Wilson was broken, politically and personally, in his efforts to secure the ratification of the Treaty of Versailles. Harding promised to return the country to 'normalcy'. Coolidge said that the country's business was business. Under Hoover business collapsed.

Telling the people in his first inaugural in 1933 that 'the only thing we have to fear is fear itself', Franklin D. Roosevelt secured from the Congress in his first 'hundred days' the legislation he asked for in dealing with the economic crisis. He rallied support in his radio 'fireside chats'. In his first inaugural he had said that he would, if necessary, ask the Congress for 'broad executive power to wage a war against the emergency as great as the power that would be given me if we were in fact invaded by a foreign foe'. Later he identified for Americans their foreign foes and rallied them again, after Pearl Harbor, towards victory in war. Roosevelt (and in her sphere his wife, Eleanor) exploited all the dimensions of the Presidency to the full.

Strong Presidents have been bitterly reviled by their opponents. Of the thirty-seven men who were President from Washington to Ford, four have been assassinated and attempts at assassination have been made on several others. It has been suggested that the resentments expressed against the 'usurpations' of strong Presidents (regarded as illegitimate claims to kingship: 'the strong Presidents and their haters are curiously involved in the language of monarchy') have been a factor in endangering them and other Presidents: 'The assassins may be insane; yet they act out deep convictions and resentments, shared with many of their country-men.'* The attitudes of Americans to their 'elected kings' are deeply ambiguous.

Wilson wrote in 1908 that 'it is easier to write of individual Presidents than of the presidency itself.' But the strong Presidents, and the new roles of American government at home and abroad since 1933, have made an office whose every holder is looked to for protection against threats to the security and welfare of the people. 'Whatever the Constitution says,' said former President Truman in 1954, 'he is held responsible for any disaster which may come.' Encumbered with the task of following Franklin Roosevelt, Truman had met all threats with courageous determination. His successor, Eisenhower, provided a sense of more serene (though to his critics too detached) protection.

The power to persuade

'Let me tell you something—from experience!', said President Truman, while in office, 'The President may have a great many powers given to him in the Constitution and may have certain powers under certain laws which are given to him by the Congress of the United States; but the principal power that the President has is to bring people in and try to persuade them to do what they ought to do without persuasion. That's what I spend most of my time doing. That's what the powers of the President amount to.' In 1956, in an elegant set of lectures on *The American Presidency*, Clinton Rossiter remarked that 'an entirely new theory of the presidency can be spun out of that folksy statement.'† In 1960 the theory appeared in *Presidential Power* by Richard E. Neustadt,‡ from whom an interested reader, President-elect Kennedy, was to seek advice.

Although in the 'hundred days' Franklin Roosevelt had excelled Woodrow Wilson in obtaining legislation from the Congress, the routine preparation by the executive of comprehensive and de-

* Marcus Cunliffe, *American Presidents and the Presidency* (Eyre & Spottiswoode, 1969), pp. 134 and 135.
† (Hamish Hamilton, 1957), p. 122.
‡ (John Wiley & Sons, 1960). The 1976 edition includes comments on the Kennedy, Johnson and Nixon presidencies.

tailed legislative programmes developed first under Truman and
Eisenhower. A congressional liaison office was established in the
White House, so as systematically to associate the distribution of
patronage—and such rewards as enabling a Congressman to
announce to his constituents that they were about to receive a
major defence contract—with support for key parts of the
President's programme. But in dealing with the Congress the
executive branch as a whole is not united. Despite the requirements that the heads of agencies and bureau chiefs must accept
the decisions of the President, advised by the Office of Management and Budget, on legislative clearance and budget recommendations, they cannot be prevented from lobbying against
them among their friends in the Congress (unless the President
can 'persuade them to do what they ought to do').

Nor can the President depend on support from members of his
party in the Congress. He usually tries to help keep his party's
organizations throughout the country in good repair, for any
common benefit that may accrue to candidates running on the
party's ticket and because, while party lines may not mean much,
they do mean something. In 1964 President Lyndon Johnson, who
had as Vice-President succeeded President Kennedy in 1963, was
re-elected in a landslide, along with the largest majorities for the
President's party in the two Houses of the Congress since Franklin
Roosevelt's first two terms. 'Johnson in 1965 presided over more
legislative innovations on the home front than any other President
in any other single session of Congress in the twentieth century.'*
But the President seeks the electorate's endorsement as 'President
of all the people': it is not worth his while risking some of his
popular support for the sake of the party. Conversely, members
of his party in the Congress do not take major political risks for
him. In any case, in eight of the fifteen two-year Congresses from
that meeting after the mid-term elections of 1946 (the first after
Vice-President Harry Truman succeeded to the Presidency) to
that meeting after the mid-term elections of 1974 (the first after
Vice-President Gerald Ford succeeded to the Presidency) majorities in both Houses were not of the President's party.

---

* Louis W. Koenig, *The Chief Executive*, 3rd ed. (Harcourt, Brace, 1975),
p. 153.

To reach beyond the Congress for support, Theodore Roosevelt brought the press into the White House and Woodrow Wilson started the practice of holding press conferences. Franklin Roosevelt fully exploited press conferences to say what he wanted to say—and to hear what it was well for him to hear. Since his day the President may reach into American homes on television as well as radio, though no successor has matched his genius for communication to the audience.

However, the press serves its own purposes. When deceptions and manipulations of the press became continuous in the Vietnam war, the press was instrumental in establishing the 'credibility gap' which destroyed President Lyndon Johnson politically. President Nixon regarded 'the media' as among the worst of his many enemies. In 145 months as President, Franklin Roosevelt had held 1,011 press conferences; in 67 months, President Nixon held 37.

To try to persuade members of the Congress to do what the President thinks they ought to do, the President exaggerates threats, especially from abroad, and reduces long-term problems to 'crises' requiring instant solutions. When Truman wanted to secure congressional support for aid to Greece and Turkey in 1947, Senator Vandenberg, the leading Republican supporter of a bipartisan foreign policy, advised him to scare hell out of the country.

The Congress fails to offer alternative leadership. In 1964, on the basis of very selected information from President Johnson about alleged attacks on American destroyers off the coast of Vietnam, the Congress gave overwhelming approval to the Tonkin Gulf resolution, which was later cited as justifying the dispatch of large numbers of American troops to fight in Vietnam. When this use of the resolution was challenged by Senator Fulbright and others in 1967, the President dared the Congress to rescind it. Because of Vietnam, Johnson withdrew from the contest for his party's nomination in 1968. The Tonkin Gulf resolution was not rescinded by the Congress until January 1971.

Despite the failure of the 'presidential war' in Vietnam, when the problems of inflation became of major concern, the Congress, with Democratic majorities in both Houses, passed the Economic

Stabilization Act of 1970, granting the Republican President standby powers to introduce wage and price controls: any war against inflation was also to be presidential. Although President Nixon had not wanted the Act's authorization, he invoked it in 1971 to impose a ninety-day wage and price freeze, followed for a time by other controls. Members of the Congress assumed responsibility only for criticism.

There is, indeed, now much enabling statutory authority which the President may invoke, largely in circumstances of his own choosing. But, as President Truman explained, constitutional and legislative authority is only the context—though a very important context—in which the President exercises his power to persuade.

In 1962 the Kennedy administration persuaded steelworkers to accept a modest wage increase, on the implicit understanding that this would prevent an inflationary rise in steel prices. Yet within a few days major steel companies began to announce price increases. President Kennedy set about persuading them to do what they ought to do. The Attorney General (his brother Robert) launched an investigation into whether there had been a violation of anti-trust legislation. Democrats in the Congress promised their own investigations. The Secretary of Defense prepared to shift contracts from companies that had raised their prices. The Democratic national party headquarters placed calls to Democratic governors asking them to issue public statements supporting the administration. In his televised press conference the President made a blistering attack on a 'tiny handful of steel executives' who pursued private power and profit, at a time of 'grave crises in Berlin and Southeast Asia'. Companies that had not raised their prices announced they would not. Those that had cancelled the increases.

Federal administrators, members of the Congress, members of the President's party in those two groups and in the country, and members of interest groups want the President to do things for them and not to do things against them. The lesson of Neustadt's book was that the President must act so as to make their wants serve his needs. The President's power to persuade is the power to make them offers they cannot refuse.

In all but the shortest run, the power of the President to lead depends not on the force of law but on the force of public opinion. All the strong and would-be strong Presidents have known that they must capture the hearts and minds of the people. 'The presidency', President-elect Franklin Roosevelt said in 1932, 'is not merely an administrative office. That is the least of it. It is pre-eminently a place of moral leadership.' 'I run for the presidency of the United States', said John F. Kennedy on the eve of the 1960 election, 'because it is the centre of action, and, in a free society, the chief responsibility of the President is to set before the American people the unfinished public business of our country.'

Theodore Roosevelt, the first of the twentieth-century Presidents, said that 'people used to say of me that I was an astonishingly good politician and divined what the people were going to think. . . . I did not "divine" how the people were going to think; I simply made up my mind what they ought to think, and then did my best to get them to think it.' Presidential leadership consists, above all, of making the people offers they cannot refuse.

FOR FURTHER READING:

Stanley Bach and George T. Sulzer, eds., *Perspectives on the Presidency* (Heath, 1974).

Rowland Egger, *The President of the United States*, 2nd ed. (McGraw-Hill, 1972).

Joseph E. Kallenbach, *The American Chief Executive* (Harper & Row, 1966).

Harold Seidman, *Politics, Position, and Power*, 2nd ed. (O.U.P., 1975).

Aaron Wildavsky, ed., *The Presidency* (Little, Brown, 1969).

8: The Congress

A: CONGRESSIONAL ROLES AND MEMBERSHIP

The Constitution of the United States, as drafted in 1787, provided that members of two Houses of Congress, the House of Representatives and the Senate, were to be the direct representatives of the people and the States in the national government. Representatives were to be chosen by the voters in the several States for two-year terms; Senators by the State legislatures for six-year terms, one-third retiring every two years. In 1913 the Seventeenth Amendment made Senators directly elected by the voters. With the Presidency soon regarded as a popularly elective office, the President claimed to represent the nation as a whole as against Congress, representing its parts.

Indeed, members of Congress more vigorously exercise the representation of the parts of the country which they serve than do members of the British Parliament. Members of Congress frequently 'vote their constituents' because local constituency conditions are more influential than in Britain as determinants of congressional election results, except in landslides such as 1964 or 1974 when one overriding concern, anxiety over the potential behaviour of Goldwater and anger at the actual behaviour of Nixon, may have swayed voters throughout the nation. The shorter House term forces Representatives to start campaigning for re-election about ten months after taking their seats at the commencement of one Congress in order to arrange for the organization, finance and petitions needed to campaign in the primary elections preceding the general election to the next Congress. A leading contemporary student of Congress has emphasized that the need for re-election not only downgrades the role of party in Congress but has also contributed to the development of such prominent features of congressional structure as the powers of committees and the proliferation of sub-committees which benefit incumbents enormously at the polls.*

The two chambers possess essentially equal constitutional powers in the legislative process. Bills raising revenue must originate in the House of Representatives, but all bills must pass both Houses in the same form before being sent to the President for his approval. Lawmaking has survived as a significant congressional function despite the President's acknowledged role as chief legislator. The Congress does not act merely as an automatic rubber stamp for legislative proposals initiated by the President or by majority party leaders on Capitol Hill.

Article I, Section 9, of the Constitution requires: 'No Money shall be drawn from the Treasury, but in Consequence of Appropriations made by Law; and a regular Statement and Account of the Receipts and Expenditures of all public Money shall be published from time to time.' Today budgetary initiatives, like major legislative initiatives, come mainly from the President. But Congress's control of the purse is exercised to subject executive budgetary proposals to exacting scrutiny.

Congressional oversight of administration is also buttressed by the constitutional requirement, in Article II, Section 2, Clause 2, that the most important administrative appointments receive senatorial consent (as do the appointments of Federal judges— see Chapter 9, Section C). From the Senate's powers in relation to appointments emerged the practice of 'senatorial courtesy' with respect to Federal offices at State level. The President consults any Senators of his own party from the State where a Federal Officer appointed by him is to serve. If the President persists with a nomination which is offensive to the Senator, for whatever reason, the Senate as a whole will normally reject the nomination.

The Senate has refused to confirm Presidential nominations for the highest national offices, though only eight Cabinet

---

* David R. Mayhew, *Congress: The Electoral Connection* (Yale University Press, 1974).

nominations have been rejected outright. At this level questions of policy or personal fitness, rather than senatorial courtesy, are at issue. The Watergate crisis led to close scrutiny by the Senate of nominations made by Presidents Nixon and Ford. In 1973 the Senate Foreign Relations Committee chaired by Senator W. J. Fulbright, long an opponent of the administration's Vietnam policy irrespective of the incumbent President's party, voted to postpone consideration of the nomination of a career diplomat, G. McMurtrie Godley, as assistant secretary of state for East Asian affairs because he had been ambassador to Laos at a time when the CIA had been directing the effort to prevent a communist take-over. President Ford withdrew four nominations in 1974, including two made by his predecessor, because the individuals concerned were associated with Nixon's re-election campaign, and for that reason attracted adverse criticism even though no charges were brought against them.

The Constitution also grants Congress a potential influence in the choice of President and Vice President. The House elects the President if no candidate receives a majority of electoral college votes, a function not exercised since 1825. The Senate elects the Vice President in similar circumstances, though only Vice President Richard Johnson in 1837 has been chosen in this way. The Twenty-fifth Amendment (1967) requires that a majority of both House and Senate confirm the President's nominee as Vice President if a vacancy in that office occurs. In 1973 President Nixon nominated and Congress confirmed House Minority Leader Gerald Ford as Vice President following the resignation of Spiro Agnew, accused of corruption and evasion of income tax during his term as Governor of Maryland. Immediately after he resigned Agnew was fined $10,000 in a Federal court for evasion of income tax on 'payments received' in 1967. The corruption investigation against Agnew was then dropped. Vice President Ford succeeded to the Presidency in August 1974 and Congress was again required under the Twenty-fifth Amendment to confirm the President's choice as Vice President, in this case Governor Rockefeller.

The House enjoys 'the sole power of impeachment' while the Senate is assigned 'the sole power to try all impeachment', i.e., it is the House which must decide whether a public official is to be tried and defines the charges, and it is the Senate which acts as judge and jury. Up to 1974 thirteen officials had been impeached, of whom four were convicted.

The impeachment process is the only element of constitutional responsibility in the relationship between President and Congress. It has been fully invoked once only against a President—in 1868 when the Senate acquitted President Andrew Johnson by one vote. President Nixon's resignation in August 1974 was determined by the assumptions that the House would move to impeach him and that the Senate would find him guilty on one or more articles of impeachment recommended to the House by its Judiciary Committee. Articles I and II charging obstruction of justice and abuse of presidential powers were recommended in the Judiciary Committee by more than two-thirds of its members, including six or seven Republicans. Article III citing contempt of Congress for failing to hand over tapes and papers was passed by a much narrower majority. The fact that over one-third of the Republicans on the Judiciary Committee joined with all the Democrats in recommending impeachment largely defused any charges that the Democrats were indulging in a vendetta against an unloved Republican President because he was a Republican, and thus effectively sealed Nixon's fate.

President and Congress are constitutionally and electorally separate apart from impeachment, an institutional condition of fundamental importance to the American political system because, irrespective of other influences on party structure, it makes for some indiscipline within the congressional parties and for tension between the executive and legislative branches. The fact that the President cannot dissolve Congress and its converse, that the President does not resign if the House and Senate reject his legislative and executive policies, frees Congressmen from party loyalties in order to pursue their own beliefs or those of their constituents.

The Constitution includes some regulation of the composition of Congress. Representatives must be at least twenty-five years of age when elected, at least seven years a citizen of the United States, and an inhabitant of the State from which elected. The

Representatives are apportioned among the States strictly according to population. Senators must be at least thirty years of age, at least nine years a citizen, and must reside in the State. With two Senators each irrespective of population, which in 1970 ranged from just over 300,000 in Alaska to nearly 20 million in California, States are equally represented.

The Founding Fathers envisaged the Senate as fulfilling three functions: advisory council to the President; protection of States with small populations; and a conservative check on the popularly elected House. Hence the provision in the Constitution for a smaller chamber of older citizens indirectly elected, equal representation of the States irrespective of population, and the 'advise and consent' clauses. As explained in Chapter 2, Section C above, the Senate has not been a genuinely advisory body. Rather the Congress has functioned as an actively bicameral legislature.

The provision of equal representation of States as such has not led to a deliberate alliance of the States with small populations against the large States. But certain rural and regional minorities are generally considered to have benefited from equal representation, particularly farming, mining and Southern white interests. Nevertheless the Senate is generally regarded as the more liberal and the more prestigious of the two houses despite its conservative origins, and this was borne out when the Senate occasionally overrode Nixon vetoes which were sustained in the House. The explanation of the greater conservatism of the House lies in the difference in constituency. Many Senators must satisfy Statewide electorates in many of which an urbanized, industrial majority decides elections. In contrast House constituencies are smaller (except in Alaska, Delaware, Nevada, Vermont and Wyoming which each have a single Representative) and therefore more homogeneous with respect to social and political conditions. Many are located in mainly rural or suburban areas and return conservative candidates mindful of their conservative electorate. There is also a lower turnover in House than in Senate seats. However, the growing representation of the Democratic party in non-Southern districts since 1958 and landslide Democratic victories in 1964 and 1974 have contributed to a liberalization of

House organization by reducing the powers of committee chairmen.

Congress is rather conservative in composition. It is overwhelmingly male, white, middle-aged and middle-class. Localism is readily evident. Custom ensures that Representatives reside in their districts not only after election but for considerable periods before election. Over 70 per cent of Representatives in the Ninety-first Congress (1969–70) were born in the State in which they were elected. All but five of New York's Representatives in the 92nd Congress were born in the State; the Brooklyn Representatives were born in Brooklyn; the Staten Island Representative was born in Staten Island. Election defeat usually means that re-entry into the House or Senate requires winning back the lost district or State.

Almost all national legislators are native-born Americans and two-thirds are veterans. The average age of Representatives has fallen from 52 years at the commencement of the Ninety-third Congress in 1973 to 46·8 years in 1977 so that the Ninety-fifth Congress (1977–78) was distinguished by the youngest House since the Second World War. The average age of Senators in the Ninety-fifth Congress was 54·6 years. Senators are older because of the Constitution's age requirements and because membership of the House is frequently an apprenticeship to serving in the Senate. There has been no female Senator since Margaret Chase Smith of Maine was defeated in 1972. However, the number of women serving in the House reached an all-time high in 1974 when eighteen, including twelve incumbents, were elected. (The 1974 elections also produced the first female Governor to be elected without previously succeeding her deceased husband: Ella T. Grasso of Connecticut.) One black Senator and fifteen black Representatives were elected to the Ninety-fourth Congress.

Although there are more Roman Catholics in Congress than any one of the Protestant denominations, Protestants are strongly represented. In the Ninety-fourth Congress slightly over 50 per cent of the membership belonged to four Protestant denominations: Methodist, Presbyterian, Episcopalian and Baptist.

The legal profession predominates in the Congress. Two hundred and twenty-one Representatives and sixty-seven Senators in the Ninety-fourth Congress had law degrees. Businessmen and bankers, farmers and teachers were also strongly represented. In contrast very few members had worked in manual occupations. Only three—all Democrats and all in the House—described themselves as 'labour leaders'. Two former astronauts have also reached the Senate: John Glenn (Democrat, Ohio) and Harrison R. Schmitt (Republican, New Jersey).

B: THE STRUCTURE OF CONGRESS

Two rival yet interdependent institutions—political party and committee system—organize the congressional political process and determine its output. Members of Congress now belong with rare exceptions to the Democratic and Republican parties. The majority party in each house is in control of the formal structure because its members vote unanimously at the commencement of each Congress to ensure the election of its nominees to the key offices such as the Speakership of the House and standing committee chairmanships. Party leaders elected by their colleagues attempt to rally fellow party members behind a legislative strategy designed to support, or to oppose in a responsible though partisan fashion, the President's policy programme. But the majority party viewpoint does not prevail to the extent of ensuring the comprehensive enactment of presidential policies when he is of the same party, or their outright rejection when he is not.

There are clear differences in the voting records of most Democrats compared to most Republicans. *Congressional Quarterly* reports that in 1974 37 per cent of the 1,081 recorded votes in House and Senate together were party votes in which a majority of Democrats were opposed by a majority of Republicans (63 per cent of the recorded votes were bipartisan in that a majority of Democrats agreed with a majority of Republicans). This is consistent with the frequent conclusion in studies of voting behaviour in Congress that 'party remains the single most important factor in roll-call voting.'* Party conflict is not the con-

* Julius Turner and Edward V. Schneier, Jr., *Party and Constituency*, rev. ed. (The John Hopkins Press, Baltimore, 1970), p. 239.

sequence of strong discipline being enforced within the congressional parties. It emerges from the tendency of most individual Congressmen to establish fairly consistent voting records which are heavily dependent upon political circumstances in their home constituencies, at least on issues which are important to their constituents. The high proportion of safe congressional seats (on average about 90 per cent of incumbents are re-elected to the House) accounts for the consistency in voting behaviour on the part of Congressmen who can ensure re-election by satisfying 'the folks back home'. The Congressmen who establish highly liberal or high conservative positions reflect constituencies with clear leanings one way or the other.

There are more than the two partisan voting positions implied by the two-party composition of Congress and the majority party's domination of congressional offices. Both congressional parties are characterized by distinctive but fluid liberal and conservative wings and, on occasions, important votes are decided by coalitions which cut across party lines. More than half of the party votes in 1974 were characterized by the appearance of a conservative coalition, i.e., a majority of Northern Democrats were confronted by an alliance of a majority of Republicans and a majority of Southern Democrats. (*Congressional Quarterly* defines the South as the eleven Confederate States along with Kentucky and Oklahoma.) The significance of the conservative coalition varies according to the political composition of Congress following the biennial elections. In 1974 the conservative coalition was successful 67 per cent of the time in the House and 54 per cent in the Senate. But following the mid-term elections in 1974, which led to an increase in the number of Northern Democrats, the success rate of the conservative coalition fell in 1975 to 52 per cent in the House and 48 per cent in the Senate. Between 1961 and 1974 the conservative coalition achieved an annual over-all success rate in Congress of 59 per cent ranging from 33 per cent in 1965 following the 1964 Democratic landslide to 83 per cent in 1971.

There is also a liberal coalition in so far as the majority of Northern Democrats frequently require for success the support of some liberal Republicans in order to offset the loss of a majority of Southern Democrats. The group of liberal Republicans is smaller and less cohesive than the Southern Democrats in the conservative coalition, but it occupies a critical role on occasions such as the Senate's rejection of two of President Nixon's Supreme Court nominations in 1969 and 1970 and the congressional overriding of Nixon and Ford vetoes.

Party may be 'the single most important factor' but it clearly is not the dominant factor it is in Britain, unless it is argued that there are three parties in Congress—on the assumption that Southern Democrats merit the status of an independent legislative party, allying itself with a majority of Republicans on some issues and with a majority of Northern Democrats on others. Even so, Republicans and Northern Democrats also disagree with the majority view of their respective parties more or less frequently. The decentralization of the congressional parties has led one commentator to argue that 'the fact is that no theoretical treatment of the United States Congress that posits parties as analytic units will go very far.'*

The weakness of party has had profound consequences for the structure of Congress. The decentralization of structure which is the most characteristic feature of the party system in general is evident within Congress in the decisive procedural and legislative powers vested in committees, and in particular their chairmen. The weakness of party has also led to the development of such celebrated and often maligned conventions as the seniority rule for selecting committee chairmen and the filibuster in the Senate, by which a determined minority can talk out offending measures that are supported by a majority. In the House, which requires much tighter organization than the Senate because of its size, political influence is divided between the Speaker, who is the leader of the majority party as well as chief presiding officer of the House itself, and the 'control' committees, those of Rules and of Ways and Means, on which conservative majorities transcending party lines often dominate. It has been argued that Congress is little more than the sum of its committees.

The powers of committees and their chairmen and the conventions such as the seniority rule and the filibuster are substitutes

* Mayhew, *op. cit.*, p. 27.

for party discipline, which has usually been too weak to enable the majority party leaders backed by their normal followers to organize the political process in Congress and to determine its outcomes. However, the relative influence of party and committee system has been changing in favour of party since 1970, helped by the growing demand for reform which has profoundly affected the Democratic party in and out of Congress. The reforms of Congress which have been achieved and their significance are analysed below, following accounts of party organization and the committee system.

Party organization

The Democratic leader in the Senate, formally described as the Majority Floor Leader when there is a Democratic majority, is elected by the Conference of Democratic Senators. The Democratic Floor Leader is also chairman of the party's Policy Committee, which establishes the legislative timetable, and of the Steering Committee, which makes Democratic committee assignments. He is advised by a Whip, sometimes referred to as Assistant Floor Leader, who is elected by the Democratic Conference, and by four Assistant Whips. Republican leadership positions in the Senate are more widely distributed. The Minority Floor Leader is aided by a Whip and five Assistant Whips. The Republican Conference elects its own Chairman, and the chairmen of two party committees: the Policy Committee, which attempts to establish policy positions which all Republican Senators can support, and the Committee on Committees which makes Republican committee assignments.

The formal presiding officer of the Senate is the Vice-President of the United States, who has a casting vote in the event of a tie. The Vice-President seldom appears in the Senate, which elects as alternative presiding officer a President pro tempore, usually a senior member of the majority party. In practice freshman Senators, who are expected to be seen and seldom heard, act as presiding officers. Compared to the House of Representatives the parties in the Senate, and therefore the Senate itself, are much more loosely organized. The Conferences and the Policy Committees frequently exercise little influence: e.g., the Democratic Conference met only once a year when Johnson was Majority Floor Leader, in order to re-elect, usually without objection, the Floor Leader himself and the President pro tempore and to ratify the committee assignments made by the Democratic Steering Committee. The Policy Committee belies its name in so far as little or no time is spent attempting to arrive at a legislative policy agreeable to all or most party members.

The Democratic party leadership in the House of Representatives comprises the Speaker of the House who is the overall party leader, the Floor Leader, the Chairman of the Democratic Caucus, and the Chief Whip supported by one Chief Deputy Whip, and eighteen Assistant Whips. The Speaker is the presiding officer of the House and is thus formally elected by the House; but the effective choice is made in the majority party caucus, which also elects the Floor Leader, who is second in rank to the Speaker. The Floor Leader appoints the Whip, who selects his own deputies. The assistant whips are chosen on a regional basis, either by the appropriate 'dean', i.e., the longest-serving member from the region, or by the Democrats from the eighteen regional zones. There is also an increasingly important Democratic Steering and Policy Committee chaired by the Speaker. On it are represented the party leaders (Speaker, Majority Leader and Chairman of the Democratic Caucus), eight members appointed by the Speaker, and twelve members elected by regional delegations.

The House Republican leadership includes the Minority Floor Leader, a position once held by President Ford (1965–1973), the Chairman of the Republican Conference, and the Minority Whip in charge of one deputy whip, three regional whips and twelve assistant whips. The Conference elects the Minority Leader, its own Chairman and the Minority Whip. Republican party committees included the Committee on Committees, which makes Republican committee assignments and is chaired by the Minority Leader, and the Policy Committee, chaired by Del Clawson (California), which discusses the Republican position on policy issues before the House.

The whips act as liaison between party leaders and their colleagues. They acquaint the leaders with the views and likely votes of party members and they make sure that members know what is expected of them. But the whip organization does not attempt to impose party discipline and some of the whips may themselves have low indices of party loyalty. Their most important function is ensuring that all members supporting the views of the party leadership turn out to vote when required. When active the whips do increase the number of Congressmen turning out to vote.

Congressional committees

Congress has developed an elaborate committee system to facilitate a more extensive and timely performance of its legislative and supervisory functions than would be possible were the House and Senate each to act collectively at all times. About forty Representatives serve on House committees and fifteen Senators on Senate committees. Parties are represented in proportion to their overall strength, though several committees tend to be liberal or conservative in their attitudes to legislation, depending upon the attitudes of the chairman or the dominant alliance (which may cut across party lines). Committees enable Congressmen to develop specialized knowledge and legislative expertise in policy areas of particular interest to themselves personally or their constituents.

There are four types of congressional committee—standing, select and special, joint and conference. The permanent standing committees, established either by each House individually or by Act of Congress, are chiefly concerned with examining bills in detail and with deciding which to 'report out', i.e. report back to the floor for final acceptance or rejection. The standing committees are also directly involved in the congressional oversight of administration and executive policy making. The latter is the major role of the Senate Foreign Relations committee. The standing committees conduct public hearings and question experts, civil servants and executive politicians on policy and administrative matters within the committee's jurisdiction. The investigatory functions of standing committees received especially dramatic publicity in 1974, when the House Judiciary Committee was assigned the task of investigating whether there were grounds for the impeachment of President Nixon.

Select and special committees, which are not normally granted legislative functions, are set up on an *ad hoc* basis to carry out investigations into particular fields or specific matters. Select committees occasionally establish a permanent existence and are then promoted to the status of standing committees: the Senate Veterans' Affairs Committee and the House Small Business Committee made this transition. In 1973 the Senate established a Select Committee on Presidential Campaign Activities (the 'Watergate Committee') to investigate allegations that illegal campaign activities had been covered up by Administration officers including the President himself. In 1975 the Senate and the House established select committees to investigate the activities of the F.B.I. and C.I.A. in the United States and in foreign states. The Senate Select Committee on Government Intelligence Gathering Agencies has issued reports in which the C.I.A. stands accused of attempting to assassinate foreign leaders such as Fidel Castro and Patrice Lumumba. In 1975 the Senate maintained five other select or special committees covering Standards and Conduct, Small Business, Nutrition and Human Needs, Ageing, and National Emergencies and Delegated Emergency Powers. The House operated only two select committees in 1975, on Intelligence and on Ageing.

Joint committees, comprising members of House and Senate, also perform supervisory and investigatory rather than legislative functions. The Joint Committee on Atomic Energy, which does report out legislation, is one of the most powerful of all congressional committees, with a considerable influence over executive policy making in its field. There were seven joint committees in the Ninety-fourth Congress. Conference committees are a special type of joint committee composed of selected members of House and Senate standing committees which have dealt with similar legislative proposals. In order to get a common proposal to send to the President for his approval, the conference committee has to eliminate discrepancies between the two versions.

The 1946 Legislative Reorganization Act established fifteen standing committees in the Senate and nineteen in the House. By

I

Table 8.1:

Standing committees in the 95th Congress 1977–78

SENATE			HOUSE		
Committee	Members	Chairman	Committee	Members	Chairman
Agriculture, Forestry and Nutrition	14	Talmadge (Georgia)	Agriculture	43	Foley (Washington)
Appropriations	26	McClellan (Arkansas)	Appropriations	55	Mahon (Texas)
Armed Services	16	Stennis (Mississippi)	Armed Services	40	Price (Illinois)
Banking, Housing and Urban Affairs	13	Proxmire (Wisconsin)	Banking, Currency and Housing	43	Reuss (Wisconsin)
Budget	14	Muskie (Maine)	Budget	25	Giaimo (Connecticut)
Commerce, Science and Transportation	18	Magnuson (Washington)	Interstate and Foreign Commerce	43	Staggers (W. Virginia)
			Science and Technology	36	Teague (Texas)
Energy and Natural Resources	14	Jackson (Washington)	Interior and Insular Affairs	43	Udall (Arizona)
Environment and Public Works	14	Randolph (W. Virginia)	Public Works and Transportation	40	Johnson (California)
Finance	18	Long (Louisiana)	Ways and Means	37	Ullman (Oregon)

Foreign Relations	17	Sparkman (Alabama)	International Relations	37	Zablocki (Wisconsin)
Governmental Affairs	14	Ribicoff (Connecticut)	Government Operations	43	Brooks (Texas)
			District of Columbia	25	Diggs (Michigan)
			Post Office and Civil Service	28	Nix (Pennsylvania)
Human Resources	15	Williams (New Jersey)	Education and Labour	40	Perkins (Kentucky)
Judiciary	15	Eastland (Mississippi)	Judiciary	34	Rodino (New Jersey)
Rules and Administration	8	Cannon (Nevada)	Rules	16	Delaney (New York)
			House Administration	25	Thomson (New Jersey)
			Standards of Official Conduct	12	Flynt (Georgia)
Veterans Affairs	9	Cranston (California)	Veterans Affairs	28	Roberts (Texas)
			Merchant Marine and Fisheries	40	Murphy (New York)
(Select Committee on Small Business)			Small Business	25	Smith (Iowa)

1976 there were eighteen standing committees in the Senate and twenty-two in the House. The Senate added Aeronautical and Space Sciences in 1958, Veterans' Affairs in 1970 and Budget in 1975. The House added Science and Astronautics in 1958 (changed to Science and Technology in 1975), Standards of Official Conduct in 1968, and Budget in 1975. The House has also elevated Small Business (1975) from select committee to standing committee status. The House voted in 1975 to abolish the Internal Security Committee, better known as the Un-American Activities Committee, which investigated the political background of individuals accused of subversive actions. In February 1977 the Senate adopted some of the reforms of committee structure and jurisdictions recommended by a select committee chaired by Senator Adlai E. Stevenson III (Illinois). Three standing committees (Aeronautical and Space Sciences, District of Columbia, and Post Office and Civil Service) were abolished and their concerns distributed among the remaining committees.

Committee structure is similar in the two Houses. Most committees exercise legislative and supervisory functions in carefully defined policy areas indicated by the names of committees listed in Table 8.1. The House has three internal committees which regulate its procedure and the behaviour of members: Rules, House Administration and Standards of Official Conduct. The more loosely organized Senate requires only one such committee, Rules and Administration. The House has two subject committees which are not repeated in the Senate: Merchant Marine and Fisheries, and Small Business.

Committees differ in importance, both formally and inforally. The most sought after assignments are to Senate Foreign Relations, House Rules and the financial committees, which are Appropriations in both Houses, Finance in the Senate and Ways and Means in the lower House. Assignments are not strenuously sought to the committees on the District of Columbia, House Administration or Senate Rules and Administration. There is strong competition for the more influential committees, which is recognized formally by restrictions on the number of such posts to be held by individual Representatives and Senators. The

House distinguishes between exclusive (Appropriations, Rules, and Ways and Means), semi-exclusive (the committees dealing with agriculture, armed services, banking, education, foreign affairs, commerce, judicial matters, the post office, public works and scientific affairs), and non-exclusive committees. Representatives assigned to an exclusive committee hold no other committee posts. No Representative can be appointed to more than one semi-exclusive committee, though many hold two committee assignments, one from each of the semi-exclusive and non-exclusive categories. The Senate distinguishes between major and minor committees. Since the Senate is much smaller than the House there are more committee assignments to go round. Senators may not serve on more than two major committees and one minor committee.

Assignments are made by the various 'committees on committees', which comprise the Republican committees so designated in House and Senate, the Democratic Steering Committee in the Senate and, since 1975, the Democratic Policy and Steering Committee in the House. Before 1975 Democratic assignments in the House were made by the Democratic members of the Ways and Means Committee. All assignments are nominally subject to the approval of each party as a whole. The Speaker appoints members of the House Ways and Means Committee. Committee assignments are governed by several customary rules. Subject to the restriction imposed by the representation of parties in proportion to the composition of House or Senate, appointment to the most important committees requires a certain amount of seniority. Freshmen Congressmen seldom get appointed immediately to the most sought after committees, especially Appropriations and Rules in the House.

The committees on committees usually attempt to obtain some form of regional balance. In the House requests for assignments are channelled through the senior member of each state party delegation and each Democratic member on Ways and Means is responsible for handling requests from a particular zone, i.e. a set of contiguous States including his own. Preference is given to congressmen who have acquired the reputation of being 'responsible' legislators: hard working and respectful of the rules and customs of Congress. Constituency pressures sometimes determine the assignments requested and granted, as when members from rural areas seek and obtain places on the Agriculture committees, while members from Western States opt for the Interior and Insular Affairs committees. Assignments are used as rewards for good behaviour; troublesome members have difficulty in obtaining places on the more influential committees.

Committee chairmen are formally elected by the House and the Senate at the commencement of each Congress. The candidates of the majority party always win. The choice of committee chairmen thus appears to lie with the majority party. But for most of the twentieth century until the 1970s, both parties chose not to exercise the power to designate chairmen. Instead, chairmen were chosen by means of the seniority rule whereby the committee member of the majority party with the longest continuous service was automatically adopted as the party's candidate unless he was already chairman of another committee. The ranking minority member of each standing committee was chosen in a similar fashion.

The chairman is credited with being 'usually in virtual control of his committee'.* Not all chairmen attempt to dominate their committee. But they all can acquire for themselves, if they are inclined, considerable influence in respect of which bills from the many submitted to the committee are chosen for serious consideration, the decision whether to report out a bill to the floor, and the content of bills so reported. Committees change many legislative proposals almost out of recognition. They may also produce a compromise bill from several bills covering similar ground. Chairmen possess particularly effective executive powers, such as the appointment of sub-committee chairmen, the establishment of the committee's timetable and the selection of witnesses for committee hearings.

The seniority rule has been a favourite target of liberal critics of Congress because of their belief that it puts the strategic but largely negative policy making powers of committee chairmen in

* R. K. Huitt, 'The Internal Distribution of Influence: The Senate', in R. K. Huitt and R. L. Peabody, *Congress: Two Decades of Analysis* (Harper and Row, New York, 1969), p. 193.

the hands of individuals who are frequently more conservative than the average legislator. Seniority rewards the holders of safe seats, particularly Southern Democrats, Northern Democrats from urban constituencies and Midwestern Republicans. Certainly there are more Southern chairmen than the South would merit on grounds of population or even representation within the Democratic party in Congress. Six Senate chairmen and nine House chairmen in the Ninety-fourth Congress represented Southern constituencies, though the number of Southern chairmen in the House fell to five in 1977. The average age of committee chairmen is considerably higher than the average for each branch of Congress, 66 years in the Senate (compared to 54·6 for the entire Senate) and 63 years in the House (compared to 46·8 years for the House as a whole). In addition many chairmen have given more than average support to the conservative coalition.

Reform

Several important, though not fundamental, reforms of the congressional committee system have been introduced since 1970, by the parties and by Congress itself acting upon the recommendations of bipartisan committees. The main targets for reform have been the seniority rule, the committee system, and the budgetary process. The principal political issue has centred on a sustained attempt by liberal members of the House Democratic caucus to make standing committees and their chairmen more responsive to the caucus and the party leadership. Seniority is regarded as a cause as well as a symptom of the relative weakness of party in Congress.

The first modification of the seniority rule was introduced by Republican Representatives in 1970 when they decided to vote by secret ballot on their Committee on Committee's proposals as senior Republican member on each standing committee. The change became operational at the beginning of the Ninety-second Congress in January 1971. At the same time the House Democratic caucus also decided to modify the automatic workings of seniority by allowing a challenge to any chairman recommended by the Democratic members of the Ways and Means Committee if ten members of the chairman's standing committee so requested. An unsuccessful attempt was made to unseat the seventy-two-year-old chairman of the District of Columbia committee, John McMillan of South Carolina. In 1973 the Democratic caucus went a stage further by allowing for a caucus vote by secret ballot on all chairmen if 20 per cent of the caucus demanded a vote. Every chairman was then accepted without difficulty.

The reform movement was much more successful in 1975, following the substantial rise in Democratic representation in the House brought about by the 1974 mid-term elections dominated by Watergate. One quarter of the Democratic caucus was new to the House. The caucus, meeting in December 1974 with the seventy freshmen present, many of whom were liberals, adopted a number of reforms designed to increase the influence of the party leadership and the caucus itself at the expense of committees and their chairmen.

The committee assignment powers of Democratic members of the Ways and Means Committee were transferred to the Democratic Steering and Policy Committee, which is more likely to pay attention to the wishes of the party leaders. The Steering and Policy Committee was given the task of recommending to the caucus the party's candidates as committee chairmen. The caucus also attempted to lessen the influence of conservative Democrats in the two 'control' committees. The membership of the Ways and Means Committee was increased from twenty-five to thirty-seven. The Speaker was assigned the responsibility of appointing all members of the Rules Committee.

Thus, the caucus brought to an end the automatic resort to seniority to fill all committee chairmanships. The Steering and Policy Committee made the first move by voting to depose two incumbent chairmen—Wright Patman (Texas, eighty-one years of age, Banking, Currency, and Housing) and Wayne Hays (Ohio, sixty-three, Rules and Administration). The Steering and Policy committee recommended the remaining twenty chairmen to the caucus along with Reuss (Wisconsin, sixty-two), the fourth ranking Democrat on the Banking Committee, and Thompson (New Jersey, fifty-six), the second ranking Democrat on Rules and Administration. The caucus rejected four of the Steering and

Policy Committee's recommendations, viz., Reuss, Thompson and two elderly Southerners, W. Poage (Texas, seventy-six, Agriculture) and F. Hebert (Louisiana, seventy-three, Armed Services). The Steering and Policy committee then recommended the two chairmen it had earlier turned down—Patman and Hays —and the second ranking Democrats on Agriculture and Armed Services. The caucus rejected Patman, but accepted the others.

Three elderly Southern chairmen thus lost their positions as chairmen of important House committees in 1975 as a result of deliberate action on the part of the Democratic caucus. Another Southern chairman, Wilbur Mills (Arkansas) of Ways and Means, was persuaded not to seek re-election following a highly publicized series of escapades with a striptease dancer. In the summer of 1976 Wayne Hays was forced to resign both his position as Chairman of the Committee on Rules and Administration and his House seat following the revelation that he had given a sinecure job on the staff of the House Administration Committee at a salary of $14,000 per annum to Miss Elizabeth Ray in return, according to Miss Ray, for 'her sexual favours'. Hays was replaced as Chairman of the Committee by Thomson, who had opposed him for the post in January 1975.

Although the seniority rule now no longer applies automatically to the selection of committee chairmen, the 1975 developments were strictly limited. Reuss was the only new chairman not to have been the second ranking Democrat at the time of his promotion. The new chairmen were not clearly more liberal in their policy tendencies than those they replaced. The Democratic caucus voted against an age limit of seventy years for committee chairmen and against requiring chairmen to step down after three terms in office. But the liberal members of the caucus believe that chairmen will become more responsive to the will of the majority because the threat of demotion is now there.

There have been fewer changes in the Senate. However, the Democratic Conference decided in 1975 to permit in future years a vote by secret ballot on the chairmen recommended by the Steering Committee. This reform was duly implemented in February, 1977 at the commencement of the Fifteenth Congress, when the Democratic Conference determined the nominees for committee chairmen. However, there were no serious challenges to the recommendations of the Steering Committee.

The Legislative Process

More than 26,000 bills were introduced in the Ninety-third Congress (1973–4), of which 528 passed into law. Senators introduce their bills directly from the floor. Representatives introduce their bills merely by placing them in the 'hopper'—a box on the clerks' table. All bills are then referred without debate by the presiding officer to an appropriate standing committee.

A bill has to clear four hurdles in Congress before reaching the President. The bill must first be reported back as amended by the standing committee. In fact most bills 'die' in committee or suffer drastic rewriting. The committees rather than party leaders or the majority party caucus determine which bills will be granted serious examination. About 10 to 15 per cent of bills are reported by standing committees back to the floor. The bill must then be found a place on the legislative timetable of the House or Senate. Thirdly, each House sits in judgement on the committee's recommendations. Finally, identical bills must emerge from House and Senate—if necessary by way of a conference committee to resolve discrepancies between House and Senate versions.

The jurisdictions of standing committees are clearly defined in the legislation or resolutions under which the committees are established. The referral of bills to standing committees based on the primary subject matter of each particular bill is usually automatic and non-controversial. However, bills can be drafted so as to overlap the jurisdictions of two committees which differ in their political leanings. The presiding officer may have some discretion regarding the referral of a particularly sensitive bill. Its supporters may be able to gain some advantage by first introducing a bill in the House where the appropriate committee is more favourable than its counterpart in the other House. The 1964 Civil Rights Act was introduced first in the lower House because its Judiciary Committee, chaired by Emmanuel Celler of New York, was considerably more liberal than the Senate Judiciary Committee, chaired by Senator Eastland of Mississippi.

Once bills are passed on by the standing committees, political control of the legislative timetable in the House of Representatives is shared among the Speaker as presiding officer and majority party leader, the Rules Committee and the House itself. Private bills, which amounted to about 35 per cent of the legislation adopted by the Eighty-eighth Congress (1963–4), and non-controversial bills on the Consent Calendar are considered on three or four days each month; such bills require near-unanimous support, or at least the absence of any opposition, in order to pass through Congress. Money bills from the Appropriations and Ways and Means committees are also privileged business which do not need to be considered by the Rules Committee. Pension bills from the Veterans' Affairs committee and rivers and harbours legislation from Public Works are privileged business too.

The Rules Committee considers non-privileged bills, i.e., most of the controversial bills. The committee decides on when individual bills are to be considered by the House and the conditions of debate. The Rules Committee can secure changes in the contents of bills by threatening not to grant a rule. Otherwise the committee can also influence the content of legislation by issuing an open rule or a closed rule. Under open rules bills can be amended without restriction on the House. Closed rules specify the types of amendment which may be brought during House debate. Less than 10 per cent of rules issued are of the closed variety.

Procedures are available to the House to secure the release of bills held up in committee. If a majority of the House membership signs a discharge petition, which is then supported on the floor of the House, the committee—including the Rules Committee—must release the proposed legislation. This procedure, of which there is a similar version in the Senate, is rarely used. The House can also suspend the rules and proceed to accept or reject bills in the pipeline, if two-thirds of Representatives present and voting so decide.

The political powers of committees, especially the House 'control' committees, are a function of the relative strengths of the liberal and conservative coalitions in any Congress. If congressional elections return a determined liberal majority, as in

1948, 1964 and 1974, the control committees lose power. In 1949 the House adopted a twenty-one-day rule which took power away from the Rules Committee by allowing committee chairmen to bring to the floor any bills languishing in Rules for more than twenty-one days. The rule was dropped in 1951 but reappeared briefly in 1965–6.

The legislative timetable in the Senate is determined mainly by the Policy Committee of the majority party, dominated by the Majority Leader, who appoints twelve of its fifteen members. But the relaxed customs of the Senate are evident in the practice whereby the Minority Leader is consulted before the decision to clear a particular bill for floor consideration is taken. The most dramatic indication of the inability of a Senate majority to control the legislative process has been the filibuster, which was first curbed only in 1917, after a filibustering attempt was made to prevent President Wilson from acquiring the right to arm American merchant ships. Then the Senate adopted Rule 22, the closure rule, which defines the conditions under which debate can be ended and filibusters defeated. In its present form the Rule specifies that sixteen Senators must sign a petition calling for an end to debate. Two days later a vote is held. Debate is cut off if two-thirds of Senators present and voting so decide. The closure rule was even more conservative from 1949 to 1959, when the required two-thirds majority was calculated against the entire membership of the Senate.

There has been a steep increase in the use of Rule 22. Twenty-two closure motions were decided from 1917 to 1959, of which only four were successful, all of these in the 1920s. Twenty-three closure motions were put in the 1960s; only three were successful but two of these enabled the Senate to adopt the 1964 Civil Rights Act and the 1965 Voting Rights Act against the wishes of the most successful exponents of the filibuster, the Southern Democrats. (Senator Strom Thurmond of South Carolina had spoken for over twenty-four hours against a civil rights bill in 1957.) Liberal Senators have failed so far in their attempt to reduce the required majority for closure to 60 per cent of those present and voting. But liberals have themselves made use of the filibuster to prevent the passage of anti-'busing' legislation.

Fifty-four closure motions were noted by the Senate between 1970 and 1974, of which eleven were adopted. The increase was largely due to a decision by Democratic leaders to use Rule 22 to prevent the attachment of 'non-germane' amendments to legislative measures. The practice of tacking on amendments which are not strictly related to the subject matter of the bill is permitted in the Senate. It is a favourite method of making political capital, or indirectly killing the main proposals of the bill. However, once Rule 22 is invoked, 'non-germane' amendments are not allowed.

Congress passed the Budget Reform Act in 1974 to take effect in 1976. This legislation was a response to the demand that Congress put its own house in order regarding consideration of the presidential budget. Congress tended to concentrate on individual items increasing or cutting the President's requests for appropriations, ignoring total expenditures. The Budget Reform Act was designed to encourage fiscal responsibility—a major battle-cry of Republican Presidents confronting a Democratic Congress—by introducing a framework for congressional consideration of the budget. Congress is required to establish total expenditure levels as well as authorizations for specific items and then ensure that the two are compatible. A new standing committee—the Budget Committee—was established in the Senate and in the House. The House Budget Committee must include representatives of both party leaderships and five members each of the two financial committees, Appropriations and Ways and Means. The Budget Committee's membership will be kept flexible by the requirement that no member can serve for more than four years in ten. As explained in Chapter 7, the 1974 Budget Reform Act also struck at presidential impoundment of funds appropriated for particular purposes.

C: CONGRESS AND THE PRESIDENT

The effective distribution of policy making powers between President and Congress has become a controversial issue among students of American politics. Policy formulation is principally the function of the political executive in most modern political systems. But the Constitution assigns the national legislative powers to the Congress. The separation of powers and the decentralization of party structure in the United States prevent outright presidential domination of the Congress and vice versa. The President is widely acknowledged as the 'Chief Legislator' because the presidential office and not the majority party in Congress is the only source of national policy proposals in any coherent, integrated form. The reaction of Congress to the President's legislative programme is determined by a number of variables, of which the most influential are the party identity and personality of the President, his institutional conception of the Presidency, the distribution of seats in Congress between liberals and conservatives as much as between Democrats and Republicans, and the extent to which public opinion encourages individual congressmen to support or to oppose presidential initiatives. Party is a significant force in the organization and voting alignments in Congress, but Senators and Representatives act more as judges of the President's legislative requests than as initiators of comprehensive policy programmes.

It has been argued that Congress has genuinely initiated only three major pieces of national legislation since 1932: the 1938 Fair Labor Standards Act, the 1948 Taft-Hartley Act, and the 1973 War Powers Act.* One school of thought therefore assigns Congress an essentially negative role in policy formulation, that of enlarging or cutting down presidential initiatives. This view has been challenged, most bluntly in the assertion that 'the orthodox generalization that the President is both chief initiator and chief legislator is simply wrong.'† This calls attention to the fact that presidential legislative leadership is not automatic.

Presidential-congressional relations from 1960 to 1976 varied enormously, ranging from President Johnson's effective control over Congress in 1965–6 to President Nixon's fight for survival in 1973–4. President Kennedy faced a Democratic Congress in

---

* Several views of the congressional role in the legislative process are reported in J. R. Johannes, 'The President Proposes and Congress Disposes . . . But Not Always: Legislative Initiative on Capitol Hill', *The Review of Politics*, Vol. 36, 1974, pp. 356–70.

† R. M. Pious, 'Sources of Domestic Policy Initiatives', *Proceedings of the Academy of Political Science*, Vol. 32, No. 1, p. 108.

which a conservative coalition enjoyed considerable political strength because the 1960 elections brought a decline in the representation of Northern Democrats. On Kennedy's death, Lyndon Johnson, one of the most successful party leaders in Senate history, took over as Chief Executive. Then the landslide Democratic victory of 1964 in presidential and congressional elections returned the new President, who now believed he had a clear mandate for decisive action, and a liberal Congress prepared to support his domestic programme. The Vietnam war soured the relationship between Johnson and a Congress which had lost some of its liberal members in the 1966 elections.

Even before Watergate, the relationship between Republican President Nixon and the Democratic Congress was marked by considerable hostility based on policy differences and on Nixon's belief that congressional obstruction unduly weakened the Presidency. The passage of the War Powers Act over a Nixon veto in 1973 may have imposed severe restrictions upon the President's freedom of action in international politics, but this remains to be seen. The mid-term 'Watergate' elections of 1974 returned a strongly liberal Democratic caucus, which turned its attention to reform of Congress without attempting to challenge seriously the new President, Ford, in the execution of the now expected presidential roles as chief diplomat, chief legislator and so on.

To return in more detail to the beginning of the period under discussion, the weakness of Kennedy's relationship with the Congress elected in 1960 was revealed when the new Administration's legislative tactics started in January 1961 with only a narrowly successful attempt to increase the size, and hopefully thereby change the political leanings, of the House Rules Committee. Chaired by a long-serving Southern Democrat, 'Judge' Howard Smith of Virginia, the Rules Committee had been acting in a conservative fashion since the late 1930s, holding up and watering down liberal legislative proposals. In the late 1950s the twelve members of the committee—eight Democrats, four Republicans— frequently divided evenly, with six Democrats frustrated by a conservative coalition of the four Republicans supported by Smith and by William Colmer of Mississippi, who was to succeed Smith as Chairman in 1967.

Though the Democrats enjoyed a nominal House majority of eighty-nine in the Eighty-seventh Congress (1961–2), the proposal to enlarge the Rules Committee was adopted by only five votes, 217 against 212. The supporters of the move to enlarge the Rules Committee, which was organized by the powerful Speaker Sam Rayburn (Texas) on behalf of the Kennedy Administration, included all but two of the 159 Northern and Border Democrats. The opposing conservative coalition included 148 Republicans and sixty-two Southern Democrats. The critical supporting votes defeating the conservative coalition were cast by twenty-two Republicans and thirty-six Southern Democrats. Eighteen of the twenty-two liberal Republicans represented districts in the Northeast. The Southern Democrats supporting the Administration's attempt to increase the chances of its legislative programme clearing the House on the whole represented urban districts with relatively small black populations.

The subsequent appointment of two liberal Democrats and one Republican to the Rules Committee did not open the way to the adoption of liberal legislation. Indeed Kennedy was forced 'to set his sights low'* because of the inherent strength of the conservative coalition. The Rules Committee opposed administration policy on Federal aid to education. Administrative proposals on minimum wages, Medicare and civil rights were either severely reduced in Congress or introduced in a less radical form than the administration would have liked. When the Eighty-seventh Congress ended in 1962 'the Kennedy domestic programme was in shambles'.†

Yet the period from 1963 to 1966 was to see the enactment of the most far-reaching policy programme since the New Deal. The improvement in the administration's record with Congress began before Kennedy's death. But it became much more pronounced in the two years which followed, partly because of Kennedy's assassination and, perhaps more significantly because of the huge Democratic gains in 1964. The significance of changes in political forces at work on and beyond Capitol Hill for the content of

* L. Koenig, *The Chief Executive*, 3rd ed. (Harcourt, Brace and World, Inc., New York, 1975), p. 151.

† J. L. Sundquist, *Politics and Policy* (The Brookings Institution, Washington, D.C., 1968), p. 474.

policies approved by the Congress is vividly illustrated by the passage of the 1964 Civil Rights Act.

Congress did not play a major role in the civil rights movement until the 1960s, because Southern Democrats were able to make full use of the obstructionist tactics available in congressional structure and procedure, particularly the filibuster in the Senate. A weak Civil Rights Act, passed in 1957, inspired Strom Thurmond to make his famous speech lasting over twenty-four hours. But that filibuster was not continued by the Southern Democrats because of the fear that the closure rule would be applied, weakening their bargaining position on details.

President Kennedy was widely criticized when he did not introduce a major civil rights bill in 1961, even though the reason for inaction was clear: the implicit strength of the conservative coalition in the Eighty-seventh Congress. However, the civil rights movement had been growing in strength since the mid-1950s, when Martin Luther King led a Negro boycott of buses in Montgomery, Alabama. King's Southern Christian Leadership Conference of blacks and whites led a campaign of direct action against racial discrimination in public places such as buses and lunch counters. The campaign climaxed in a 'March for Jobs and Freedom' when 200,000 people, 90 per cent of them black, gathered in Washington on 28 August 1963.

Kennedy sent a civil rights bill to Congress in June 1963. Chairman Celler of the House Judiciary Committee allocated the bill to a particularly liberal sub-committee, which amended it to make it much stronger. The Judiciary Committee itself had to water down its own sub-committee's proposals because Southern Democrats on the full committee were in favour, believing that the bill was now extreme enough to ensure defeat in the House. The bill, still stronger than the Administration's original proposals, was in the Rules Committee when Kennedy was assassinated in Dallas in November 1963. Howard Smith, the conservative Democratic Chairman of the Rules Committee, held up the bill until the House approved a discharge petition. It then passed the House with the support of 92 per cent of Northern and Border Democrats, 80 per cent of Republicans and 11 per cent of Southern Democrats.

The House bill was introduced to the Senate in March 1964, sparking off the longest-running filibuster in American history. Two procedural moves were critical. Firstly, the House bill was not sent to a Senate standing committee but was instead considered in the full Senate to keep it from the Senate Judiciary Committee chaired by Senator Eastland of Mississippi. Secondly, on 6 June, the Senate passed a closure motion and the bill was then accepted over the opposition of twenty-seven Senators, mainly Southern Democrats. The Civil Rights Act was signed by President Johnson on 2 July 1964.

A strong Voting Rights Act was passed in 1965. But in 1966 President Johnson failed to persuade Congress to accept another civil rights bill aimed at discrimination in housing in the North as well as the South.

The 1964 Democratic landslide was followed by the enactment of legislation providing for aid to education, Medicare and an anti-poverty programme. The House Ways and Means Committee had refused to report favourably on proposals for financing medical care for over-sixty-fives introduced by the Kennedy Administration. But in 1965, after an increase in representation on the committee of Northern Democrats as a result of the 1964 elections, Ways and Means proceeded to report out a more liberal bill than the Administration was requesting. Wilbur Mills, the Ways and Means Chairman, moved from operating as a conservative check on Medicare legislation to the position of liberal spokesman on behalf of liberal measures in order to avoid a defeat for himself and his committee. The Medicare Act was signed by President Johnson on 30 July 1965.

Three sources of tension dominated presidential-congressional relations during Nixon's period in office. Party conflict was inevitable in the confrontation between a Republican President and a Democratic Congress. The constitutional separation of executive and legislature as a source of tension was particularly significant because the President was preoccupied with safeguarding the office of the Presidency against congressional encroachments, especially in foreign affairs. The Watergate crisis added a third element in 1973-4.

Nixon's first significant defeat at the hands of Congress occurred when he failed to secure the consent of the Senate to two of his nominations to the Supreme Court. The President was granted two opportunities early in his first term to make appointments to the Court. The Senate confirmed by seventy-four votes to three in June 1969 his nomination of Warren Burger to replace Earl Warren as Chief Justice. In May 1969 Justice Abe Fortas, a Johnson appointee, resigned from the Court and the President nominated Clement Haynesworth (South Carolina) in August. But the Senate rejected Haynesworth by fifty-five votes to forty-five in November. In January 1970 the President nominated Harold Carswell (Florida). But the Senate again refused, by fifty-one votes to forty-five, to confirm the nomination.

The President was influenced by two political motives when he made his nominations. He said he wished to restore the constitutional balance of the Supreme Court by making it more conservative, a reaction against the liberal Supreme Court presided over by Earl Warren. In so doing he was acting in the manner established by earlier Presidents. A second motive may have been the 'Southern strategy' whereby the Republican party hoped to attract the permanent allegiance of the South, already in electoral revolt against Democratic presidential candidates as a protest against the party's desegregation policies. Unfortunately for the President both nominees were suspect: Haynesworth because he had failed to disqualify himself from a case involving a firm in which he had a financial interest; and Carswell because he appeared to many to be a segregationist and because too many of his judgements were overturned by superior courts.

The issues raised by the nominations of Haynesworth and Carswell split both parties into liberal and conservative sections. Both divided on a two-to-one basis, the Democrats opposing and the Republicans supporting the President's nominees. The Democrats who supported the President were almost exclusively from the fifteen Southern and Border States; the only exceptions were Senator Gravel (Alaska) who voted for Haynesworth and Senator Bible (Nevada) who voted for Carswell. Two Southern Democrats, Gore (Tennessee) and Yarborough (Texas), voted against both Haynesworth and Carswell, and Senators Spong (Virginia) and Fulbright (Arkansas) voted against Carswell. Subsequently

Yarborough lost his seat when he failed to win the Democratic primary in 1970; Gore was defeated by a Republican in 1970; and Spong was defeated by a Republican in 1972. The Republican Senators opposed to their President's nominees were more widely distributed across the nation, though a majority on both occasions came from the Northeast States.

Policy differences between a Republican President and a Democratic majority in Congress were explicit in President Nixon's largely successful use of the veto power. During his first term Congress overrode four out of thirteen regular vetoes in order to maintain Federal financing of programmes on education, construction of medical facilities, pensions for railroad workers and water pollution control. The party conflict and Nixon's concern regarding the power of the Presidency led him to veto nine bills in 1973, of which Congress managed to override only one. Five vetoes reflected the President's desire to cut down expenditures proposed by the Democratic Congress for programmes on vocational rehabilitation, emergency medical services, disaster relief, a minimum wage, and rural water and sewer grants. The presidential success rate in Congress in 1973 was the lowest since *Congressional Quarterly* started keeping detailed records in 1952. Nevertheless the successful use of the veto to restrict programmes inspired by the Democrats indicated the inability of Congress to dictate policy terms to the President. *Congressional Quarterly*, in a review of the congressional legislative record in 1973, concluded that 'on major domestic issues Congress either accepted compromises or bowed to a determined President over willing to use his veto.'

Four of President Nixon's vetoes in 1973 were prompted by his belief that Congress was encroaching on powers which properly belonged to the executive branch. Congress duly sustained the vetoes of legislation which would have enlarged congressional right of access to U.S.I.A. documents and required Senate confirmation of the President's appointment of the Director of the Office of Management and Budget. Nixon also successfully vetoed an amendment to an appropriations bill which, if passed, would have disallowed the use of funds to support combat activities in Cambodia and Laos. But in September 1973 President Nixon was unable to prevent the enactment over his veto of the War Powers Bill, which Congress demanded in the belief that American involvement in Vietnam and Cambodia, under Democratic President Johnson and Republican President Nixon, necessitated a curtailment of the presidential warmaking power.

Nixon's veto of the War Powers Bill was easily overridden in the Senate by seventy-five votes to eighteen, with all but three Democrats and twenty-five of forty Republicans opposing the President. In the House 87 per cent of Democratic Representatives, including forty-nine of sixty-nine Southern Representatives, and 46 per cent of Republican Representatives combined to override the veto by four votes more than the required two-thirds majority of those present and voting. All ten Republican Representatives from New England supported the War Powers Bill. And fewer than 60 per cent of Republican Representatives from other regions, except the Outer South (68 per cent) and the Mountain States (63 per cent), voted to sustain Nixon's veto.

The War Powers Act can be regarded as the symbolic end to an era of American military intervention abroad. It remains to be seen whether the President's options in foreign policy have been effectively restricted. The controversy over the significance of the War Powers Act was most vividly illustrated by the actions of a few Democrats like Senator Eagleton of Missouri and the black Representative from Oakland, California, Ron Dellums, who voted to sustain the Nixon veto because they believed that the Act enlarged rather than reduced the presidential warmaking power.

The balance of policy making power between President and Congress appeared in the 1973–6 period to be in a state of flux. The resignation of one President, and the loss of authority implicit in his successor's non-elective status, made the Presidency vulnerable to a reassertion of congressional powers. The discontent in Congress, particularly in the Senate, over the conduct of the Vietnam war and the liberalization of the Democratic caucus following the 1974 mid-term elections provided the Congress with strong motives for taking a more positive role in policy making.

Party differences were uppermost in the relationship between President Ford and the Ninety-fourth Congress elected in November 1974. Ford vetoed almost twice as many bills as Nixon, though he was in office for only two years and five months. And Congress overrode a higher proportion of Ford's vetoes than of any President in the period since 1913. But the veto is a formidable presidential weapon because, as indicated in Table 8.2, it is unusual for Congress to produce the two-thirds majority required to override the President.

Table 8.2:

The presidential veto 1913–1975

President	Pocket vetoes	Regular vetoes	Congressional overrides	% regular vetoes overridden
Wilson	11	33	6	18
Harding	1	5	0	0
Coolidge	30	20	4	20
Hoover	16	21	3	14
Roosevelt	263	372	9	2·4
Truman	70	180	12	6·7
Eisenhower	108	73	2	2·7
Kennedy	9	12	0	0
Johnson	14	16	0	0
Nixon	16	25	5	20
Ford	16	45	12	26·7
Total	554	802	53	6·6

Seldom does one party win two-thirds of the seats in either the Senate or the House of Representatives. The Democrats won a bare two-thirds majority of House seats in 1974, the first time since 1938. But the Democrats have not held two-thirds of the Senate since 1966, though they did so following the elections of 1956, 1962 and 1964. The extensive Democratic gains in the House following the 1974 elections gave rise to speculation concerning a 'veto-proof' Congress. Yet the Ninety-fourth Congress failed to override almost three-quarters of President Ford's thirty regular vetoes in 1975–6. It remains to be seen whether the 1973

War Powers Act and the 1974 Congressional Budget and Impoundment Control Act represent the beginning of an enlargement of congressional powers *vis-à-vis* the Presidency.

The President's powers are endangered most when the chief executive belongs to one party and two-thirds of the House and of the Senate belong to the opposing party. The American electorate, despite its volatility in the past two decades, does not frequently produce such an extreme result. Jimmy Carter criticized President Ford during the 1976 campaign for not providing the strongly Democratic Congress with 'adequate leadership'. Carter was quite explicit about the roles of President and Congress. 'Congress is inherently incapable of unified leadership. That leadership has got to come from the White House'.* In November 1976 the American electorate narrowly elected Carter to the Presidency, along with a Congress in which the Democrats held over two-thirds of seats in the House and 62 per cent of seats in the Senate. In so doing the electorate provided Carter with the opportunity for an effective relationship with the Congress, reminiscent of Roosevelt's effective New Deal years from 1933 to 1938 and Johnson's most productive period in 1965–6.

FOR FURTHER READING:

D. M. Berman, *In Congress Assembled* (Macmillan, New York, 1964).

D. R. Mayhew, *Congress: The Electoral Connection* (Yale University Press, New Haven, 1974).

T. P. Murphy, *The New Politics Congress* (D. C. Heath, Lexington, 1974).

R. L. Peabody and N. W. Polsby (eds.), *New Perspectives on the House of Representatives*, 2nd ed. (Rand McNally, Chicago, 1969).

L. K. Pettit and E. Keynes, *The Legislative Process in the U.S. Senate* (Rand McNally, Chicago, 1969).

L. N. Rieselbach, *Congressional Politics* (McGraw-Hill, New York, 1973).

* *Congressional Quarterly Weekly Report*, 4th September 1976, p. 2379.

9: The Courts and the Law

A: LAWYERS IN POLITICS

In any developed system of government the courts, along with the police and other executive agencies of what is referred to in the United States as 'law enforcement', are the specialized institutions of society for preserving law and order. This chapter is mainly concerned with describing the organization of these institutions in the United States.

In a system of constitutional government, such as that in the United Kingdom or the United States, the courts also have sufficient independence from the other governmental authorities to act as a check upon their actions. Where there is such a 'government of laws' or 'rule of law', the courts protect the legal rights of persons, particularly those relating to arrests and trials, from abridgement by the police and other law enforcement agencies.

In the United States, moreover, the constitutional definitions of the powers of the Federal and the State governments and the constitutional provisions for the separation of powers and the protection of personal rights furnish grounds for turning issues of public policy into questions of legal competence to be decided by the courts. 'Scarcely any political question arises in the United States', wrote Alexis de Tocqueville in *Democracy in America* in the 1830s, 'that is not resolved, sooner or later, into a judicial question. Hence all parties are obliged to borrow, in their daily controversies, the ideas and even the language, peculiar to judicial proceedings.' The doctrine that accords to the courts the authority to make the final interpretation of constitutional provisions and the exercise of that authority by the Supreme Court of the United States, especially with respect to civil liberties (including the procedural rights of accused persons), are the subjects of the next chapter.

It might seem that the chief explanation for the large numbers of lawyers among American political office holders lies in a need for lawyers to run governments in which legal considerations play so large a part. The presence of the lawyers has certainly contributed to the legalistic cast of American politics. 'As most public men are or have been legal practitioners,' concluded de Tocqueville, 'they introduce the customs and technicalities of their profession into the management of public affairs.' But the chief explanation for their presence lies in the affinities between careers in law and politics in American society.

Three-fifths of the delegates to the Philadelphia Convention in which the Constitution of the United States was drafted were lawyers associated, by and large, with the mercantile and planter classes. Both politics and the professions were democratized in the Jacksonian era. The spoils of office were spread among the victors of an electoral process in which the great majority of adult white males might participate. Entry into the professions became easier. While in medicine the trend was decisively reversed at the start of this century, the training of lawyers continued to be fairly simple and widely available. Apprenticeship in law offices, of which there were an ample number, was the main method of training until after the First World War. Careers in politics and the law, often in conjunction, were especially important to children of immigrants as means of getting ahead in American society.

Politicians and lawyers are both concerned with the law, and both advocate causes of those whom they represent. Yet studies of the performances of politicians, as members of State legislatures for example, have found no significant differences between lawyers and non-lawyers. On the other hand, political activity helps lawyers as lawyers. Professional ethics prohibit advertising. Lawyers in politics obtain publicity. Once they have established their legal practices, most lawyers in politics leave politics; but theirs is one of the few occupations in which at any point in a career a period in public office is apt to produce occupational benefits.

Political nominations for public offices tend to go to people well settled in the areas to be served. Typically, politicians work themselves up from one office to another through local and State and perhaps on to national politics. While there are more exceptions lately, these have always been the basic rules of political recruitment in the United States.

The great majority of lawyers practise locally in the States, each of which has its own law and bar, training for which is now usually undertaken in one of the law schools of the universities in the State. By way of contrast, the executives of the large corporations of interstate (and international) scope move about the country as they rise in their careers. In the practice of politics, lawyers are usually much more eligible for nominations.

In recent decades the leading executives and other top people associated with the corporate economy have constituted a loose national élite from which many political executives of the Federal Government have been drawn. The graduates from 'national' law schools, like those of Harvard and Yale Universities, who enter 'Wall Street' firms or their equivalents in the other main business centres, become part of this governing élite. All levels of American government regulate much more than they did, enacting the kinds of laws likely to give rise to litigation in their enforcement; but new dominant issues of national policy relating to defence and foreign affairs and the management of the economy are much less of a legal nature. Again the presence of large numbers of lawyers in American political offices is not to be explained primarily by a need for lawyers in government. They are there because they are available in large numbers—the American legal profession is, on a *per capita* basis, more than three times as numerous as England's—at key points of political recruitment.

B: THE JUDICIAL SYSTEMS

Basically, the American courts and the law which they apply are like those of England. American judges, like English judges, are drawn from the legal profession, not from a career service as in a continental European country. There is not, alongside the ordinary courts, a separate hierarchy of administrative courts enforcing a separate body of administrative law, though there are now many administrative tribunals whose findings are protected in varying degrees from reconsideration by the ordinary courts. Public officials sue and are sued in the ordinary courts. The general principle is that if their acts are *ultra vires* (without legal authority) they lose their official standing. The hardship resulting from the doctrine of Anglo-American law that the sovereign may not be sued in the sovereign's courts, for redress of damages done by public officials acting within their authority, has now been largely removed at both the Federal and State levels in the United States (as in England) by legislation consenting to such suits in the general or special courts. In both countries the 'rule of law' rests on the separateness of the ordinary courts from the executive and the comprehensiveness of their function, in deciding the cases before them, to 'declare' the law of the land.

The basic similarity of the courts and the law in the two countries is, of course, the result of the derivation of American judicial institutions from those established in the English colonies that became the first States. At the time of independence the colonial courts became State courts without fundamental change. The development of the common law in their jurisdictions continued unbroken by the transfer of sovereignty. The first systems have provided guidelines for the rest, Federal and State.

The Federal judiciary is described in Section C. The State judiciary, which is simply the collective name for the courts and judges of the several States, is described in Section D. The remainder of this section is concerned with first identifying and explaining the relations among the several judicial systems.

In each State there is a judicial system established by the State Constitution and statutes to apply State law: the Constitution, statutes, administrative regulations, local ordinances and common law (in Louisiana also the code of civil law) of the State. The United States has its law arising from the Constitution, laws and treaties of the United States. There is, strictly speaking, no Federal common law. The State and Federal bodies of law are placed in a single hierarchy of law by Article VI of the Constitution of the United States, which declares that the law of the United States 'shall be the supreme Law of the Land; and the Judges in every State shall be bound thereby, any Thing in the Constitution or Laws of any State to the contrary notwithstanding.'

While the Constitution thus provides for a dual system of law, nothing in it necessitates a dual system of courts. It specifies, in Article III, Section 1, that there shall be 'one supreme Court' of the United States, without determining the number of its members. It empowers but does not require the Congress to establish courts inferior to the Supreme Court. It defines, in Article III, Section 2, the extent of the judicial power of the United States, as reaching all cases: involving the Constitution, laws and treaties of the United States; involving diplomatic and consular personnel; of admiralty and maritime jurisdiction; in which the United States is a party; and—to summarize several clauses—in which there is a diversity of citizenship, international or interstate, between the parties. Among the cases embraced by this Federal judicial power, some are put within the original jurisdiction of the Supreme Court (under which comparatively few cases have arisen) and the rest within its appellate jurisdiction, 'with such Exceptions, and under such Regulations as the Congress shall make'.

A ruling of the Supreme Court in 1793 that the definition of the extent of the Federal judicial power permitted a State to be sued by a citizen of another State was set aside by the Eleventh Amendment to the Constitution, adopted in 1798, explicitly protecting a State's sovereign immunity from suit by private persons. However, in 1976 the Supreme Court held that the scope of the Eleventh Amendment was limited by the enforcement clause of the Fourteenth, adopted in 1868, so that Congress may in passing civil rights legislation under the Fourteenth provide for private suits against States and State officials that would be constitutionally inadmissible in other contexts.

It would be consistent with the Constitution for the Congress to leave all cases arising under the judicial power of the United States to be tried in the State courts, except those dealt with by the Supreme Court under its limited original jurisdiction. From the outset, however, the Congress, in the Judiciary Act of 1789, established a system of Federal courts alongside the State courts. It divided the cases for trial arising under the Federal judicial power into three categories: those within the exclusive jurisdiction of the Federal courts; those within the exclusive jurisdiction of the State courts; and those within the concurrent jurisdiction of both. (In the concurrent field the party bringing suit makes the original choice of forum but the other party then has, with some exceptions, the right to insist on a Federal trial.) While the precise definitions of the categories have been changed and the Federal courts have over time taken a greater share of the much increased number of cases involved, the basic decision of the First Congress about the division of jurisdiction has always been adhered to. It means that, although there is a full system of Federal courts, the State courts deal with many of the cases within the scope of the Federal judicial power as well as all of the much more numerous cases arising under the judicial power left to the States.

It would also be consistent with the wording of the Constitution for the Congress to prevent the Supreme Court of the United States from reviewing the decisions of the State courts in cases involving 'Federal questions'—that is to say, claims founded upon the Constitution, laws and treaties of the United States. But again the First Congress, in the Judiciary Act of 1789, took a fundamental decision that has always been adhered to, by confirming a broad appellate jurisdiction of the Supreme Court in cases raising Federal questions, whether decided in lower Federal or the State courts.

Federal questions arise not only in matters of substantive law, as in alleged conflicts between the provisions of State and Federal statutes, but also from the actions of the law enforcement agencies and courts in dealing with cases. During the last half-century the Supreme Court has imposed on the States constitutional requirements relating to police and judicial procedures that it had previously applied only at the Federal level. Thus cases in the State courts which originally have no Federal element may in the course of proceedings give rise to Federal questions bringing them within the appellate jurisdiction of the Supreme Court of the United States. (They may also give rise to 'habeas corpus' proceedings in a Federal court on the ground that a State that violates the Federal constitutional rights of the accused forfeits jurisdiction.) However, the Supreme Court does not as a general rule take an appeal from a State decision (nor does a case come into the Federal judicial system in a 'habeas corpus' proceeding) until the judicial processes of the State, with their opportunities for appeal and disposal of an issue, have been exhausted.

The nature of the federal division of powers, as affirmed by the Tenth Amendment, means that no Federal court may be granted original or appellate jurisdiction over cases not coming within the scope of the Federal judicial power at all. With respect to them, the State courts make up fifty separate judicial systems, among which Article IV, Section 1, of the Federal Constitution requires that 'full faith and Credit shall be given in each State to the public Acts, Records, and judicial Proceedings of every other State.' The Congress is empowered to prescribe by general laws the manner of proof. Since the end of the nineteenth century, the enactment by States of uniform legislation relating to both the substance and procedures of law has mitigated some of the effects of maintaining the separate legal systems of the States in an increasingly integrated nation. But there are still many diversities in law, as in marriage and divorce law, sometimes giving rise to difficulties in the implementation of legal reciprocity.

Article IV, Section 2, of the Federal Constitution requires one State to extradite upon demand a person charged with a crime in another. The Supreme Court has ruled that a State Governor cannot be compelled to extradite under this clause, but in practice extradition is usually granted as a matter of routine under State law. Moreover, the Congress, invoking its interstate commerce power, has made fleeing from a State in cases involving any of a list of crimes dealt with by the States into a Federal offence, requiring Federal officers to return the fugitive to the State to face the Federal charge. Once there, he may be turned over to the State authorities.

C: THE FEDERAL JUDICIARY

The Federal courts

The Judiciary Act of 1789 set the membership of the Supreme

Court at six Justices. It divided the country into Federal judicial districts (none of which has—with one trivial exception—ever contained parts of more than one State), grouped in Federal judicial circuits. A District judge held the District Court and, together with two Supreme Court Justices riding circuit, made up the Circuit Court when it met in his District. Both District and Circuit Courts had an original jurisdiction. Circuit Courts had a limited jurisdiction over appeals from the District Courts: a District Judge did not vote on an appeal from his own decision. As described in the previous section, the Judiciary Act also gave the State courts jurisdiction in some classes of Federal cases and the Supreme Court of the United States a broad final appellate jurisdiction in cases from both the lower Federal and the State courts raising Federal questions.

The net changes since 1789 in the organization of the courts of the Federal districts and circuits have produced two largely, though not entirely, separately organized levels of courts, one of general original and the other of general appellate jurisdiction: the District Courts and the Courts of Appeals. The number of Supreme Court Justiceships has been varied between five and ten, but kept at nine since 1869. The Justices were relieved of the need to ride circuit in 1891. An Act of 1925 put the exercise of the Supreme Court's appellate jurisdiction very largely at the Justices' discretion. The details that follow are as at mid-1975.

There are eighty-nine Federal judicial districts distributed among the fifty States, each district having a District Court with an establishment of one to twenty-seven judgeships. There is also a District Court in the District of Columbia, with an establishment of fifteen judgeships. The District Courts try Federal criminal cases and the great majority of the civil actions arising in the Federal courts. They review and enforce orders of some Federal administrative agencies.

For 'a capital, or otherwise infamous crime' the Fifth Amendment to the Constitution requires 'a presentment or indictment of a grand jury'. Normally a case is tried by a single District Judge, with a (petit) jury for criminal prosecutions and civil suits at common law, as required by Article III, Section 2, of the Constitution and the Sixth and Seventh Amendments, unless jury trial is waived by both parties. In certain cases, as when an injunction is sought to restrain the enforcement of a Federal or State statute on grounds of its conflict with the Constitution of the United States, a District Court is required by statute to consist of three judges, at least one of whom is from a Court of Appeals. In such cases, cases in which a Federal statute or treaty has been held unconstitutional and a Federal agency or official has been a party, and cases arising under certain Acts of the Congress or of 'such imperative public importance as to justify the deviation from normal appellate process', the Supreme Court has direct appellate jurisdiction over the District Courts. Otherwise appeals lie to the Courts of Appeals.

There are ten numbered Federal judicial circuits, each of which includes the Federal judicial districts in more than one State, and a separate circuit for the District of Columbia. Each circuit has a Court of Appeals with an establishment of from three to fifteen judgeships. Besides acting as general appellate courts for the District Courts, the Courts of Appeals review and enforce orders of many Federal agencies exercising quasi-judicial functions. Three to nine judges may sit *en banc* to hear a case: in practice, usually three; a quorum is two.

The 'one supreme Court' consists of the Chief Justice of the United States and eight Associate Justices, who sit together to hear a case: the quorum is six. They are still assigned to circuits, two of them to two circuits each. They act individually on certain pleas that arise from court actions, particularly dispositive orders, in their circuits. The business of the Supreme Court is described in the next sub-section.

Article III, Section 1, of the Constitution vests the judicial power of the United States in the Supreme Court and 'in such inferior Courts as the Congress may from time to time ordain and establish'. The courts mentioned so far are deemed to be established under that clause. They are therefore 'constitutional' courts because, while all but the Supreme Court have been created by legislation, their 'judicial Power' (as distinct from the 'legislative Powers' and 'executive Power' vested in the other branches of the Federal Government by Articles I and II) has its source in the Constitution. The Congress also has the legislative power, enumerated in Article I, Section 8, 'to constitute Tribunals inferior to the supreme Court'. When it invokes that power, in association with the 'necessary and proper' clause of Article I, Section 8, in order to provide for adjudications relating to the non-judicial functions of the Federal Government, the courts it establishes are 'legislative' courts.

The one certain difference made by this distinction between the 'constitutional' and 'legislative' Federal judiciary relates to the tenure of judges. The judges of all Federal courts are appointed by the President with the advice and consent of the Senate, though the Constitution (Article II, Section 2) absolutely requires this only for judges of the Supreme Court. Article III provides that the judges of the courts organized under its authority 'shall hold their Offices during good Behaviour', which means that they cannot be removed or required to retire except on conviction by a two-thirds majority of the Senate on impeachment by the House of Representatives. This constitutional requirement of life tenure does not apply to the members of 'legislative' courts. Sometimes the Congress gives them life tenure, sometimes not.

The first 'legislative' courts were established in pursuance of the Federal Government's authority to govern the Territories, such courts exercising both 'Federal' and 'local' jurisdiction. Originally, therefore, the Supreme Court regarded all of the judiciary in the District of Columbia as 'legislative'; but it now regards the District Court and Court of Appeals there as 'constitutional', too, which means their judges must have life tenure. There is at present a District Court in each of the Territories of Puerto Rico, Guam, the Canal Zone, and the Virgin Islands: in Puerto Rico, the District Judges have life tenure (there are separate local 'Commonwealth' courts); in the other Territories, they are appointed for eight years. The four districts are included in the numbered Federal judicial circuits, so that all told there are ninety-four District Courts in eleven circuits.

From the second half of the nineteenth century the Congress has established Courts of specialized jurisdiction to adjudicate matters that might otherwise be dealt with by legislative or executive bodies. The United States Court of Claims (against the

K

Federal Government), created in 1855, the United States Court of Customs and Patent Appeals, created in 1909, and (under the latter) the United States Customs Court, created in 1926, were originally 'legislative' courts; but in the 1950s the Congress formally gave them 'constitutional' status. At the present time two 'legislative' courts of specialized jurisdiction are the United States Court of Military Appeals, created in 1950, whose three judges are appointed from civilian life for staggered terms of fifteen years, and are removable by the President for neglect of duty or because of a mental or physical disability, and the United States Tax Court (concerned with income and estate taxes), a former administrative tribunal organized as a court of record under Article I in 1969.

Judges of courts with 'constitutional' status may be temporarily transferred, to exercise 'the judicial power' of other 'constitutional' courts of the appropriate level. But 'constitutional' courts refuse to perform 'non-judicial' duties, such as rendering decisions which do not relate to particular, genuine controversies or which are of an advisory nature. In assigning duties to 'legislative' courts, the Congress need not strictly adhere to the separation of powers, though if a decision of any tribunal is merely advisory, the Supreme Court does not recognize it as a judicial action at all.

The business of the Supreme Court

A case filed in the Supreme Court is placed on one of its three dockets: Original, Appellate and Miscellaneous. In most of the cases on the Original Docket two or more States are the parties. (Legislation confers concurrent original jurisdiction on the Federal District Courts in most of the other kinds of cases in which the Constitution confers original jurisdiction on the Supreme Court.) In its 1974–5 term the Supreme Court disposed of four cases on its Original Docket, denying leave to file complaint in three and deciding one on its merits.

Cases from other courts for review, on the Appellate Docket, reach the Supreme Court by application for writ of appeal, petition for writ of certiorari, or certification of 'any question of law in any civil or criminal case as to which instructions are desired' (usually by a Federal Court of Appeals or the Court of Claims). Certification is seldom used. An appeal lies: when a State court of last resort or a lower Federal court (provided in the latter case that a Federal agency or official is a party) declares an Act or Treaty of the United States unconstitutional; when, in a case involving a claim that a provision of a State statute or Constitution conflicts with Federal law, a State court of last resort upholds or a Federal Court of Appeals invalidates the State provision; or when the Act under which a case arises provides for direct appeal from the decision of a Federal District Court. In other cases involving 'a Federal question of substance' a party adversely affected by a decision of a State court of last resort, a Federal Court of Appeals, the Court of Claims, or the Court of Customs and Patent Appeals, may petition for a writ of certiorari.

In theory an appeal, when validly raised, ought to secure review for the appellant as a matter of right. In practice the Supreme Court exercises discretion to dismiss an appeal for want of a substantial Federal question. Review on writ of certiorari is in both theory and practice a matter of discretion for the Supreme Court. It is granted on the vote of four Justices, though a majority of the nine may later decide that it was improvidently granted. In its 1974–5 term the Supreme Court disposed of 1,877 cases on its Appellate Docket, denying or dismissing appeals or petitions for review in 1,594 cases and deciding 283 cases on their merits.

Cases on the Miscellaneous Docket include petitions for the extraordinary writs, like that of habeas corpus (which may be granted initially by a single Justice). A large number of petitions come from prisoners challenging the legality of their convictions under the Federal *in forma pauperis* statute, which allows an indigent citizen to enter proceedings in any Federal court. In its 1974–5 term the Supreme Court disposed of 1,966 cases on its Miscellaneous Docket, denying or dismissing appeals or petitions for review in 1,914 cases and deciding 52 cases on their merits.

Cases decided on their merits are disposed of either after hearing argument or, in most instances, simply on their records. After hearing argument (and discussing and voting on a case or set of cases in conference), the Court usually disposes of the case or cases heard by a signed Opinion of the Court. The task of writing it is assigned to a Justice among the majority agreed about the disposition by the Chief Justice if he is among the majority, otherwise by the Senior Associate Justice among them. Others of the majority may write concurring opinions, differing from the (Opinion of the) Court on one or more points of law or reasoning. If there is a dissenting minority, one or more of its members usually write dissenting opinions.

Other cases are disposed of by unsigned Per Curiam opinions, setting forth the unanimous or majority decisions of the Court. Some Per Curiam opinions are written after hearing argument and may contain sufficient legal reasoning to be regarded, along with signed Opinions of the Court, as full opinions. However, the great majority of them are memorandum orders, summarily disposing of the cases on their records—e.g. 'affirmed' or 'reversed'.

All told, the Supreme Court disposed of 3,847 cases in its 1974-5 term. Of the 336 decided on their merits, 159 cases were disposed of by 137 full opinions: 144 cases by 123 signed Opinions and 15 cases by 14 Per Curiam opinions. In 63 of the full opinions the principal issue dealt with was constitutional. These made up the Supreme Court's annual contribution to the constitutional law of the United States.

An Act of 1922 empowered the Chief Justice of the Supreme Court to convene a Judicial Conference of senior and representative Federal judges at least once a year for the purpose of surveying the conditions of business in the Federal courts and planning the temporary reassignment of judges to cope with it. An Act of 1939 set up the Administrative Office of the United States Courts to perform housekeeping functions for the lower courts and to advise on the handling of business. Former President William Howard Taft, who had become Chief Justice in 1921, provided the impetus for both the Act of 1922 and that of 1925 which, by curtailing the right of appellants to apply for a review of their cases by the Supreme Court, enabled the Court to get abreast of its business.

Federal judges

The President uses his power to appoint Federal judges with the advice and consent of the Senate to nominate lawyers who are, with few exceptions, members of his own party. The appointment of a District Judge is governed by 'senatorial courtesy': it is subject to the veto of any Senator of the President's part from the State in which the Federal judicial district is located. This means that the initiative in suggesting names for nominations often comes from the Senators. Since no Federal judicial circuit is limited to a single State, the influence of Senators is more diffuse on appointments to the Courts of Appeals. The President may seek to confine suggested names to those of persons with judicial or other particularly relevant professional experience. For a nomination to the Supreme Court the emphasis is much less on obtaining Senators' prior advice than on securing their subsequent consent; and senatorial consideration of the politics of the President's nominee is directed much more to trying to predict his future opinions as a judge than to assessing his past services as a partisan.

The President asks his Attorney General, as head of the Department of Justice, to investigate the suitability of persons suggested for judicial nominations. In the 1950s the practice developed of the Attorney General's referring the name of anyone being seriously considered to a committee of the American Bar Association for a rating of professional competence. However, Presidents occasionally act against, or without obtaining, the committee's advice.

By the end of Gerald Ford's presidency 101 men had sat on the Supreme Court. Ninety-one were of the President's party at the time of their appointments to the Court. Appointments to the lower Federal Courts have been even more partisan. Of the ten exceptions among the 101 Supreme Court Justices, two were appointed at the end of a President's term when the President-elect was of the other party; two were generally regarded as closer to the President in their thinking than to their own party leaders; three were appointed to widen the President's political appeal; two (as well as one or two already accounted for) were personal friends of the President; and Benjamin Cardozo, appointed by President Hoover early in 1932, was, as the Chief Judge of the highest court of New York State and the author of several books on the law, so widely reputed to be the best qualified jurist in the country as to make his choice almost inevitable. (He turned out to be an undistinguished Justice.) Thus an examination of the exceptions to partisan appointments serves mainly to demonstrate further that to political victors belong the judicial spoils.

Most Presidents have looked upon appointments to the Supreme Court as chances to influence the Court's interpretation of the Constitution to accord with their general views on public policy. At the time of appointment to the Court, forty-two of the 101 Justices had had no previous judicial experience, but almost all of the 101 had been active in public affairs. In recent decades many appointees have been high executive officials, especially of the Department of Justice. (Republicans look somewhat more to the bench, Democrats more to the executive and other political posts, for appointees.) Personal friendship with the President or his closest advisers is frequently decisive: it increases the likelihood that the President will guess correctly about an appointee's broad judgements on constitutional issues. While there have been some gross miscalculations, of which President Eisenhower's appointment of Governor Earl Warren of California as Chief Justice in 1953 is the outstanding instance, a student of all appointments through those of President Kennedy concluded that about three-fourths of the Justices have 'conformed to the expectations of the Presidents who appointed them to the Supreme Court'.*

When the Justices rode circuit, it was customary to appoint them from the appropriate areas of the country. In this century, more attention is paid to whether there are Justices of the Catholic and Jewish as well as Protestant faiths. President Johnson's appointment of Thurgood Marshall as an Associate Justice in 1967 was instantly recognized as establishing the principle that there ought usually to be at least one Negro on the Court. In filling any particular vacancy, however, there are many considerations but (except for the convention that judges must be lawyers) no rules.

Nearly one in five presidential nominations for Supreme Court

* Robert Scigliano, *The Supreme Court and the Presidency* (Free Press, 1971), p. 146.

posts have been rejected by the Senate, either directly by an adverse vote or indirectly by a refusal to act. Most nominations made in the last year of a President's term of office have been rejected when the other party has had a majority in the Senate. Most rejections have occurred in one, the other or both of those circumstances. Each rejection, like each nomination, has its particular history; but the general pattern is obvious: the check the Senate exercises with respect to Supreme Court appointments is strongest when the President's hold on the Senate is weakest. The Senate may force a postponement: in the summer of 1968 it refused to confirm President Johnson's nomination of Justice Abe Fortas to succeed Earl Warren as the Chief Justice; Warren held over his retirement until the next summer, when he was replaced by President Nixon's appointee, Warren Burger. (Fortas was the first nominee for a Supreme Court appointment to be rejected since 1930.) The Senate may force the President to find a more acceptable nominee than his first, or second, choice: in 1969–70 the Senate, with a Democratic majority, voted down two nominees of Republican President Nixon for a vacant Associate Justiceship, though the Senators divided more on regional than party lines.

Only one Supreme Court Justice has been impeached: Samuel Chase in 1804–5. Following the first partisan change of the Presidency in 1801, which had been accompanied by the replacement of an extreme Federalist by a Democratic-Republican majority in the Congress, the Jeffersonians sought to break the Federalist hold on the Court. The attempt was abandoned when, on the several roll calls in the Senate, the vote most adverse to Chase (nineteen to fifteen for conviction) still fell four short of the necessary two-thirds majority. In 1969 revelations about the salaries that Justices Fortas and William O. Douglas had been drawing from posts with private foundations set up by financiers named in a stock fraud case led Fortas to resign from the Court and Douglas from his outside post. Eight judges of lower Federal courts have been impeached, of whom four were convicted and one resigned; nine more have resigned under the threat of impeachment.

D: THE STATE JUDICIARY

The State courts

In the States the constitutional provision for the judiciary is usually comprehensive and elaborate, in contrast to the paucity of direct provision for the Federal courts in the Federal Constitution. The ensuing summary description of the State courts (as at the end of 1975, unless otherwise indicated) omits most of the many variations from State to State, and also much of the complexity that characterizes most State systems.

Broadly speaking, there are in each State two sets of trial courts, one for minor and one for more important cases, and one or more levels of appellate courts:

Justices of the Peace or magistrates and municipal courts (under such names as 'city court' and 'police court') deal with misdemeanours, minor traffic offences, small claims and the like, and perhaps hold preliminary hearings in cases involving felonies. The typical J.P. is a non-lawyer who serves as a notary public, performs civil marriages and dispenses petty justice, obtaining all or most of his remuneration from the fees and sometimes the fines he collects, though the trend has been to curtail his judicial functions. In urban areas, magistrates are much more likely to be salaried and with legal training. A municipal court handles somewhat more important cases than a magistrate's court. It is normally the first 'court of record' presided over by a 'judge', sometimes with a jury. Otherwise there are no juries in the minor trial courts.

County or district courts try the more important criminal and civil cases. Nine States (as at 1972) require that all felony cases be initiated by grand jury indictment. Fifteen States authorize the defendant to waive grand jury indictment and twenty-six allow the public prosecutors discretion to submit charges in a procedure known as information: however, grand jury indictment may still be required for a few crimes, such as homicide and political corruption. Typically, a county court is presided over by a single judge, sitting with a (petit) jury in criminal cases and in many civil cases.

Appellate courts provide a general right of appeal to convicted persons and the losing parties in civil actions. In practice, not more than 5 per cent of the cases decided in the major trial courts are appealed. In half the States, there are intermediate appellate courts between the trial courts and the highest court, with restrictions on appeals to the latter. Cases in the appellate courts are heard by three or more judges, sitting without a jury.

The highest court of a State, usually known as the Supreme Court, is composed of from three to nine judges. It is the final interpreter within the State of the State Constitution and laws, in carrying out the judicial function of deciding cases. In some States it is also required to render advisory opinions on questions of law.

There may be separate courts for criminal and civil cases. A very few States retain the general separation of common law and equity courts introduced into English America at a time when they were separate in England. Besides the courts of more or less general jurisdiction, there are special courts to deal, for example, with minor traffic offences, juvenile delinquency or the probation of wills. There are also administrative tribunals for adjudicating between the State and a private party—about licences or benefits, for example—or between two private parties: in almost every State, for instance, about workmen's compensation claims. The ordinary courts always exercise at least a minimum of jurisdiction over the conduct of administrative justice.

In recent decades the advocates of reform of the State judicial systems have been most agreed in wanting a fairly simple general structure of courts, in which the magistrates or judges of each level may be assigned to those courts or divisions of courts where they can be of most help, either temporarily so as to cope with fluctuations in the distribution of work or for longer periods because of specialist knowledge. The fact that the business of the State courts is much heavier and more complex than that of the Federal courts increases the need for achieving in the States at least as much flexibility in deploying judicial personnel as is now available in the Federal system. Formerly, judicial administration was a matter only of domestic concern for the several courts, with their clerks and bailiffs. Reform requires submitting the judges themselves to administrative supervision. The separation of

powers usually requires that the responsibility for such supervision be vested in members of the judiciary, at the top the chief
judge of the highest court in the judicial hierarchy.

Reform has been opposed by many politicians and lawyers who
fear a reduction in the opportunities for influence, patronage and
profitable legal business which the complicated, unintegrated
systems sometimes lavishly provide. Opponents of change have
been assisted by the entrenchment of details of judicial organization in State Constitutions. However, the extreme congestion of
many court calendars has helped generate the support for reform
among at least a few leaders of the bench and bar which is essential
to its success. Especially when there is a major constitutional
revision, considerable improvements are now often effected. The
achievements of Chief Justice Arthur Vanderbilt of New Jersey in
obtaining a highly integrated system of courts and extensive
administrative powers for the Chief Justice, when the State
adopted a new Constitution in 1947, gave him a deserved
reputation as the ablest State judge of his generation.

State judges

The term 'State judges' refers here to the judges of the major trial
and appellate courts of the States. In Rhode Island they, like
Federal judges, serve for life. In Massachusetts and New Hampshire the members of all courts serve to the age of seventy. In New
Jersey, the judges of the superior trial and appellate courts serve
first for seven years and then, if reappointed, for life; the judges of
county courts are first appointed for five years and take longer to
be given tenure. Otherwise the members of all courts in the States
are chosen for fixed terms: justices of the peace or magistrates,
usually for two, four or six years; judges of major trial courts,
usually for from four to eight years; and judges of the appellate
courts, usually for from six to ten years.

In four of the original thirteen States all or the most important
judges are chosen by the legislature. Vermont (the fourteenth
State) changed recently from legislative election to gubernatorial
appointment with senatorial consent from a list of persons designated as qualified by a Judicial Selection Board: but after the

initial term, retention in office is by vote of the legislature. In seven other States, all of which except Hawaii (the fiftieth State) are in the Northeast, the Governor appoints the judges, with the consent of the State Senate or an Executive Council; or, in Maryland, subject to subsequent election on a non-partisan ballot. In New York judges are elected on a partisan ballot, but the Governor designates which general trial court judges constitute the intermediate appellate court of the State. Thus, among the oldest States both the original predominance of the legislature and the early strengthening of the independence of the other branches in American Constitutions are still evident in the selection and tenure of judges.

In most States the principle of popular election associated particularly with Jacksonian democracy is adhered to for all or part of the judiciary, though the terms of office for judges are longer than for comparable office holders in the legislative and executive branches. In twenty-four States all or almost all judges are elected: in eleven on a partisan and in thirteen on a non-partisan ballot. The non-partisan ballot was one of the devices by which Progressive reformers sought to reduce the influence of 'machine politics'. The most recent fashion, reflecting the greater influence of the bar associations, has been the 'Missouri Plan', first adopted in that State in 1940, whereby initially the Governor appoints judges from among the nominees of a commission of bench, bar and 'lay' members and thereafter the judges 'run on their records' in plebiscites determining whether they remain in office. This system is used for at least the judges of higher courts in twelve States. California has a mixture of methods: under the 'California Plan' adopted in 1934, initially the Governor appoints the judges of the appellate courts, with the approval of a Commission on Judicial Appointments, and thereafter the judges run on their records for re-election; all other members of the judiciary are elected on a non-partisan ballot.

Practice often blurs the distinctions among the methods of selection. When judges are appointed by the Governor with the approval of the Senate, the equivalent of Federal 'senatorial courtesy' often does not prevail; but the chamber as a whole has more influence, with the result that when Governors and senatorial majorities are of different parties, many appointments are made from the party in control of the Senate. In about half the States with the non-partisan ballot party influences operate informally. On the other hand, in some States in which judges are elected on a partisan ballot the parties agree not to oppose each other's incumbents (in two the incumbents formally run on their records). Many more judges are first appointed than the formal provisions indicate because their predecessors resign before the end of the terms for which they have been elected and the Governors fill the casual vacancies. Incumbents who stand for re-election are usually returned.

For all that, there are significant differences between the judges elected on partisan ballots and the others. The former are likely to reach the bench after serving as an elected prosecuting attorney, in which office they gain the notice of the public or at least a section of it. The latter are more dependent on the support of State legislators or bar associations, and usually have a better educational background.

Whatever the methods of selection, State judges are on the whole more involved in politics than Federal judges. Most of them are closer to the people than their Federal counterparts. Continuance in office usually depends at least to some extent on political support. These factors operate even more strongly on the minor judiciary. Moreover, the detailed regulation of the machinery of government in State Constitutions and the constitutional and statutory regulation by the States of the political parties involve State judges in adjudicating many disputes between and within the parties over power and its objects.

For removing a judge before the expiry of his term, impeachment is available in all but one of the States, and the only method in more than one-third of them. Other methods are: removal by joint legislative resolution, sometimes requiring two-thirds or three-fourths majorities of the two houses; recall by the electorate; and removal by the highest court or special judicial council. With the exception of a couple of the variations upon the last of these methods, they have all proved too cumbersome for effective use.

E: LAW ENFORCEMENT

The policing and prosecuting authorities

The general power to govern reserved to the States under the Constitution of the United States is known in American constitutional law as the police power. It is the power to regulate in order to protect the public peace, health, safety, morals and general welfare. It must be exercised within the constraints set by the Federal Constitution as interpreted by the Supreme Court of the United States. There is now a great deal of Federal regulatory legislation, which takes precedence when Federal and State laws conflict. There is also a large measure of 'co-operative federalism' in promoting the general welfare. But the States remain primarily responsible for preserving the law and order of the community; policing in the narrower, more familiar sense of the term. Within the States, in turn, this responsibility is primarily discharged by local agencies of law enforcement.

In rural areas and the fringes of urban areas, local sheriffs (who are elective office holders in every State except Rhode Island) and sheriffs' deputies perform the policing function. In urban areas, where the great majority of Americans live, they have been superseded by (in 1972) more than 40,000 police departments, employing on average ten policemen each. By far the largest departments are in the largest central cities, which have much higher crime rates than the country as a whole. At the start of 1972 New York City's department employed 30,700 policemen and 2,300 civilians; Chicago's 13,200 and 1,700; Los Angeles' 7,000 and 2,400; and Philadelphia's 7,600 and 900. It was reported in 1976 that private security firms in the United States had 800,000 people in uniform.

The States' militia or National Guard units of civilians prepared for armed service in emergencies—whether mobilized by the Governors or, under legislation implementing the clause of the Constitution of the United States which empowers Congress 'to provide for calling forth the Militia to execute the Laws of the Union, suppress Insurrections and repel Invasions', 'federalized' by the President—are used to cope with a variety of situations beyond the capacity of the regular police. (A Congressional Act of 1916 reorganized the militia as the National Guard to make them a more effective national defence reserve.) They deal with emergencies arising, for example, from natural disasters or serious rioting. They have sometimes been used by a Governor to displace a corrupted local police administration, or by the President to overcome State defiance of Federal authority (see Chapter 7, Section A). In December 1975 the Army Guard strength was 392,000, the Air Guard strength 94,000, constituting a total National Guard of 486,000 members.

The need for Governors to send in National Guard contingents to deal with the numerous black riots in the nation's cities in the 1960s led to an intensification of U.S. Army training of Guardsmen to handle civil disturbances. Their record of increasing effectiveness and restraint was marred in 1970 when Guardsmen killed four students at Kent State University, Ohio, during a demonstration against the incursion of American and South Vietnamese forces into Cambodia.

With the advent of the motor car State highway patrols were formed. In twenty-three States (as at 1974) there are general State police forces (incorporating the highway patrols). Only Hawaii has neither a State police nor highway patrol. Generally, State governments increasingly provide facilities to aid local law enforcement. But ordinary policing is still very predominantly a local government activity.

The police bring many of the minor prosecutions. Otherwise in American law enforcement prosecutions are brought by general prosecuting attorneys or administrative agencies charged with the enforcement of particular laws.

The chief law officer of a State is its Attorney General. In six States he is chosen by the Governor with the consent of the State Senate or other body; in Maine, by the legislature; and in Tennessee, by the highest court. In the other forty-two States he is elected. The only duty common to every Attorney General is the rendering of advisory opinions on questions of law. In Rhode Island he acts as the local prosecutor. In the other States there are local (county or district) prosecuting attorneys. In six States some or all of them are appointed officials: in two the appointing power is vested in the Attorney General. In forty-three States, however, all are elected. In most States, the Attorney General has little or no control over original prosecutions, but he usually has more say about appeals.

In the Federal Government the Judiciary Act of 1789 provided for an Attorney General and for a District Attorney in each Federal judicial district. In 1870 the office of the Attorney General was expanded into the Department of Justice, with a Solicitor General put in charge of representing the Government in the Supreme Court. The Attorney General, Solicitor General and District Attorneys are appointed by the President with the consent of the Senate: District Attorneys are, like District Judges, patronage appointees subject to 'senatorial courtesy'. Unlike the Judges, however, the D.A.s are appointed for only a four-year term concurrent with the President's and may be removed at any time.

The Justice Department allows District Attorneys considerable discretion in bringing prosecutions, except in matters of particular concern to the Department. The Solicitor General must approve an appeal.

Federal law enforcement services have been created piecemeal as required by particular departments and agencies in carrying out their functions and implementing Federal legislation. Thus the Department of the Treasury established law enforcement forces to combat smuggling, counterfeiting and evasion of the internal revenue laws. The Revenue Marine, authorized by the Congress in 1790, is no longer in the Treasury: as the United States Coast Guard, it is now in the Department of Transportation in peacetime and in the Navy in time of war. The anti-counterfeiting Secret Service, founded in 1865, acquired the additional responsibility of protecting the President in 1901.

Within the Department of Justice are: the Immigration and Naturalization Service with its Border Patrol; the Drug Enforcement Administration; and the Federal Bureau of Investigation, founded in 1908 but acquiring its present pre-eminence among Federal law enforcement agencies under the long directorship (1924–72) of Mr. J. Edgar Hoover. The F.B.I. is charged with investigating all violations of Federal laws other than those whose investigation is specifically assigned to another agency. It provides services, such as fingerprint identification, for all law enforcement agencies in the United States.

Following the report of President Johnson's Commission on Law Enforcement and the Administration of Justice in 1967, the Congress enacted the Omnibus Crime Control and Safe Streets Act of 1968, which provided block grants to the States according to their populations, with a guaranteed 'pass-through' of at least 75 per cent of the money for projects to local governments, for the purpose of improving law enforcement. The first use of block grants to initiate a Federal aid programme and the 'pass-through' formula (which was subsequently modified to help State governments already contributing heavily to the costs of local law enforcement) reflected the concern of the Congress that Federal aid should not result in Federal or State control of this traditionally local function. It may well be that with adequate financial support the decentralized system can be made to deal as well as any possible alternative with the general increase in crime.

On the other hand, the growth of organized crime since the Prohibition era and the ease with which it is able to corrupt police, prosecutors and courts in particular localities and sometimes in State governments probably create insoluble problems for the present system. Like the great business corporations formed in the late nineteenth century, the organized crime syndicates seem too powerful for the localities and States alone. However, invoking the Federal power, not only to help fight against crime but also to supervise the lower law enforcement agencies sufficiently so as to make them reasonably corruption-free, is thought to be fraught with the dangers of a centralized police state. The revelations arising from the Watergate affair, but not confined to the Nixon Administration, about the pressures put on Federal law enforcement agencies by White House officials to harass the latter's political enemies and to interfere with the course of justice, followed by admissions of abuses of power by the F.B.I. (and the Central Intelligence Agency), have reinforced the case for caution.

The dispensing of justice

Surveys have indicated that about half the major crimes committed in the United States are not reported to the police. Of those reported, about a quarter lead to arrests. Following about half the arrests, charges are dropped. Perhaps as many as nine-tenths of the other half of the arrests lead to pleas of guilty. Major crimes are over a hundred times more numerous than those resulting in trials.

However, both minor and major offences congest the courts. This is especially true of the State courts, because most of the kinds of offences that produce large numbers of cases come within their jurisdiction. Motoring offences produce the great majority of all cases before American courts. Drunkenness accounts for one-third of all arrests. Ordinary crime generally is dealt with by State justice.

One consequence of the congestion in the courts is that large numbers of defendants are in effect punished without trial. It was reported in the 1970 census that 52 per cent of the inmates of city and county jails on census day had not yet been tried. Particular investigations in large cities have shown that most defendants not out on bail spend more than a month in jail between arraignment and trial. While the time thus spent is taken into account by judges when sentencing the guilty, the innocent also suffer, as they do when they must resort to professional bail bondsmen to avoid remand—at a fee of 5–10 per cent of the amount of bail.

Minor offences creating a large volume of routine business are normally disposed of by the courts with great dispatch. A traffic court may deal with minor motoring offences without requiring the appearance of defendants willing to accept a standard penalty. A magistrate may regularly get through 250 drunk and disorderly cases a day.

On the other hand, the ease with which adjournments are obtained and the opportunities for multiple appeals enable defending counsel sometimes to drag contested cases out for many years. In recent decades rulings of the United States Supreme Court about defendants' rights have increased the burden on the judiciary of pre-trial motions and post-conviction proceedings. Yet it takes only a comparatively few cases absorbing more than the minimum of judicial time to clog the courts.

Therefore, even cases arising from major crimes can be barely coped with only because the great majority of defendants plead guilty. Instrumental in achieving this result is the practice of plea bargaining, whereby prosecutors agree to bring lesser charges in return for the co-operation of the accused. This practice is openly acknowledged, though where there is judicial discretion in sentencing, the prosecutors cannot guarantee leniency. However, the pressure of business leaves judges little time to question recommendations: 'it is customary for the lawyers on both sides to get together and decide what punishment, if any, is appropriate in a particular case, and for the judge to go along with whatever arrangement is made.'*

Likewise, only a small minority of civil issues are decided by the courts. Many commercial disputes are settled by arbitration. Most divorces are uncontested. Judges sometimes play a considerable part in arranging settlements in civil cases on their dockets in pre-trial conferences with the parties, but most cases are settled out of court by the parties themselves. However, congested dockets and delays, often of several years, before cases are reached for trial are usual. Contributing to the congestion is the practice of lawyers' taking personal injury and similar cases for contingent fees: only winning clients pay them (often one-third of the amounts recovered). Contributing to the delays are, again, the opportunities for them which counsel exploit. The most effective defence against a claim is often to hold out until witnesses forget or disappear.

The existence of the courts and the law that they declare conditions the other ways of disposing of cases. Predictions about the behaviour of judges and juries largely determine the settlements reached in civil suits. Decisions about the procedural rights of the accused may affect the balance of power in plea bargaining. But justice is negotiated by litigants much more than it is administered by the courts. Moreover, 'discretion in law enforce-

---

* Delmar Karlen, *Judicial Administration—The American Experience* (Butterworths, 1970), p. 79.

ment and judicial agencies increases as one moves *down* the administrative hierarchy. . . . The patrolman, the lowest-ranking police officer, has the greatest discretion. . . . In many prosecution offices, . . . the deputies are able to decide which cases to accept from the police and the charges to be made. . . . without the control or guidance of the prosecutor.'* There is, as an old saying puts it, a good deal of law at the end of a policeman's nightstick—or on a deputy prosecutor's desk.

FOR FURTHER READING:

Henry J. Abraham, *The Judicial Process*, 3rd ed. (O.U.P., 1975).

George F. Cole, *Politics and the Administration of Justice* (Sage, 1973).

Herbert Jacob, *Justice in America*, 2nd ed. (Little, Brown, 1972).

Delmar Karlen, *Judicial Administration—The American Experience* (Butterworths, 1970).

---

* George F. Cole, *Politics and the Administration of Justice* (Sage, 1973), pp. 32–3.

10: The Supreme Court and Civil Liberties

A: THE AMERICAN DOCTRINE OF JUDICIAL SUPREMACY

Chief Justice John Marshall enunciated the doctrine of judicial supremacy, as the basic principle of the constitutional law of the United States, in the Opinion which he wrote for the unanimous Supreme Court in the case of Marbury v. Madison in 1803: '. . . all those who have framed written constitutions contemplate them as forming the fundamental and paramount law of the nation, and consequently, the theory of every such government must be, that an act of the legislature, repugnant to the constitution is void. . . . It is, emphatically, the province and duty of the judicial department, to say what the law is. Those who apply the rule to particular cases, must of necessity expound and interpret that rule. If two laws conflict with each other, . . . the court must determine which of these conflicting rules governs the case: this is of the very essence of judicial duty. If then, the courts are to regard the constitution, and the constitution is superior to any ordinary act of the legislature, the constitution, and not such ordinary act, must govern the case to which they both apply.' In Marbury v. Madison a provision of the Judiciary Act of 1789 extending the original jurisdiction of the Supreme Court within the Federal judicial power beyond those cases specifically mentioned in the Constitution was held to be in conflict with the Constitution—that is to say, unconstitutional—and, therefore, not valid law.

The proposition that, when two laws conflict, the courts must apply the higher is inherent in the notion of a legal system. The extent to which the invalidity of a particular provision of the lower law is held to render its other provisions void varies: the usual rule of construction in American constitutional law is to preserve as much law as possible; but it may be held that the several provisions of an act are so interconnected that they must fall together.

The two other propositions from which Marshall drew his conclusion are more peculiarly Anglo-American: first, that to the extent that a constitution is written it is law (not convention or a declaration of principles) higher than any other law; and second, that what makes a law law (not convention or a declaration of principles) in a 'government of laws' is that it is 'declared'—expounded and interpreted—by the ordinary courts. Put that way these propositions may seem unexceptionable (which is why the courts put them that way). What they mean is that when the requisite majority of the judges of the court of last resort in the judicial system come to a conclusion about the meaning of a constitutional provision, their interpretation is binding on the legislature, the executive and the lower courts, however general the belief among the latter that the provision means something else.

While in England, since there is no written constitution, an Act of Parliament is the supreme law, in America legislative enactments have always been subject to higher law. Acts of colonial assemblies were set aside by colonial courts and the Privy Council in London as contrary to colonial charters or English law. After independence, in the period before the adoption of the Constitution of the United States, acts of State legislatures were set aside by State courts as contrary to the State Constitutions, though no State Constitution explicitly empowered the courts to review the acts of the co-ordinate legislative branch, and the State legislatures sometimes protested vigorously. The Constitution of the United States was—and is—similarly inexplicit; but the framers (most of whom were lawyers) expected Anglo-American practice to be followed. The often-repeated charge that the doctrine of judicial supremacy is a 'usurpation' of power by the courts has no warrant in the historical evidence about the 'intention of the framers'.

From the start Justices of the Supreme Court assumed that they had the right to declare Acts of the Congress to be unconstitutional. Marbury *v.* Madison is generally referred to as the first case in which a Federal Act was declared void; but there was an earlier case, United States *v.* Yale Todd, in 1794, which was not reported at the time. The supremacy of the courts in constitutional interpretation is a feature of the Federal and every State constitutional system in the United States.

While every court, high or low, may exercise judicial supremacy in constitutional interpretation against the claims of the legislative and executive branches of government, a court does so only when required to, in deciding a case before it or, in some States, when the highest court in the State is asked by the appropriate authorities for an advisory opinion. The American doctrine of judicial supremacy thus differs from the English doctrine of parliamentary sovereignty, which describes a general competence to make law. However, once the highest court competent to interpret a constitutional provision has interpreted it, that interpretation can be changed only by a constitutional amendment (which in turn is given its authoritative interpretation by the courts) or by a reversal on the part of the court in a subsequent decision. 'We are under a Constitution,' said Charles Evans Hughes (Associate Justice of the United States Supreme Court, 1910–16, and Chief Justice, 1930–41) in 1907 and again while running for President in 1916, 'but the Constitution is what the judges say it is.'

Unless the context indicates otherwise, the term 'judicial review' in American constitutionalism refers specifically to the power of the courts to review legislation for its conformity with the Constitution under which it has been enacted. The courts of each State review acts of the State legislature with respect to the State Constitution. (In three States the Constitution requires an unusual majority among the members of its highest court before a statute is finally held invalid.) Both Federal and State courts review Acts of the Congress with respect to the Federal Constitution, because, as explained in Section B of Chapter 9, cases involving Federal Acts are tried in both Federal and State courts. However, as also explained in that section, the Supreme Court has a broad appellate jurisdiction over cases involving Federal questions, whether decided in lower Federal or State courts. Thus, it controls the interpretation of the Federal Constitution through-out the dual judicial system of Federal and State courts: at any given time the Constitution of the United States is what a majority of Supreme Court Justices have last said it is. They have, all told (as at July 1976), declared Acts of the Congress unconstitutional 112 times.

Moreover, in American federalism the supremacy of Federal law, provided for in Article VI of the Constitution, gives rise to judicial review of State actions for their compatibility with that supreme law. Again the supremacy is enforced by both Federal and State courts: Article VI explicitly binds 'the Judges in every State' in this respect. Any provision of a State Constitution or law in conflict with the Constitution or a valid law or treaty of the United States must be held invalid. In interpreting both the State and Federal provisions in cases of alleged conflict, the final word rests with the Supreme Court of the United States.

Since there is no direct Federal executive or legislative veto over the actions of State governments, Federal supremacy can be regularly maintained only by the courts. 'I do not think', said Mr. Justice Holmes, 'the United States would come to an end if we lost our power to declare an Act of Congress void. I do think the Union would be imperilled if we could not make that declara-tion as to the laws of the several States. For one in my place sees how often a local policy prevails with those who are not trained to national views.'

Other aspects of American constitutionalism would be at risk if the courts could not review the actions of the coordinate branches of government. In opposition to Chief Justice Marshall, Presidents Jefferson and Jackson argued that each branch—legislative, executive or judicial—should be guided by its own interpretation of the Constitution in the exercise of its respective powers. The courts have themselves declared that there are 'political questions' with respect to which they do not review the actions of the other branches. In Federal constitutional law, for example, whether a State has a republican form of government, whether an amendment to the Constitution has been duly ratified and whether a particular territory belongs to the United States have been held to be 'political questions'.

The courts preserve over-all judicial supremacy: they decide which questions are 'political' and may change their minds (either way). Perhaps 'political questions' are best defined as those matters with respect to which the courts, under current canons of interpretation, are least likely to set aside the determination of the other branches. As a general principle, however, to allow each branch to decide for itself what is constitutional would be incompatible with the 'rule of law'. It would destroy the check on executive action which an independent judiciary is intended to provide.

To leave the final word to the legislative branch, which would superficially resemble the English arrangement, would be incompatible with the American separation of powers. In the United States acts of the Congress or the State legislature, unlike those of the British Parliament, may become law over executive veto. Treating acts of the legislature as the supreme law would endanger the independence of the executive.

The framers of the Constitution of 1787 provided for the independent presidency of the United States. Andrew Jackson created the concept of the President as the 'tribune of the people', especially *vis-à-vis* the representatives of the more particular interests in the Congress. After Jackson, Presidents disagreeing with the Supreme Court have sought, not to question its supremacy in constitutional interpretation, but to induce it to change the contents of its decisions, especially by taking (or making) opportunities to appoint new members with (they believe) the right views.

B: THE SUPREME COURT'S EXERCISE OF JUDICIAL SUPREMACY

The Dred Scott decision of 1857 and the Reconstruction amendments

The first case after Marbury *v.* Madison in which an Act of the Congress was declared unconstitutional by the Supreme Court was Dred Scott *v.* Sandford in 1857. By seven votes to two the Justices held that the Missouri Compromise of 1820 had violated the clause of the Fifth Amendment of the Bill of Rights which prohibits the Federal Government from depriving any person of life, liberty, or property, without due process of law. For by making the then remaining northern Louisiana Territory 'free soil', that Act had operated to deprive a slave owner moving there of his property in slaves. In the Opinion of the Court Chief Justice Taney wrote that such a deprivation 'could hardly be dignified with the name of due process of law'. This was the first use by the Supreme Court of the due process limitation on governmental action to protect a substantive, as distinct from a procedural, right. Taney also declared that blacks, slave or free, were not citizens of the United States and had no rights under its Constitution.

President Buchanan had, in his inaugural address of 1857, commended the Dred Scott decision in advance, as an aid to settling controversies about slavery and 'free soil', whatever the decision might be (he had prior knowledge of it). Instead, by reducing the possibilities of compromise, the Dred Scott case helped precipitate the Civil War. Its decision and *dicta* were overruled by the three postwar Reconstruction amendments to the Constitution.

The Thirteenth Amendment, adopted in 1865, prohibited slavery. The Fourteenth Amendment, adopted in 1868, made all persons born or naturalized in the United States, and subject to its jurisdiction, citizens of the United States—and therefore with the constitutional rights of citizens—and provided moreover for the protection of personal rights from State action: no State may 'deprive any person of life, liberty, or property, without due process of law; nor deny to any person within its jurisdiction the equal protection of the laws'. The Fifteenth Amendment, adopted in 1870, prohibited racial discrimination in the suffrage.

1865–1885: political interference, judicial review and judicial restraint

During the Civil War the Supreme Court had prudently avoided a clash with President Lincoln over his use of martial law to intern Southern sympathizers in the non-seceding States. However, in *Ex Parte* Milligan in 1866 it condemned the use of military commissions to try cases in Indiana. The decision cast doubt on the legal validity of the military rule being imposed on the Southern States by the Reconstruction Acts. In 1868, after the case of *Ex Parte* McCardle, challenging the constitutionality of the Acts, had been argued before the Court under its appellate jurisdiction, the Congress passed a Bill, over President Andrew Johnson's veto, one of whose provisions withdrew this type of case from that jurisdiction.

A majority of the Justices contrived not to decide the McCardle case until the Bill became law. In 1869 a unanimous Court upheld the power of the Congress, so to make exceptions to the Court's appellate jurisdiction. This has been the only instance of the Congress's using that power in order to prevent the Supreme Court from rendering a decision on the constitutionality of an Act.

In 1837 the membership of the Supreme Court had been set at nine. In 1863 a tenth place was added. Then, before a vacancy arising in May 1865 had been filled, an Act of 1866 stipulated that no further appointments were to be made so long as there were at least seven incumbent Justices. Finally, at the end of 1869, an Act restored the number of places to nine, at which figure it has since remained.

In February 1870, when the number of Justices had fallen to seven as the consequence of the Act of 1866, the Court decided, by four votes to three, that provisions of the wartime legislation under which the Federal Government had, for the first time, issued paper money as legal tender were beyond the powers of the Congress. On the same day, President Grant, who had been forewarned of the decision, nominated to the Court, under the Act of 1869, two men who believed the legal tender legislation to be constitutional. Not all of the Legal Tender Cases had been disposed of by the Supreme Court. In 1871 the two new Justices joined the three dissenters in the first case, to reverse the ruling of the previous year and sustain the legislation. This has been the only instance of a direct connection between appointments to the Supreme Court and an immediate reversal, desired by the President, of a recent invalidation of an Act.

Despite the weak position of the Supreme Court during the

Reconstruction period, the invalidation of Federal as well as State legislation became a routine feature of judicial review at this time. Prior to 1865 provisions of State Constitutions, State statutes or municipal ordinances had been held to conflict with the Federal Constitution in about forty cases, but provisions of Acts of the Congress had been declared unconstitutional in only three cases: the first unreported, the second relating to the Court's own jurisdiction and the third disastrous in its political effects. Between 1865 and 1885 Acts of the Congress were declared unconstitutional in fourteen cases (including the first Legal Tender Case), and State and local provisions in about eighty-five cases.

With respect to the federal division of powers Chief Justice Marshall (who served from 1801 to 1835) had led the Court in a sweeping definition of the powers of the Congress. The Court under Chief Justice Taney (who served from 1836 to 1864) had given more emphasis to States' rights. But in the sixty years before the Civil War, governments, especially the Federal Government, had used their powers sparingly. In the period of somewhat more active government thereafter, the Court's role as umpire of the federal division of powers grew apace.

However, in retrospect the Court's exercise of judicial review can be seen to have been governed until the late 1880s by a policy of judicial self-restraint. By far the greater part of governmental activity remained State and local; and, on the whole, the Court upheld State (including local) action against claims that it burdened interstate commerce or that it infringed constitutionally protected private rights. In Munn v. Illinois in 1877 the Court sustained the State's regulation of grain-warehouse charges against both claims, the latter invoking the reference to property in the due process clause of the Fourteenth Amendment. In his Opinion of the Court Chief Justice Waite held that property devoted to a public use becomes 'affected with a public interest' and may be controlled by regulatory legislation: 'For our purposes we must assume that, if a state of facts could exist that would justify such legislation, it actually did exist when the statute now under consideration was passed.' Beyond determining whether there was such a basis—usually referred to as a rational basis—for the legislation, the Court had no function: 'Of the propriety of legislative interference within the scope of the legislative power, the legislature is the exclusive judge. . . . For protection against abuses by legislatures the people must resort to the polls, not to the courts.'

The Court gave a narrow construction to constitutional protections of civil liberties: the substantive freedoms of belief and expression of opinions specified in the First Amendment of the Bill of Rights, procedural rights of accused persons and civil rights against unwarranted—in particular racial—discrimination. During Reconstruction the Congress enacted civil rights legislation to protect blacks. Its main constitutional basis was the final section of the Fourteenth Amendment empowering the Congress to enforce the provisions of the Amendment, one of which is the clause prohibiting a State from denying any person the equal protection of the laws. In 1883 the Civil Rights Acts were held unconstitutional in so far as they applied to discrimination by private persons. Likewise, judicial enforcement of the Fourteenth Amendment (and the Fifteenth) could be invoked only against direct State action.

In 1884 in the case of Hurtado v. California the Supreme Court upheld the power of the State to dispense with grand jury indictments, against the claim that the due process clause of the Fourteenth Amendment imposed on the States the requirement of grand jury indictment 'for a capital, or otherwise infamous crime' expressly imposed on the Federal Government by the Fifth Amendment of the Bill of Rights. The Court reasoned that the due process clause of the Fifth Amendment did not embrace any of the other rights specified in the Bill of Rights—for otherwise they would not have been specified—and that due process had the same meaning in the Fourteenth Amendment as in the Fifth. Therefore, the Hurtado Rule was that the due process clause of the Fourteenth Amendment did not apply to the States any of the other protections of civil liberties—substantive or procedural—of the Federal Bill of Rights.

1886–1936: 'dual federalism' and 'liberty of contract'

In 1886 the Court decided that it should no longer allow a State's regulation of railway rates to affect interstate commerce, even though there was no Federal regulation. The decision made State regulation ineffective. In 1887 the Congress entered the field by passing the first Interstate Commerce Act.

In other fields of commerce the Court created gaps in regulation which no government could adequately fill. Under Chief Justice Taney the Court had evolved a doctrine, first applied to invalidate Acts of the Congress in 1870 and 1871, to which, much later, was attached the label of 'dual federalism': not only did the constitutional grant of powers to the Congress define what had been reserved to the States, but also what had been reserved to the States defined what had been granted to the Congress. The doctrine was fully developed in the cases in 1918 and 1922 (cited in Chapter 2, Section B) in which the Court invalidated two Acts of the Congress, the first banning goods made by child labour from interstate commerce and the second taxing the employers of child labour, on the ground that the Acts invaded the reserved powers of the several States to regulate manufacturing within their borders. But a State prohibiting or penalizing the employment of child labour within its borders put its industry at a disadvantage in the common market created by the commerce clause. Thus, the 'dual federalism' decisions produced a twilight zone of economic activities which neither level of government could effectively regulate.

In 1886 the Court decided that a corporation was a 'person' protected by the due process clauses. Thereafter, it narrowed the scope of the Munn *v.* Illinois decision by setting stringent conditions for determining that a business was 'affected with a public interest' and thus susceptible to rate regulation, and by subjecting the reasonableness of the rates set by governmental regulation to judicial review. In requiring a 'fair return' on the value of the property involved, the Court created a substantive economic right protected by the due process clauses. In 1897 a substantive 'freedom' or 'liberty of contract' was also found to be protected by those clauses. Legislation setting maximum hours and minimum wages for work might be held to abridge the 'liberty of contract', as was legislation banning 'yellow dog' contracts (which required as a condition of employment that workers undertake not to join a trade union). Justice Oliver Wendell Holmes, Jr., who served on the Court from 1902 to 1932, dissenting, iterated the policy of judicial restraint.

When the political mood of the country was progressive, the decisions of the Court evoked much adverse criticism. The Court continued to hold to its main doctrines. But changes in its membership, responses to current political events and sentiments (to which Justices as members of the society can never be totally indifferent) and differences in the facts and the issues presented by counsel in the cases kept the doctrines from being so completely applied as to provoke a crisis of confidence like that following the Dred Scott decision of 1857 or that to come in 1936-7—at the cost of making the Court's decisions appear increasingly arbitrary. In defining the extent of the commerce power the Court sometimes gave a generous interpretation of the flow of commerce and the degree to which the Congress could regulate intrastate activities affecting it, and sometimes not. Munn v. Illinois was not overruled, but 'distinguished' from later cases greatly narrowing its scope—yet available to be followed when it suited the Court. In 1934 in Nebbia v. New York a bare majority of the Court held that any business might for adequate reason be regulated.

Having invalidated as contrary to the 'liberty of contract' a law setting maximum hours for men working in bakeries in Lochner v. New York in 1905 (after allowing a State's prescription of an eight-hour day for miners in 1898), the Court upheld a law setting maximum hours for women working in industrial establishments in Muller v. Oregon in 1908. Justice Brewer paid tribute in the Opinion of the Court in the Muller case to Louis D. Brandeis's brief, describing the effects of excessive labour on women. Brandeis was appointed to the Supreme Court in 1916, serving until 1939. In 1917 a State law setting maximum working hours for men and women, with provision for overtime at time-and-a-half, was upheld; and by dividing four to four (Brandeis had helped prepare the briefs before his appointment and therefore did not participate in either decision) the Court affirmed a State court decision sustaining a minimum wage law for women. But in 1923 in Adkins v. Children's Hospital the Court declared unconstitutional an Act of the Congress setting minimum wages for women and children in the District of Columbia.

To reverse decisions of the Court the Congress proposed two constitutional amendments to the States. In 1895 in the case of Pollock *v.* Farmers' Loan and Trust Company the Supreme Court, departing from precedents, found a Federal personal income tax law unconstitutional, primarily on the ground that parts of the tax were direct taxes within the meaning of Article I, Section 9, of the Constitution and had, therefore, to be apportioned among the States on the basis of population. The Sixteenth Amendment, overturning that ruling, was proposed by the Congress in 1909 and ratified by the necessary three-fourths of the States in 1913. In 1924 the Congress, having failed twice to get legislation against the use of child labour in manufacturing past the Supreme Court, proposed an Amendment permitting it to regulate or prohibit the labour of persons under eighteen years of age. The proposal failed to secure a sufficient number of ratifications among the States, and became unnecessary when the Supreme Court abandoned 'dual federalism' after 1937. The decision in the child labour case of 1918 was unanimously overruled in 1941.

1886–1936: 'separate but equal' facilities and 'fundamental' rights

In contrast with the rapid development from 1886 of the Court's protection of substantive economic rights was its continued refusal actively to protect civil liberties, in particular the civil rights of blacks, which the Fourteenth and Fifteenth Amendments had formally secured from infringement by the States. In 1896 in the case of Plessy *v.* Ferguson the Court held that a State law requiring railways to provide 'equal but separate'—later usually referred to as 'separate but equal'—facilities for whites and blacks did not violate the equal protection clause. In doing so the Court endorsed generally the policy of racial segregation that had been adopted by the former slave States; and in subsequent decisions specifically upheld segregation in other fields, such as education —even when, as in a case decided in 1899, a southern county provided assistance to high schools for whites but not for blacks.

Only from 1914 did the Court begin to look beneath the face of legislation affecting blacks. In 1914 it invalidated a State law under which railways provided grossly unequal separate facilities. In 1915 it invalidated the 'grandfather clause' of the Oklahoma Constitution, which set lower suffrage requirements for the lineal descendants of those who had voted for any form of government or lived abroad before the adoption of the Fifteenth Amendment than for other persons. In 1917 it disallowed a city zoning ordinance establishing racially exclusive residential districts, but in 1926 allowed private restrictive covenants to achieve the same effect. Likewise, in 1927 and 1932 the Court disallowed the Texas Democratic party's 'white primary' when based upon or authorized by State law, but in 1935 allowed it when maintained 'privately' by the party alone.

The First World War and the Bolshevik scare at the end of it gave rise to freedom of expression cases under the Espionage and Sedition Acts of 1917–18. The first case to reach the Supreme Court, Schenck v. United States, was decided in early 1919. Justice Holmes spoke for a unanimous Court in upholding Schenck's conviction, tested against the standard that the government must show that 'the words used are used in such circumstances and are of such a nature as to create a clear and present danger that they will bring about the substantive evils' which the government has a right to prevent. Later the same year, in Abrams v. United States, Justices Holmes and Brandeis dissented from a conviction on the ground that an immediate danger had not been proved: Holmes wrote an eloquent defence of 'free trade in ideas'. The majority of the Court did not use the 'clear and present danger' test to set aside a conviction in a freedom of expression case before 1937. Thereafter, the late Justice Holmes' advocacy of this test in that field, but only the rational basis test for governmental interference with economic activities, was taken up and broadened by the Court into a general policy of a double standard in judicial review.

In the first years of this century the Supreme Court had been called upon to decide to what extent the Constitution followed the flag into the newly acquired island territories of the United

States, with their non-Anglo-Saxon legal traditions: it was this issue that gave rise to a remark by Mr. Dooley (Finley Peter Dunne) that, whether the Constitution follows the flag or not, the Supreme Court follows the election returns. In the Insular Cases the Court ruled that constitutional protections of 'fundamental' rights, such as the prohibitions of bills of attainder and ex post facto laws, applied in all territories, but that specifications of 'formal' rights, such as the requirements of grand jury indictments and the right to trial by jury, did not apply unless and until the Congress had 'incorporated' a territory into the American system.

Two decades later the Court began to find a somewhat different set of 'fundamental' rights in the Bill of Rights, which, despite the Hurtado Rule, were henceforth to be protected from the States by the due process clause of the Fourteenth Amendment. The first intimation of this change came in a case in 1920. But the explicit breach of the Hurtado Rule was made in Gitlow *v.* New York in 1925, when Justice Sanford wrote in the Opinion of the Court that 'freedom of speech and of the press—which are protected by the First Amendment from abridgement by the Congress—are among the fundamental personal rights and "liberties" protected by the due process clause of the Fourteenth Amendment from impairment by the States.' The new approach was extended to a procedural right in Powell *v.* Alabama in 1932, when the poor, young, illiterate, black defendants charged with raping two white girls in the notorious 'Scottsboro case' were held to have been unconstitutionally denied due process of law when the State failed to provide them with counsel: the Sixth Amendment specifies a right to the assistance of counsel. (In 1935 the Supreme Court invalidated convictions in the 'Scottsboro case' a second time, because blacks had been systematically excluded from grand and petit juries in the counties where the indictment was found and the trial held.)

The breach of the Hurtado Rule has been the most important turning point in the history of constitutional law relating to substantive freedoms and procedural rights. For the States (and their localities), in exercising their 'police power' to preserve the peace, health, safety, morals and general welfare of their communities,

L

regularly impinge on substantive freedoms. Moreover, States initiate the vast majority of prosecutions, usually against the sorts of
persons most in need of protection of their procedural rights from
law enforcement agencies. There are disproportionate numbers of
the poor and especially poor blacks (such as the 'Scottsboro boys')
among defendants: there is, therefore, a strong civil rights element
in the protection of procedural rights. While the due process
clause of the Fourteenth Amendment had always been held to
require that the accused have his day in an impartial court, the
Supreme Court did not begin to set anything but the most rudimentary standards of basic due process of law for State criminal
justice until it started also to measure it against specific procedural
requirements in the Bill of Rights. The first case in which a conviction was set aside under the due process clause on the ground
that the defendant's confession had been coerced was Brown v.
Mississippi in 1936.

The constitutional crisis of 1937 and judicial review thereafter

Between 1886 and 1933 the Supreme Court declared Acts of the
Congress unconstitutional in forty-five cases in forty-eight years.
Between 1934 and 1936 it declared Acts of the Congress unconstitutional in thirteen cases in three years—and also State and
local laws unconstitutional in thirty-six cases, an average number
per year about twice that since 1886. Major Acts of the New Deal
inaugurated by President Franklin D. Roosevelt in 1933 were
invalidated.

Two decisions in 1936 were especially provocative politically.
In United States v. Butler the Court, by six votes to three, invoking 'dual federalism' to restrict the spending power of the
Congress for the first time, declared the Agricultural Adjustment
Act of 1933 to be an unconstitutional invasion of the reserved
powers of the States. This decision destroyed the basis of the
Federal Government's agricultural policy and threatened other
major spending programmes of the New Deal. Justice Stone, in a
biting dissent, wrote that 'while unconstitutional exercise of
power by the executive and legislative branches of the govern-

ment is subject to judicial restraint, the only check upon our own exercise of power is our own sense of self-restraint. . . . Courts are not the only agency of government that must be assumed to have capacity to govern.' In Morehead *v*. New York *ex rel*. Tipaldo the Court, by five votes to four, followed the Adkins case of 1923 in invalidating a law setting minimum wages for women and children. Expectations that recent cases like Nebbia *v*. New York indicated a re-emergence of Chief Justice Waite's policy of judicial restraint in reviewing governmental regulation of private economic activities were thus disappointed.

Since becoming President in 1933, Roosevelt had not had a chance to appoint a member of the Supreme Court. He was the only President other than James Monroe, over a century before, to serve a full four years after first taking office without making even a single appointment. The normal process that ensures that the Supreme Court does not get too far behind (or ahead) of the election returns had thus not operated at all since major changes had taken place in American government and politics.

In 1937 the President proposed that the Congress provide for the appointment of six new Justices to sit with the existing nine, six of whom were over seventy years of age and had served for more than ten years, or to replace any of those six who could be induced to retire under new, generous pension arrangements. This Court-'packing' Plan was defeated in the Senate. But in the midst of the constitutional crisis produced by it, the Court, in the case of West Coast Hotel Company *v*. Parrish, upheld a minimum wage law for women and children, overruling the Adkins case in a five to four decision, with Justice Roberts on the other side from the year before: 'A switch in time saved nine.' In the Opinion of the Court Chief Justice Hughes declared that 'the Constitution does not speak of freedom of contract.' Furthermore, one of the anti-New Deal Justices announced his retirement.

The membership of the Court changed rapidly thereafter. By the end of 1941 seven of the eight Associate Justices were Roosevelt's appointees; and the Chief Justice was Harlan F. Stone, appointed to the Supreme Court by President Coolidge as an Associate Justice in 1925 and appointed by Roosevelt to succeed Hughes upon the latter's retirement in July 1941. By that time 'dual federalism', 'liberty of contract' and the judicial protection of other substantive economic rights had all gone.

With respect to the federal division of powers, the Court went back to the judgements of Chief Justice Marshall, rendered when governments made very little use of their powers, in a situation in which governments were making much more use of their powers than ever before. In 1942 in Wickard v. Filburn Justice Jackson spoke for a unanimous Court in holding that an Ohio dairy and poultry farmer who raised wheat most of which was consumed on his own farm was nevertheless subject to the commerce power of the Congress to regulate wheat. For, even if none of the wheat had been 'intended for interstate commerce or intermingled with the subjects thereof', the farmer's activity affected, however minutely, the supply-demand nexus for wheat in the United States. This decision was based on the case of Gibbons v. Ogden in 1824, in which, by declaring that the commerce power extended to any activity affecting more than one State, 'Chief Justice Marshall described the Federal commerce power with a breadth never yet exceeded. . . . He made emphatic the embracing and penetrating nature of this power by warning that effective restraints on its exercise must proceed from political rather than from judicial processes.'

While judicial restrictions on the extent to which the Congress might exercise its regulatory, taxing and spending powers in the federal system were thus removed, the Supreme Court continued to protect interstate commerce from discriminatory or unduly burdensome regulation and taxation by the States. In the case of South Carolina State Highway Department v. Barnwell Brothers in 1938 the Court allowed the State to add to Federal regulation of interstate road hauliers restrictions on the size of vehicles and weight of loads on its highways. But in a footnote to his Opinion of the Court Justice Stone appended the *obiter dictum* (a statement not necessary for deciding the instant case) that State action must still sometimes be restrained by judicial processes, because 'when the regulation is of such a character that its burden falls principally on those without the State, legislative action is not likely to be subjected to those political restraints which are normally exerted on legislation where it affects adversely some interests

within the State.' In 1945 in Southern Pacific Company *v.*
Arizona the Court did not allow the State to add to Federal
safety measures for interstate railways limits on the lengths of
trains within its boundaries. In the Opinion of the Court Chief
Justice Stone wrote that 'where Congress has not acted, this
Court, and not the State legislature, is under the commerce
clause the final arbiter of the competing demands of State and
national interests.' However, since 1937 the Court has on the
whole permitted State regulation and non-discriminatory taxation
to impinge more than previously on interstate commerce and
other concerns of the Federal Government, subject to the power
of the Congress, representing the people of all the States, to
redefine the boundaries of the permissible either way.

With respect to governmental actions affecting private persons,
the Court adopted a policy of a double standard in judicial
review—also enunciated as *obiter dictum* in a footnote to an Opinion
of the Court by Justice Stone in 1938—in accordance with which
the Court has distinguished between general economic and social
regulation on the one hand and actions impinging on civil
liberties on the other. In sustaining an Act of the Congress prohibiting the shipment of adulterated milk, in the case of United
States *v.* Carolene Products Company in 1938, Stone wrote for the
Court that 'regulatory legislation affecting ordinary commercial
transactions is not to be pronounced unconstitutional unless in the
light of the facts made known or generally assumed it is of such a
character as to preclude the assumption that it rests upon some
rational basis within the knowledge and experience of the legislators.' In footnote 4 of the Opinion, attached to this statement of
the rational basis test, Stone listed the circumstances in which
legislation might be subjected to more exacting judicial scrutiny:
the circumstances involved substantive freedoms, procedural
rights and civil rights; in short, civil liberties.

Between 1937 and 1942 there were no cases in which the
Supreme Court declared Federal legislation unconstitutional. Between 1943 and July 1976 (the end of the 1975–6 term) there
were thirty-seven. In most instances the initiative for the invalidated provisions had come from within the Congress rather
than, as is now usual for major Federal legislation, from the

President. In all cases but two legislative provisions were invalidated on the ground that they infringed the Bill of Rights or civil liberties specified or implied elsewhere in the Constitution (such as the right to retain citizenship acquired under the Fourteenth Amendment). The two exceptions were: the declaration in Oregon *v.* Mitchell in 1970 that the provision of the Voting Rights Act of that year lowering the voting age to eighteen in State and local elections exceeded the powers of the Congress—the Twenty-sixth Amendment, adopted in 1971, accomplished the result invalidly anticipated by the Act; and the declaration in National League of Cities *v.* Usery in June 1976 that the 1974 amendments extending the requirements of an otherwise valid national minimum wage and maximum hours statute to almost all employees of State and local governments interfered unconstitutionally with the functioning of those governments in the federal system. Moreover, in Buckley *v.* Valeo in January 1976, in which some parts of Federal legislation controlling expenditures in campaigns for presidential nominations and elections were held unconstitutional on civil liberty grounds, the composition of the regulatory Federal Election Commission as created in 1974—its six voting members nominated two each by the President, the Speaker of the House of Representatives and the President pro tempore of the Senate, and subject to confirmation by both Houses of Congress—was held to violate the constitutional separation of powers.

State (including local) actions continue to give rise to the great majority of cases involving claims that civil liberties have been impaired. The Supreme Court's protection of civil liberties has become by far the most frequently invoked aspect of its exercise of judical supremacy over the States.

C: THE SUPREME COURT'S
PROTECTION OF CIVIL LIBERTIES

In footnote 4 of his Opinion of the Court in the Carolene Products

Company case in 1938 Justice Stone defined three circumstances in which the Supreme Court might be expected to qualify its normal presumption of the constitutionality of legislation. The first was 'when legislation appears on its face to be within a specific prohibition of the Constitution, such as those of the first ten amendments, which are deemed equally specific when held to be embraced within the Fourteenth'. The second was when 'legislation . . . restricts those political processes which can ordinarily be expected to bring about repeal of undesirable legislation'. Examples of the political processes to be protected were the suffrage and the dissemination of information. The third circumstance was when legislation is 'directed at particular religious . . . or national . . . or racial minorities'. For 'prejudice against discrete and insular minorities . . . tends seriously to curtail the operation of those political processes ordinarily to be relied upon to protect minorities.'

Regard for the specific provisions—the words—of the Constitution, like the doctrine of *stare decisis* (following precedent), guides the Justices' conduct so as to make constitutional law more certain and stable, and not simply what at any given moment they say it is. But, in adapting the law of a Constitution difficult to amend to changing circumstances, the Supreme Court has directly over-ruled its own decisions nearly as many times as it has set aside Acts of the Congress; and it has not consistently related the stringency of judicial review of governmental actions to the specificity of the prohibitions of the Constitution which the actions are alleged to violate. In enforcing the specific prohibition against a State passing any 'Law impairing the Obligation of Contracts' the Court now allows any legislation that is 'reasonable'. It protects absolutely the right of a woman to request an abortion during the first three months of pregnancy, as an aspect of a 'right to privacy' not mentioned in the Constitution.

Stone's reference to the specific prohibitions of the Bill of Rights gave the impression that the Court would continue to protect the 'human' rights of individuals, such as the freedoms of belief and expression and the procedural rights of accused persons, while no longer invoking the general requirement of due process of law to protect substantive 'property' rights. However, throughout footnote 4, Stone made no explicit mention of the fact that in implementing its theory of judicial review the Court would be protecting the rights of individuals. In the aftermath of the constitutional crisis of 1937 he attempted in his footnotes in the Barnwell (see the previous section) and the Carolene cases to make the definition of the exercise of judicial supremacy consonant with the democratic language of 'majority rule and minority rights'. The Supreme Court should accept the outcomes of the ordinary political processes except when the processes did not effectively operate or the outcomes jeopardized their effective operation. Therefore, except when State action affected national interests, the Court should not protect economic rights. It should enhance democracy by protecting civil liberties.

Freedom

The Supreme Court's active promotion of civil liberties in the late 1930s and 1940s largely accorded with Stone's theory. It was associated especially with the freedoms of belief and expression and the political rights of minorities. In deciding whether statutes and other governmental regulations affecting the freedom of expression dealt only with circumstances in which there was a clear and present danger of evils that governments may prevent, the Justices considered not only the instant cases but also any conceivable cases that might be brought. For 'where regulations of the liberty of free discussion are concerned . . .', Justice Murphy wrote in the Opinion of the Court in Thornhill v. Alabama in 1940, 'it is the statute, and not the accusation or the evidence under it, which prescribes the limits of permissible conduct and warns against transgression.'

Since 1938 the Jehovah's Witnesses have appealed many cases to the Supreme Court involving the exercise of their religion and their dissemination of propaganda (often virulently abusive of other religious groups). They are, indeed, a discrete and insular minority relatively unprotected by the ordinary political processes, in which they refuse to participate. They have usually won in the Supreme Court. In 1943 in West Virginia State Board of Education v. Barnette the Court declared unconstitutional a compulsory flag salute in local schools, overruling a decision the other way taken only three years before: both cases involved Jehovah's Witnesses. Justice Jackson wrote in the Opinion of the Court that 'the action of the local authorities in compelling the flag salute and pledge . . . invades the sphere of intellect and spirit which it is the purpose of the First Amendment to our Constitution to reserve from all official control.' (In applying the prohibitions of the First Amendment through the due process clause of the Fourteenth, Justices often speak as though the First Amendment applied directly to the States.)

In 1944 in the case of Korematsu v. United States the Supreme Court upheld the Federal Government's removal of American citizens of Japanese descent from the West coast for their internment in 'War Relocation Centres'. During the Chief Justiceship of Fred M. Vinson, who succeeded Stone in 1946 and was succeeded by Earl Warren in 1953, the Court weakened its protection of the freedom of expression under the pressures of the 'Cold War', most notably in the case of Dennis v. United States in 1951, upholding the conviction of eleven Communist party leaders for conspiring to teach and advocate the overthrow of the government by force. However, in 1957 the Court required that anyone charged with that offence be shown to have advocated unlawful action, not merely abstract doctrine.

Generally, the 'Warren Court' returned to applying exacting tests to governmental restrictions on the freedom of expression (though the phrase 'clear and present danger' dropped out of use). In many cases the expressions of opinion consisted largely of conduct other than pure speech. In those arising from 'sit-in' demonstrations against racial segregation in privately owned accommodations for the public, such as restaurants, the Court set aside the convictions of demonstrators. But as the demonstrations spread to other issues and took other forms the Court made it clear that there were more grounds for governments' regulating and punishing conduct than speech alone. In 1968 in United States v. O'Brien the Court affirmed O'Brien's conviction for burning his draft card as a protest against the war in Vietnam.

In 1976 in the case of Elrod v. Burns, arising from the patronage politics of Cook County, Illinois, the Supreme Court held that the discharge of a non-policymaking, non-confidential governmental employee who was satisfactorily performing his job solely on the ground of his political beliefs unconstitutionally violated the freedoms of belief and association protected by the First and Fourteenth amendments.

In 1947 the Court had completed the process begun in 1925 of embracing the prohibitions of the First Amendment in the Fourteenth, by declaring that the ban on the establishment of religion applies to the States as well as the Congress. This restricts but does not altogether prevent aid to parochial education. However, it requires governments to be neutral towards religious ideas, whether denominational or non-denominational, whereas they need not be neutral towards other ideas. There can be voluntary, though not compulsory, flag salutes and pledges in local schools. But there can be no school prayers—so held in Engel v. Vitale in 1962—or bible readings—so held in Abington School District v. Schempp in 1963.

Race

By 1944 the Court had ruled against 'private' white primaries: a State may not nullify the constitutional prohibition against racial discrimination in the suffrage by casting its electoral process in a form that permits parties effectively to discriminate. In 1948 judicial enforcement of racially restrictive covenants was prohibited: Chief Justice Vinson's Opinion of the Court in Shelley v. Kraemer marked a transition from the language of 'majority rule and minority rights', which Stone had used in defining the judicial function, to that of the claims of society and the individual, which became characteristic of the Court's approach to questions of civil liberty thereafter. It had been argued that the courts would enforce restrictive covenants against whites as well as those against blacks, so there was no discrimination against members of a particular race. Vinson noted that no case had been cited 'in which a court, State or Federal, has been called upon to enforce a covenant excluding members of the white majority. . . . But there are more fundamental considerations. The rights created by the first section of the Fourteenth Amendment are, by its terms, guaranteed to the individual. . . . Equal protection of the laws is not achieved through indiscriminate imposition of inequalities.'

The Supreme Court's growing protection of the civil rights of blacks was invoked in cases taken up by the National Association for the Advancement of Coloured People: in that of Brown *v.* Board of Education of Topeka the Justices decided unanimously in May 1954 that racial segregation in governmentally provided schools was unconstitutional. 'In these days', Chief Justice Warren wrote in the Opinion of the Court, 'it is doubtful that any child may reasonably be expected to succeed in life if he is denied the opportunity of an education. Such an opportunity, where the State has undertaken to provide it, is a right which must be made available to all on equal terms. . . . Does segregation of children in public schools solely on the basis of race, even though the physical facilities and other "tangible" factors may be equal, deprive the children of the minority group of equal educational opportunities? We believe that it does. . . . To separate them from others of similar age and qualifications solely because of their race generates a feeling of inferiority as to their status in the community that may affect their hearts and minds in a way unlikely ever to be undone.'

The Court delayed issuing decrees implementing its decision for a year. Then, in the second Brown case in 1955, it remanded the cases affected by the decision to the courts which originally heard them, 'to . . . enter such orders and decrees . . . as are necessary and proper to admit to public schools on a racially nondiscriminatory basis with all deliberative speed the parties to these cases.'

The decision in the first Brown case effectively put an end to the 'separate but equal' doctrine with respect to any facilities provided or supported by governments. In 1964 in Heart of Atlanta Motel *v.* United States the Supreme Court upheld the Civil Rights Act of that year, prohibiting discrimination in all accommodations for the public coming within the broad reach of the interstate commerce power. In 1968 in Jones *v.* Mayer it construed the Civil Rights Act of 1866 as barring all racial discrimination in the sale or rental of property, and upheld it as a valid exercise of the power of the Congress to enforce the Thirteenth Amendment outlawing slavery: indirect methods of striking at private racially restrictive covenants, as in Shelley *v.* Kraemer, were no longer necessary.

Following the second Brown case, the Supreme Court has invalidated all devices to maintain any form of '*de jure* segregation' of the races in education. Shortly after Warren E. Burger succeeded Earl Warren as Chief Justice in 1969, the Court held unanimously in Alexander *v.* Holmes County Board of Education that 'all deliberative speed' in desegregation was no longer constitutionally permissible: the school authorities must terminate any remaining dual systems at once.

In order to overcome '*de facto* segregation' in schools, arising from the existence of separate white and black residential areas in a school district or metropolitan region, lower courts have ordered school authorities to 'bus' children to schools outside their neighbourhoods so as to achieve racially mixed schools. In 1971 the Supreme Court unanimously upheld such a 'busing' order for a single school district in North Carolina against the background of a history of segregation. In 1973 and 1974 a divided Court did not sustain 'cross-district busing' orders between central cities and their suburbs involving Richmond, Virginia, and Detroit, Michigan. The Opinion of the Court in the latter case explained that it had not been shown that there was an inter-district pattern of segregation or a deliberate drawing of district lines on the basis of race. But in 1975 the Court upheld a Federal court's 'cross-district busing' order setting aside the State of Delaware's attempt to isolate the predominantly black Wilmington City School District.

Sex

In 1968 the Supreme Court held that governmental discrimination against illegitimate children was an invidious classification violating the Constitution's equal protection requirement. In 1971 in the case of Reed *v.* Reed the Court for the first time declared unconstitutional a regulatory statute discriminating against women. However, a majority of Justices, while demanding more than just a rational basis for governmental classifications by sex, do not regard them as inherently suspect or invidious, and therefore subject to the exacting standard of judicial review applied to racial classifications.

In March 1972 the Congress proposed an amendment to the Constitution that would explicitly prohibit governments from abridging equality of rights on account of sex; but it has not been ratified by three-fourths of the States, as required by the Constitution for adoption. In proposing the amendment the Congress set March 1979 as the adoption deadline.

Law enforcement

Before 1961, of the procedural rights in the Bill of Rights, only the implied underlying requirement of a fair trial and the specific rights to the assistance of counsel (though in capital cases only) and to a public trial had been held to be embraced within the due process clause of the Fourteenth Amendment. Starting in 1961, within a few years the great majority of the procedural rights were held to be embraced within it and applied fully to the States: the restriction of the right to the assistance of counsel to capital cases only was removed in Gideon v. Wainwright in 1963. Probably the only reason the whole Bill of Rights was not simply incorporated in the Fourteenth Amendment was the wish of a majority of the Justices to avoid requiring the States to use grand jury indictments and to provide the right to trial by jury in suits at common law. The Hurtado Rule has long since gone. The Hurtado decision still stands.

Since 1936 the Court had set aside coerced confessions as violations of basic due process of law. In 1964 the Fifth Amendment's specific prohibition against compelling a person to be a witness against himself was held to apply to the States. The Supreme Court laid down stringent conditions for law enforcement agencies to meet when people were—to use the British euphemism—helping the police with their enquiries. For a long train of abuses by the police, referred to by Chief Justice Warren in his Opinion of the Court in Miranda v. Arizona in 1966, led the majority of Justices to conclude that 'unless a proper limitation upon custodial interrogation is achieved . . . there can be no assurance that practices of this nature will be eradicated in the forseeable future.' The Court prohibited interrogation of a suspect in custody, without his consent, unless a defence lawyer is present.

President Nixon's appointees to the Supreme Court tipped its balance towards relaxing the standards that law enforcement agencies have to meet in obtaining convictions. In Harris *v.* New York in 1971 Chief Justice Burger wrote in the Opinion of the Court that, while the Miranda decision barred the use of a statement made by the accused in custody, before he had or had waived counsel, in the direct case against him, 'some statements in the Miranda opinion . . . indicating a bar to use of an uncounseled statement for any purpose . . . cannot be regarded as controlling': an improperly obtained statement can be used in cross-examination to impeach the credibility of the testimony of the accused in his own defence. At the end of its 1975–6 term— during which President Ford's appointee, John Stevens, joined two appointees (William Brennan and Potter Stewart) of President Eisenhower, one appointee (Byron White) of President Kennedy, one (Thurgood Marshall) of President Johnson and four appointees (Burger, Harry Blackmun, Lewis Powell and William Rehnquist) of President Nixon—the Supreme Court took another major step in its move away from rigorous review of law enforcement procedures, by ruling, six to three, in Stone *v.* Powell that the Federal courts need not grant habeas corpus relief to a State prisoner (see Chapter 9, Section B) on the ground that evidence for his trial was unconstitutionally seized, when the State has provided an opportunity for full and fair litigation of the claim of mistrial. On the other hand, the Court under Chief Justice Burger has extended the rulings of the 'Warren Court' protecting poor persons from being disadvantaged by rules and practices of the administration of justice.

Elections

In 1962 in the case of Baker *v.* Carr the Supreme Court held that the issue of whether the apportionment of electoral districts for a legislature violates the equal protection of the laws is justiciable. It had previously been regarded as a 'political question' into which the Court should not enter. By mid-1964 the Court re-

quired the States to apportion representation in each house of the
State legislature and in the United States House of Representatives so that in each scheme of apportionment the electoral
districts of the State are as nearly of equal population as is practicable. Later the requirement was extended to elections for local
authorities, although voting rights in special-purpose authorities
in which only particular groups are involved may be related to
other relevant criteria.

Of course, the Court pointed out that it was protecting the
rights of the majority from the minority rule that had been entrenched in the long-standing systems of apportionment it invalidated. But in Lucas v. Colorado General Assembly in 1964 it was
made clear that majorities no more than minorities may deprive
an individual of the right to equality in the value of his vote: the
Court struck down a scheme of apportionment for one house of
the State legislature which provided for some deliberate over-
representation of sparsely populated counties in mountainous
parts of the State, even though the scheme had been approved in
a referendum by majorities of those voting in every county of the
State and it was possible for the electorate to employ the device
of initiative against its continuance.

Privacy

In its decisions protecting civil liberties the Supreme Court
made increasing reference to a constitutionally protected sphere
of privacy for the individual. The constitutional prohibitions
against unreasonable searches and seizures and self-incrimination
have long been held to define a right of privacy in one's person
and household. 'The place of religion in our society', Justice
Clark wrote in the Opinion of the Court in the Schempp case in
1963, 'is . . . [in] the home, the church and the inviolable citadel
of the individual heart and mind. . . . it is not within the power of
government to invade that citadel.' The Court has never accorded
the dissemination of what can be defined as obscene materials the
protection of the First Amendment; but obscenity in the privacy
of one's home has been accorded the status of religious belief: 'If
the First Amendment means anything,' Justice Marshall wrote in

the Opinion of the Court in Stanley *v.* Georgia in 1969, 'it means that a State has no business telling a man, sitting alone in his own house, what books he may read or what films he may watch. Our whole constitutional heritage rebels at the thought of giving government the power to control men's minds.'

In 1965 in Griswold *v.* Connecticut the State's anti-contraceptive birth control laws were invalidated for infringing a 'right of privacy', though the Justices in the majority in this seven-to-two decision could not quite determine how to relate it to the specific prohibitions of the Constitution and their 'penumbras'. In 1973 in Roe *v.* Wade the right of privacy came definitely to rest in the most protean clause of the Constitution as an aspect of life, liberty or property protected by the requirement for due process of law. By seven votes to two the Court held, in an Opinion written by Justice Blackmun, that the right included the decision of a woman to have an abortion, which could not be restricted at all by government until 'at some point the State interests as to protection of health, medical standards, and prenatal life, become dominant'. This point, 'in the light of present medical knowledge, is at approximately the end of the first trimester' of pregnancy.

Equality

Just as several lines of decisions contributed to the right of privacy, others appeared to be establishing a constitutional requirement for governments to provide an equality of basic opportunities for their citizens. In 1966, in holding in Harper *v.* Virginia Board of Elections that a poll tax for State elections was unconstitutional, Justice Douglas wrote in the Opinion of the Court that 'wealth, like race, creed, or colour is not germane to one's ability to participate intelligently in the electoral process. . . . where fundamental rights and liberties are asserted under the equal protection clause, classifications which might invade or restrain them must be closely scrutinized and carefully confined.'

In 1969 in Shapiro *v.* Thompson a requirement of one year's residence in a State for welfare assistance was held contrary to equal protection, since the classification of welfare applicants by length of residence touched upon the fundamental right to move among the States; and in 1970 in Goldberg v. Kelley the termination of welfare benefits without a prior hearing was held contrary to due process. Justice Brennan wrote both Opinions of the Court. In Shapiro, replying to the argument that the classification took into account that old residents were more likely than new to have paid taxes to the State, he delivered the *obiter dictum* that the equal protection clause prohibits an apportionment of State services according to the past tax contributions of citizens. In Goldberg, he drew attention to the 'human' aspects of the 'right' to welfare assistance: 'Welfare, by meeting the basic demands of subsistence, can help bring within the reach of the poor the same opportunities that are available to others to participate meaningfully in the life of the community.'

Thereafter, the Court drew back in most cases from subjecting welfare regulations to exacting constitutional tests. Moreover, in 1973 in San Antonio School District v. Rodriguez the Supreme Court reversed a lower Federal court's decision that disparities in expenditure per pupil in the schools of a State, arising from a heavy reliance on local property taxes, violated the equal protection clause. Although in the first Brown case Chief Justice Warren had declared that the opportunity of an education, 'where the State has undertaken to provide it, is a right which must be made available to all on equal terms', Justice Powell in his Opinion of the Court held that education is not among the rights afforded explicit or implicit protection under the Federal Constitution. By the narrowest of margins—five votes to four, with all four of President Nixon's appointees among the majority—the Supreme Court thus refrained from another major attack on long-standing governmental practices in the exercise of its judicial supremacy to protect civil liberties. (Some State courts have subsequently held disparities in financing schools to violate provisions of their State Constitutions. In other States the legislatures have provided for more equalization.)

The impact of the Supreme Court's decisions

The lower Federal and the State courts are expected to follow the controlling decisions of the Supreme Court on Federal questions.

M

However, they may finally dispose of the cases upon which the Supreme Court has directly ruled, in the exercise of its appellate jurisdiction over them, so that the parties who successfully invoked that jurisdiction lose in the end: four of the nine defendants in the 'Scottsboro case' were ultimately convicted, with the lightest sentences for seventy-five years' imprisonment. Such outcomes are not inconsistent with accepting the Supreme Court's rulings on the issues it has decided. Other cases may be 'distinguished' from the precedents. Outright defiance is normally rare. But in a hierarchy lacking the usual administrative sanctions—in the last resort the Supreme Court can cite a defiant judge for contempt— the decisions of the highest court are fully implemented only when the lower courts really accept them, however reluctantly, as the law of the land.

That is true not only of the lower courts. When majorities in the Congress and the President continue to want legislation that has been declared unconstitutional, their typical response has been to try again, usually attempting to make the new legislation more palatable to the Supreme Court. Usually they soon succeed, often helped by changes in the membership of the Court. The longest wait was between the Supreme Court's invalidation in 1918 of the Act of 1916 banning goods made by child labour from interstate commerce and the overruling of that decision in 1941. For any constitutional doctrine of the Supreme Court to become firmly established, it must cease to be challenged by the political branches of the Federal Government.

Prior to 1937 the main impact of the Supreme Court's constitutional decisions was on legislation regulating private economic activities which, if the legislation was invalidated, continued as before. In protecting civil liberties since 1937 the Court's impact has been much more on such basic operations of governments as their permitting or restricting opportunities for expressing ideas (by speakers alleged to be 'red' or films alleged to be 'blue'), maintaining schools, conducting elections and preserving law and order. Compliance with the decisions has required changes in behaviour throughout the governmental and political systems.

The decisions of the Supreme Court on racial issues helped to lead to the first civil rights legislation passed by the Congress since Reconstruction, starting with the Civil Rights Act of 1957. But it was the new legislation, especially the Civil Rights Act of 1964 and the Voting Rights Act of 1965, which provided the Federal authorities with the sanctions—to withhold grants-in-aid to school districts; and themselves to register voters—that brought about the first substantial amount of desegregation of schools in the South and the registration of a majority of blacks of voting age in the Deep South. (The District of Columbia, the six States bordering the South and the school districts in three other States —such as Topeka, Kansas – which had segregated school systems in 1954 had quickly complied with the Brown decisions; and the registration of black voters had increased substantially, especially in the Outer South, from 1944.) By 1974 46 per cent of black schoolchildren in the South attended schools with predominantly white enrolments; elsewhere (owing to *de facto* segregation in the large metropolitan areas) fewer than 30 per cent.

By mid-1969 a proposal that a constitutional convention be called, to overrule by amendment decisions of the Supreme Court relating to the apportionment of State legislatures, had apparently obtained over the years since 1963 the support of all but one of the two-thirds of the State legislatures required by Article V of the Constitution. But spokesmen for those who would benefit electorally from reapportionment according to present population had quickly initiated proceedings, once Baker *v.* Carr had made the issue of apportionment justiciable in 1962. Even by 1966, nearly all the States had moved to comply with the apportionment rulings. The election returns followed the Supreme Court.

In contrast, the decisions banning prayers and bible readings from local schools have had few active friends. Consequently, they have been ignored in many communities, especially in the 'Bible Belt'. However, they have been more widely obeyed, usually simply because they are the law of land.

The 'Warren Court's' insistence that poor criminal defendants be provided with counsel met with a ready response. But its attempts to impose new standards in law enforcement generally met with strong resistance. Decisions 'in favour of criminals' are not popular, especially in a period of rising violence. By 1965, according to the Gallup Poll, nearly half the public thought the courts were too lenient with criminal defendants; by 1968, nearly two-thirds. In the Omnibus Crime Control and Safe Streets Act of 1968 the Congress endeavoured largely to nullify decisions like Miranda *v.* Arizona. In the 1968 presidential election Richard M. Nixon promised in his judicial appointments to redress the balance between 'the forces of peace and the forces of crime'. In 1971 in Harris *v.* New York the Supreme Court began to narrow the application of the Miranda opinion.

Some police forces attempted genuinely to comply with the 'Warren Court's' rulings. But token compliance was more common, and usually not very difficult. When a decision of the Supreme Court in 1961 made evidence inadmissible in State courts if it had been obtained by an improper search without warrant of a suspect's person and belongings, the number of cases in which the New York City police reported finding narcotics hidden on suspects was reduced by five-sixths in five years: however, the number of cases in which they reported that the drugs had been visible to them—for example, dropped by the suspect—increased very greatly. In 1968 in Terry *v.* Ohio the Supreme Court upheld the right of a police officer to stop and 'frisk' a suspect whose conduct leads the officer 'reasonably to conclude in light of his experience that criminal activity may be afoot'. In the Opinion of the Court Chief Justice Warren approached 'the issues in this case mindful of the limitations of the judicial function in controlling the myriad daily situations in which policemen and citizens confront each other on the street. . . . No judicial system can comprehend the protean variety of the street encounter . . .'. In other words, a good deal of law remains at the end of a policeman's nightstick.

FOR FURTHER READING:

Henry J. Abraham, *Freedom and the Court*, 2nd ed. (O.U.P., 1972).

Joel B. Grossman and Richard S. Wells, *Constitutional Law and Judicial Policy Making* (Wiley, 1972).

Bernard Schwartz, *A Basic History of the U.S. Supreme Court* (Van Nostrand, 1968).

H. Frank Way, Jr., *Liberty in the Balance*, 3rd ed. (McGraw-Hill, 1971).

Appendix: The Constitution of the United States

We the People of the United States, in Order to form a more perfect Union, establish Justice, insure domestic Tranquility, provide for the common defence, promote the general Welfare, and secure the Blessings of Liberty to ourselves and our Posterity, do ordain and establish this Constitution for the United States of America.

Article I

Section 1. All legislative Powers herein granted shall be vested in a Congress of the United States, which shall consist of a Senate and House of Representatives.

Section 2. The House of Representatives shall be composed of Members chosen every second Year by the People of the several States, and the Electors in each State shall have the Qualifications requisite for Electors of the most numerous Branch of the State Legislature.

No Person shall be a Representative who shall not have attained to the Age of twenty-five Years, and been seven Years a Citizen of the United States, and who shall not, when elected, be an Inhabitant of that State in which he shall be chosen.

Representatives and direct Taxes shall be apportioned among the several States which may be included within this Union, according to their respective Numbers, which shall be determined by adding to the whole Number of free Persons, including those bound to Service for a Term of Years, and excluding Indians not taxed, three fifths of all other Persons. The actual Enumeration shall be made within three Years after the first Meeting of the Congress of the United States, and within every subsequent Term of ten Years, in such Manner as they shall by Law direct. The Number of Representatives shall not exceed one for every thirty Thousand, but each State shall have at Least one Representative; and until such enumeration shall be made, the State of New Hampshire shall be entitled to chuse three, Massachusetts eight, Rhode-Island and Providence Plantations one, Connecticut five, New-York six, New Jersey four, Pennsylvania eight, Delaware one, Maryland six, Virginia ten, North Carolina five, South Carolina five, and Georgia three.

When vacancies happen in the Representation from any State, the Executive Authority thereof shall issue Writs of Election to fill such Vacancies.

The House of Representatives shall chuse their speaker and other Officers; and shall have the sole Power of Impeachment.

Section 3. The Senate of the United States shall be composed of two Senators from each State, chosen by the Legislature thereof, for six Years; and each Senator shall have one Vote.

Immediately after they shall be assembled in Consequence of the first Election, they shall be divided as equally as may be into three Classes. The Seats of the Senators of the first Class shall be vacated at the Expiration of the second Year, of the second Class at the Expiration of the fourth Year, and of the third Class at the Expiration of the sixth Year, so that one third may be chosen every second Year; and if Vacancies happen by Resignation, or otherwise, during the Recess of the Legislature of any State, the Executive thereof may make temporary Appointments until the next Meeting of the Legislature, which shall then fill such Vacancies.

No Person shall be a Senator who shall not have attained to the Age of thirty Years, and been nine Years a Citizen of the United States, and who shall not, when elected, be an Inhabitant of that State for which he shall be chosen.

The Vice President of the United States shall be President of the Senate, but shall have no Vote, unless they be equally divided.

The Senate shall chuse their other Officers, and also a President pro tempore, in the Absence of the Vice President, or when he shall exercise the Office of President of the United States.

The Senate shall have the sole Power to try all Impeachments. When sitting for that Purpose, they shall be on Oath or Affirmation. When the President of the United States is tried, the Chief Justice shall preside: And no Person shall be convicted without the Concurrence of two thirds of the Members present.

Judgment in Cases of Impeachment shall not extend further than to removal from Office, and disqualification to hold and enjoy any Office of honor, Trust or Profit under the United States: but the Party convicted shall nevertheless be liable and subject to Indictment, Trial, Judgment and Punishment, according to law.

Section 4. The Times, Places and Manner of holding Elections for Senators and Representatives, shall be prescribed in each State by the Legislature thereof; but the Congress may at any time by Law make or alter such Regulations, except as to the Places of chusing Senators.

The Congress shall assemble at least once in every Year, and such Meeting shall be on the first Monday in December, unless they shall by Law appoint a different Day.

Section 5. Each House shall be the Judge of the Elections, Returns and

Qualifications of its own Members, and a Majority of each shall constitute a Quorum to do Business; but a smaller Number may adjourn from day to day, and may be authorized to compel the Attendance of absent Members, in such Manner, and under such Penalties as each House may provide.

Each House may determine the Rules of its Proceedings, punish its Members for disorderly Behaviour, and, with the Concurrence of two thirds, expel a Member.

Each House shall keep a Journal of its Proceedings, and from time to time publish the same, excepting such Parts as may in their Judgment require Secrecy; and the Yeas and Nays of the Members of either House on any question shall, at the Desire of one fifth of those Present, be entered on the Journal.

Neither House, during the Session of Congress, shall, without the Consent of the other, adjourn for more than three days, nor to any other Place than that in which the two Houses shall be sitting.

Section 6. The Senators and Representatives shall receive a Compensation for their Services, to be ascertained by Law, and paid out of the Treasury of the United States. They shall in all Cases, except Treason, Felony and Breach of the Peace, be privileged from Arrest during their Attendance at the Session of their respective Houses, and in going to and returning from the same; and for any Speech or Debate in either House, they shall not be questioned in any other Place.

No Senator or Representative shall, during the Time for which he was elected, be appointed to any civil Officer under the Authority of the United States, which shall have been created, or the Emoluments whereof shall have been encreased during such time; and no Person holding any Office under the United States, shall be a Member of either House during his Continuance in Office.

Section 7. All Bills for raising Revenue shall originate in the House of Representatives; but the Senate may propose or concur with Amendments as on other Bills.

Every Bill which shall have passed the House of Representatives and the Senate, shall, before it become a Law, be presented to the President of the United States; If he approve he shall sign it, but if not he shall return it, with his Objections to that House in which it shall have originated, who shall enter the Objections at large on their Journal, and proceed to reconsider it. If after such Reconsideration two thirds of that House shall agree to pass the Bill, it shall be sent, together with the Objections, to the other House, by which it shall likewise be reconsidered, and if approved by two thirds of that House, it shall become a Law. But in all such Cases the Votes of both Houses shall be determined by Yeas and Nays, and the Names of the Persons voting for and against the Bill shall be entered on the Journal of each House respectively. If any Bill shall not be returned by the President within ten Days (Sundays excepted) after it shall have been presented to him, the Same shall be a Law, in like Manner as if he had signed it, unless the Congress by their Adjournment prevent its Return, in which Case it shall not be a Law.

Every Order, Resolution, or Vote to which the Concurrence of the Senate and House of Representatives may be necessary (except on a question of Adjournment) shall be presented to the President of the United States; and before the Same shall take Effect, shall be approved by him, or being disapproved by him, shall be repassed by two thirds of the Senate and House of Representatives, according to the Rules and Limitations prescribed in the Case of a Bill.

Section 8. The Congress shall have Power To lay and collect Taxes, Duties, Imposts and Excises, to pay the Debts and provide for the common Defence and general Welfare of the United States; but all Duties, Imposts and Excises shall be uniform throughout the United States;

To borrow Money on the Credit of the United States;

To regulate Commerce with foreign Nations, and among the several States, and with the Indian Tribes;

To establish an uniform Rule of Naturalization, and uniform Laws on the subject of Bankruptcies throughout the United States;

To coin Money, regulate the Value thereof, and of foreign Coin, and fix the Standard of Weights and Measures;

To provide for the Punishment of counterfeiting the Securities and current Coin of the United States;

To establish Post Offices and post Roads;

To promote the Progress of Science and useful Arts, by securing for limited Times to Authors and Inventors the exclusive Right to their respective Writings and Discoveries;

To constitute Tribunals inferior to the supreme Court;

To define and punish Piracies and Felonies committed on the high Seas, and Offences against the Law of Nations;

To declare War, grant Letters of Marque and Reprisal, and make Rules concerning Captures on Land and Water;

To raise and support Armies, but no Appropriation of Money to that Use shall be for a longer Term than two Years;

To provide and maintain a Navy;

To make Rules for the Government and Regulation of the land and naval Forces;

To provide for calling forth the Militia to execute the Laws of the Union, suppress Insurrections and repel Invasions;

To provide for organizing, arming, and disciplining, the Militia, and for governing such Part of them as may be employed in the Service of the United States, reserving to the States respectively, the Appointment of the Officers, and the Authority of training the Militia according to the discipline prescribed by Congress;

To exercise exclusive Legislation in all Cases whatsoever, over such

District (not exceeding ten Miles square) as may, by Cession of particular States, and the Acceptance of Congress, become the Seat of the Government of the United States, and to exercise like Authority over all Places purchased by the Consent of the Legislature of the State in which the Same shall be for the Erection of Forts, Magazines, Arsenals, dock-Yards, and other needful Buildings;—And

To make all Laws which shall be necessary and proper for carrying into Execution the foregoing Powers, and all other Powers vested by this Constitution in the Government of the United States, or in any Department or Officer thereof.

Section 9. The Migration or Importation of such Persons as any of the States now existing shall think proper to admit, shall not be prohibited by the Congress prior to the Year one thousand eight hundred and eight, but a Tax or duty may be imposed on such Importation, not exceeding ten dollars for each Person.

The Privilege of the Writ of Habeas Corpus shall not be suspended, unless when in Cases of Rebellion or Invasion the public Safety may require it.

No Bill of Attainder or ex post facto Law shall be passed.

No Capitation, or other direct, Tax shall be laid, unless in Proportion to the Census or Enumeration herein before directed to be taken.

No Tax or Duty shall be laid on Articles exported from any State.

No Preference shall be given by any Regulation of Commerce or Revenue to the Ports of one State over those of another: nor shall Vessels bound to, or from, one State, be obliged to enter, clear, or pay Duties in another.

No Money shall be drawn from the Treasury, but in Consequence of Appropriations made by Law; and a regular Statement and Account of the Receipts and Expenditures of all public Money shall be published from time to time.

No Title of Nobility shall be granted by the United States: And no Person holding any Office of Profit or Trust under them, shall, without the Consent of the Congress, accept of any present, Emolument, Office, or Title, of any kind whatever, from any King, Prince, or foreign State.

Section 10. No State shall enter into any Treaty, Alliance, or Confederation; grant Letters of Marque and Reprisal; coin Money; emit Bills of Credit; make any Thing but gold and silver Coin a Tender in Payment of Debts; pass any Bill of Attainder, ex post facto Law, or Law impairing the Obligation of Contracts, or grant any Title of Nobility.

No State shall, without the Consent of the Congress, lay any Imposts or Duties on Imports or Exports, except what may be absolutely necessary for executing its inspection Laws: and the net Produce of all Duties and Imposts, laid by any State on Imports or Exports, shall be for the Use of the Treasury of the United States; and all such Laws shall be subject to the Revision and Control of the Congress.

No State shall, without the Consent of Congress, lay any Duty of Tonnage, keep Troops, or Ships of War in time of Peace, enter into any Agreement or Compact with another State, or with a foreign Power, or engage in War, unless actually invaded, or in such imminent Danger as will not admit of delay.

Article II

Section 1. The executive Power shall be vested in a President of the United States of America. He shall hold his Office during the Term of four Years, and, together with the Vice President, chosen for the same term, be elected, as follows.

Each State shall appoint, in such Manner as the Legislature thereof may direct, a Number of Electors, equal to the whole Number of Senators and Representatives to which the State may be entitled in the Congress: but no Senator or Representative, or Person holding an Office of Trust or Profit under the United States, shall be appointed an Elector.

The Electors shall meet in their respective States, and vote by Ballot for two Persons, of whom one at least shall not be an Inhabitant of the same State with themselves. And they shall make a List of all the Persons voted for, and of the Number of Votes for each; which List they shall sign and certify, and transmit sealed to the Seat of the Government of the United States, directed to the President of the Senate. The President of the Senate shall, in the Presence of the Senate and House of Representatives, open all the Certificates, and the Votes shall then be counted. The Person having the greatest Number of Votes shall be the President, if such Number be a Majority of the whole Number of Electors appointed; and if there be more than one who have such Majority, and have an equal Number of Votes, then the House of Representatives shall immediately chuse by Ballot one of them for President: and if no Person have a Majority, then from the five highest on the List the said House shall in like Manner chuse the President. But in chusing the President, the Votes shall be taken by States, the Representation from each State having one Vote; A quorum for this Purpose shall consist of a Member or Members from two thirds of the States, and a Majority of all the States shall be necessary to a Choice. In every Case, after the Choice of the President, the Person having the greatest Number of Votes of the Electors shall be the Vice President. But if there should remain two or more who have equal Votes, the Senate shall chuse from them by Ballot the Vice President.

The Congress may determine the Time of chusing the Electors, and the Day on which they shall give their Votes; which Day shall be the same throughout the United States.

No Person except a natural born Citizen, or a Citizen of the United

States, at the time of the Adoption of this Constitution, shall be eligible to the Office of President; neither shall any Person be eligible to that Office who shall not have attained to the Age of thirty five Years, and been fourteen Years a Resident within the United States.

In Case of the Removal of the President from Office, or of his Death, Resignation, or Inability to discharge the Powers and Duties of the said Office, the Same shall devolve on the Vice President, and the Congress may by Law provide for the Case of Removal, Death, Resignation or Inability, both of the President and Vice President, declaring what Officer shall then act as President, and such Officer shall act accordingly, until the Disability be removed, or a President shall be elected.

The President shall, at stated Times, receive for his Services, a Compensation, which shall neither be encreased nor diminished during the Period for which he shall have been elected, and he shall not receive within that Period any other Emolument from the United States, or any of them.

Before he enter on the Execution of his Office, he shall take the following Oath or Affirmation:—'I do solemnly swear (or affirm) that I will faithfully execute the Office of President of the United States, and will to the best of my Ability, preserve, protect and defend the Constitution of the United States.'

Section 2. The President shall be Commander in Chief of the Army and Navy of the United States, and of the Militia of the several States, when called into the actual Service of the United States; he may require the Opinion, in writing, of the principal Officer in each of the executive Departments, upon any Subject relating to the Duties of their respective Offices, and he shall have Power to grant Reprieves and Pardons for Offences against the United States, except in Cases of Impeachment.

He shall have Power, by and with the Advice and Consent of the Senate, to make Treaties, provided two thirds of the Senators present concur; and he shall nominate, and by and with the Advice and Consent of the Senate, shall appoint Ambassadors, other public Ministers and Consuls, Judges of the supreme Court, and all other Officers of the United States, whose Appointments are not herein otherwise provided for, and which shall be established by Law: but the Congress may by Law vest the Appointment of such inferior Officers, as they think proper, in the President alone, in the Courts of Law, or in the Heads of Departments.

The President shall have Power to fill up all Vacancies that may happen during the Recess of the Senate, by granting Commissions which shall expire at the End of their next Session.

Section 3. He shall from time to time give to the Congress Information of the State of the Union, and recommend to their Consideration such Measures as he shall judge necessary and expedient; he may, on extraordinary Occasions, convene both Houses, or either of them, and in

Case of Disagreement between them, with Respect to the Time of Adjournment, he may adjourn them to such Time as he shall think proper; he shall receive Ambassadors and other public Ministers; he shall take Care that the Laws be faithfully executed, and shall Commission all the Officers of the United States.

Section 4. The President, Vice President and all civil Officers of the United States, shall be removed from Office on Impeachment for, and Conviction of, Treason, Bribery, or other High Crimes and Misdemeanors.

Article III

Section 1. The judicial Power of the United States, shall be vested in one supreme Court, and in such inferior Courts as the Congress may from time to time ordain and establish. The Judges, both of the supreme and inferior Courts, shall hold their Offices during good Behaviour, and shall, at stated Times, receive for their Services, a Compensation, which shall not be diminished during their Continuance in Office.

Section 2. The judicial Power shall extend to all Cases, in Law and Equity, arising under this Constitution, the Laws of the United States, and Treaties made, or which shall be made, under their Authority;—to all Cases affecting Ambassadors, other public Ministers and Consuls;—to all Cases of admiralty and maritime Jurisdiction;—to Controversies to which the United States shall be a Party;—to Controversies between two or more States; between a State and Citizens of another State;—between Citizens of different States;—between Citizens of the same State claiming Lands under Grants of different States, and between a State, or the Citizens thereof, and foreign States, Citizens or Subjects.

In all Cases affecting Ambassadors, other public Ministers and Consuls, and those in which a State shall be Party, the supreme Court shall have original Jurisdiction. In all the other Cases before mentioned, the supreme Court shall have appellate Jurisdiction, both as to Law and Fact, with such Exceptions, and under such Regulations as the Congress shall make.

The Trial of all Crimes, except in Cases of Impeachment, shall be by Jury; and such Trial shall be held in the State where the said Crimes shall have been committed; but when not committed within any State, the Trial shall be at such Place or Places as the Congress may by Law have directed.

Section 3. Treason against the United States, shall consist only in levying War against them, or in adhering to their Enemies, giving them Aid and Comfort. No Person shall be convicted of Treason unless on the Testimony of two Witnesses to the same overt Act, or on Confession in open Court.

The Congress shall have Power to declare the Punishment of Treason,

but no Attainder of Treason shall work Corruption of Blood, or For-
feiture except during the Life of the Person attainted.

Article IV

Section 1. Full Faith and Credit shall be given in each State to the public
Acts, Records, and judicial Proceedings of every other State. And the
Congress may by general Laws prescribe the Manner in which such Acts,
Records and Proceedings shall be proved, and the Effect thereof.

Section 2. The Citizens of each State shall be entitled to all Privileges
and Immunities of Citizens in the several States.

A Person charged in any State with Treason, Felony, or other Crime,
who shall flee from Justice, and be found in another State, shall on
Demand of the executive Authority of the State from which he fled, be
delivered up, to be removed to the State having Jurisdiction of the Crime.

No Person held to Service or Labour in one State, under the Laws
thereof, escaping into another, shall, in Consequence of any Law or
Regulation therein, be discharged from such Service or Labour, but shall
be delivered up on Claim of the Party to whom such Service or Labour
may be due.

Section 3. New States may be admitted by the Congress into this
Union; but no new State shall be formed or erected within the Jurisdiction of any other State; nor any State be formed by the Junction of two
or more States, or Parts of States, without the Consent of the Legislatures
of the States concerned as well as of the Congress.

The Congress shall have Power to dispose of and make all needful Rules
and Regulations respecting the Territory or other Property belonging to
the United States; and nothing in this Constitution shall be so construed
as to Prejudice any Claims of the United States, or of any particular
State.

Section 4. The United States shall guarantee to every State in this
Union a Republican Form of Government, and shall protect each of
them against Invasion; and on Application of the Legislature, or of the
Executive (when the Legislature cannot be convened) against domestic
Violence.

Article V

The Congress, whenever two thirds of both Houses shall deem it necessary, shall propose Amendments to this Constitution, or, on the Application of the Legislatures of two thirds of the several States, shall call a
Convention for proposing Amendments, which, in either Case, shall be
valid to all Intents and Purposes, as Part of this Constitution, when ratified by the Legislatures of three fourths of the several States, or by
Conventions in three fourths thereof, as the one or the other Mode of
Ratification may be proposed by the Congress; Provided that no Amend-

ment which may be made prior to the Year One thousand eight hundred and eight shall in any Manner affect the first and fourth Clauses in the Ninth Section of the first Article; and that no State, without its Consent, shall be deprived of its equal Suffrage in the Senate.

Article VI

All Debts contracted and Engagements entered into, before the Adoption of this Constitution, shall be as valid against the United States under this Constitution, as under the Confederation.

This Constitution, and the Laws of the United States which shall be made in Pursuance thereof; and all Treaties made, or which shall be made, under the Authority of the United States, shall be the supreme Law of the Land; and the Judges in every State shall be bound thereby, any Thing in the Constitution or Laws of any State to the Contrary notwithstanding.

The Senators and Representatives before mentioned, and the Members of the several State Legislatures, and all executive and judicial Officers, both of the United States and of the several States, shall be bound by Oath or Affirmation, to support this Constitution; but no religious Test shall ever be required as a Qualification to any Office or public Trust under the United States.

Article VII

The Ratification of the Conventions of nine States, shall be sufficient for the Establishment of this Constitution between the States so ratifying the Same.

AMENDMENTS

Amendment 1

Congress shall make no law respecting an establishment of religion, or prohibiting the free exercise thereof; or abridging the freedom of speech, or of the press; or the right of the people peaceably to assemble, and to petition the Government for a redress of grievances.

Amendment 2

A well regulated Militia, being necessary to the security of a free State, the right of the people to keep and bear Arms, shall not be infringed.

Amendment 3

No Soldier shall, in time of peace be quartered in any house, without the consent of the Owner, nor in time of war, but in a manner to be prescribed by law.

Amendment 4

The right of the people to be secure in their persons, houses, papers, and effects, against unreasonable searches and seizures, shall be not violated, and no Warrants shall issue, but upon probable cause, supported by Oath or affirmation, and particularly describing the place to be searched, and the persons or things to be seized.

Amendment 5

No person shall be held to answer for a capital, or otherwise infamous crime, unless on a presentment or indictment of a Grand Jury, except in cases arising in the land or naval forces, or in the Militia, when in actual service in time of War or public danger; nor shall any person be subject for the same offence to be twice put in jeopardy of life or limb; nor shall be compelled in any criminal case to be a witness against himself, nor be deprived of life, liberty, or property, without due process of law; nor shall private property be taken for public use, without just compensation.

Amendment 6

In all criminal prosecutions, the accused shall enjoy the right to a speedy and public trial, by an impartial jury of the State and district wherein the crime shall have been committed, which district shall have been previously ascertained by law, and to be informed of the nature and cause of the accusation; to be confronted with the witnesses against him; to have compulsory process for obtaining witnesses in his favor, and to have the Assistance of Counsel for his defence.

Amendment 7

In Suits at common law, where the value in controversy shall exceed twenty dollars, the right of trial by jury shall be preserved, and no fact tried by a jury, shall be otherwise re-examined in any Court of the United States, than according to the rules of the common law.

Amendment 8

Excessive bail shall not be required, nor excessive fines imposed, nor cruel and unusual punishments inflicted.

Amendment 9

The enumeration in the Constitution, of certain rights, shall not be construed to deny or disparage others retained by the people.

Amendment 10

The powers not delegated to the United States by the Constitution, nor prohibited by it to the States, are reserved to the States respectively, or to the people.

Amendment 11

The Judicial power of the United States shall not be construed to extend to any suit in law or equity, commenced or prosecuted against one of the United States by Citizens of another State, or by Citizens or Subjects of any Foreign State.

Amendment 12

The Electors shall meet in their respective states and vote by ballot for President and Vice-President, one of whom, at least, shall not be an inhabitant of the same state with themselves; they shall name in their ballots the person voted for as President, and in distinct ballots the person voted for as Vice-President, and they shall make distinct lists of all persons voted for as President, and of all persons voted for as Vice-President, and of the number of votes for each, which lists they shall sign and certify, and transmit sealed to the seat of the government of the United States, directed to the President of the Senate;—The President of the Senate shall, in the presence of the Senate and House of Representatives, open all the certificates and the votes shall then be counted;—The person having the greatest number of votes for President, shall be the President, if such number be a majority of the whole number of Electors appointed; and if no person have such majority, then from the persons having the highest numbers not exceeding three on the list of those voted for as President, the House of Representatives shall choose immediately, by ballot, the President. But in choosing the President, the votes shall be taken by states, the representation from each state having one vote; a quorum for this purpose shall consist of a member or members from two-thirds of the states, and a majority of all the states shall be necessary to a choice. And if the House of Representatives shall not choose a President whenever the right of choice shall devolve upon them, before the fourth day of March next following, then the Vice-President shall act as President, as in the case of the death or other constitutional disability of the President.—The person having the greatest number of votes as Vice-President, shall be the Vice-President, if such number be a majority of the whole number of Electors appointed, and if no person have a majority, then from the two highest numbers on the list, the Senate shall choose the Vice-President; a quorum for the purpose shall consist of two-thirds of the whole number of Senators, and a majority of the whole number shall be necessary to a choice. But no person constitutionally ineligible to the office of President shall be eligible to that of Vice-President of the United States.

Amendment 13

Section 1. Neither slavery nor involuntary servitude, except as a punishment for crime whereof the party shall have been duly convicted, shall exist within the United States, or any place subject to their jurisdiction.

Section 2. Congress shall have power to enforce this article by appropriate legislation.

Amendment 14

Section 1. All persons born or naturalized in the United States, and subject to the jurisdiction thereof, are citizens of the United States and of the State wherein they reside. No State shall make or enforce any law which shall abridge the privileges or immunities of citizens of the United States; nor shall any State deprive any person of life, liberty, or property, without due process of law; nor deny to any person within its jurisdiction the equal protection of the laws.

Section 2. Representatives shall be apportioned among the several States according to their respective numbers, counting the whole number of persons in each State, excluding Indians not taxed. But when the right to vote at any election for the choice of electors for President and Vice-President of the United States, Representatives in Congress, the Executive and Judicial officers of a State, or the members of the Legislature thereof, is denied to any of the male inhabitants of such State, being twenty-one years of age, and citizens of the United States, or in any way abridged, except for participation in rebellion, or other crime, the basis of representation therein shall be reduced in the proportion which the number of such male citizens shall bear to the whole number of male citizens twenty-one years of age in such State.

Section 3. No person shall be a Senator or Representative in Congress, or elector of President and Vice-President, or hold any office, civil or military, under the United States, or under any State, who, having previously taken an oath, as a member of Congress, or as an officer of the United States, or as a member of any State legislature, or as an executive or judicial officer of any State, to support the Constitution of the United States, shall have engaged in insurrection or rebellion against the same, or given aid or comfort to the enemies thereof. But Congress may by a vote of two-thirds of each House, remove such disability.

Section 4. The validity of the public debt of the United States, authorized by law, including debts incurred for payment of pensions and bounties for services in suppressing insurrection or rebellion, shall not be questioned. But neither the United States nor any State shall assume or pay any debt or obligation incurred in aid of insurrection or rebellion against the United States, or any claim for the loss or emancipation of any slave; but all such debts, obligations and claims shall be held illegal and void.

Section 5. The Congress shall have power to enforce, by appropriate legislation, the provisions of this article.

Amendment 15

Section 1. The right of citizens of the United States to vote shall not be denied or abridged by the United States or by any State on account of race, color, or previous condition of servitude.

Section 2. The Congress shall have power to enforce this article by appropriate legislation.

Amendment 16

The Congress shall have power to lay and collect taxes on incomes, from whatever source derived, without apportionment among the several States, and without regard to any census or enumeration.

Amendment 17

The Senate of the United States shall be composed of two Senators from each State, elected by the people thereof for six years; and each Senator shall have one vote. The electors in each State shall have the qualifications requisite for electors of the most numerous branch of the State legislatures.

When vacancies happen in the representation of any State in the Senate, the executive authority of such State shall issue writs of election to fill such vacancies: *Provided,* That the legislature of any State may empower the executive thereof to make temporary appointments until the people fill the vacancies by election as the legislature may direct.

This amendment shall not be so construed as to affect the election or term of any Senator chosen before it becomes valid as part of the Constitution.

Amendment 18

Section 1. After one year from the ratification of this article the manufacture, sale, or transportation of intoxicating liquors within, the importation thereof into, or the exportation thereof from the United States and all territory subject to the jurisdiction thereof for beverage purposes is hereby prohibited.

Section 2. The Congress and the several States shall have concurrent power to enforce this article by appropriate legislation.

Section 3. This article shall be inoperative unless it shall have been ratified as an amendment to the Constitution by the legislatures of the several States, as provided in the Constitution, within seven years from the date of the submission hereof to the States by the Congress.

Amendment 19

The right of citizens of the United States to vote shall not be denied or abridged by the United States or by any State on account of sex.

Congress shall have power to enforce this article by appropriate legislation.

Amendment 20

Section 1. The terms of the President and Vice President shall end at noon on the 20th day of January, and the terms of Senators and Representatives at noon on the 3d day of January, of the years in which such terms would have ended if this article had not been ratified; and the terms of their successors shall then begin.

Section 2. The Congress shall assemble at least once in every year, and such meeting shall begin at noon on the 3d day of January, unless they shall by law appoint a different day.

Section 3. If, at the time fixed for the beginning of the term of the President, the President elect shall have died, the Vice President elect shall become President. If a President shall not have been chosen before the time fixed for the beginning of his term, or if the President elect shall have failed to qualify, then the Vice President elect shall act as President until a President shall have qualified; and the Congress may by law provide for the case wherein neither a President elect nor a Vice President elect shall have qualified, declaring who shall then act as President, or the manner in which one who is to act shall be selected, and such person shall act accordingly until a President or Vice President shall have qualified.

Section 4. The Congress may by law provide for the case of the death of any of the persons from whom the House of Representatives may choose a President whenever the right of choice shall have devolved upon them, and for the case of the death of any of the persons from whom the Senate may choose a Vice President whenever the right of choice shall have devolved upon them.

Section 5. Sections 1 and 2 shall take effect on the 15th day of October following the ratification of this article.

Section 6. This article shall be inoperative unless it shall have been ratified as an amendment to the Constitution by the legislatures of three-fourths of the several States within seven years from the date of its submission.

Amendment 21

Section 1. The eighteenth article of amendment to the Constitution of the United States is hereby repealed.

Section 2. The transportation or importation into any State, Territory, or possession of the United States for delivery or use therein of intoxicating liquors, in violation of the laws thereof, is hereby prohibited.

Section 3. This article shall be inoperative unless it shall have been ratified as an amendment to the Constitution by conventions in the several States, as provided in the Constitution, within seven years from the date of the submission hereof to the States by the Congress.

Amendment 22

Section 1. No person shall be elected to the office of the President more than twice, and no person who has held the office of President, or acted as President, for more than two years of a term to which some other person was elected President shall be elected to the office of the President more than once. But this Article shall not apply to any person holding the office of President when this Article was proposed by the Congress, and shall not prevent any person who may be holding the office of President, or acting as President, during the term within which this Article becomes operative from holding the office of President or acting as President during the remainder of such term.

Section 2. This article shall be inoperative unless it shall have been ratified as an amendment to the Constitution by the legislatures of three-fourths of the several States within seven years from the date of its submission to the States by the Congress.

Amendment 23

Section 1. The District constituting the seat of Government of the United States shall appoint in such manner as the Congress may direct:

A number of electors of President and Vice President equal to the whole number of Senators and Representatives in Congress to which the District would be entitled if it were a State, but in no event more than the least populous State; they shall be in addition to those appointed by the States, but they shall be considered, for the purposes of the election of President and Vice President, to be electors appointed by a State; and they shall meet in the District and perform such duties as provided by the twelfth article of amendment.

Section 2. The Congress shall have power to enforce this article by appropriate legislation.

Amendment 24

Section 1. The right of citizens of the United States to vote in any primary or other election for President or Vice President, for electors for

President or Vice President, or for Senator or Representative in Congress, shall not be denied or abridged by the United States or any State by reason of failure to pay any poll tax or other tax.

Section 2. The Congress shall have power to enforce this article by appropriate legislation.

Amendment 25

Section 1. In case of the removal of the President from office or of his death or resignation, the Vice President shall become President.

Section 2. Whenever there is a vacancy in the office of the Vice President, the President shall nominate a Vice President who shall take office upon confirmation by a majority vote of both Houses of Congress.

Section 3. Whenever the President transmits to the President pro tempore of the Senate and the Speaker of the House of Representatives his written declaration that he is unable to discharge the powers and duties of his office, and until he transmits to them a written declaration to the contrary, such powers and duties shall be discharged by the Vice President as Acting President.

Section 4. Whenever the Vice President and a majority of either the principal officers of the executive departments or of such other body as Congress may by law provide, transmit to the President pro tempore of the Senate and the Speaker of the House of Representatives their written declaration that the President is unable to discharge the powers and duties of his office, the Vice President shall immediately assume the powers and duties of the office as Acting President.

Thereafter, when the President transmits to the President pro tempore of the Senate and the Speaker of the House of Representatives his written declaration that no inability exists, he shall resume the powers and duties of his office unless the Vice President and a majority of either the principal officers of the executive department or of such other body as Congress may by law provide, transmit within four days to the President pro tempore of the Senate and the Speaker of the House of Representatives their written declaration that the President is unable to discharge the powers and duties of his office. Thereupon Congress shall decide the issue, assembling within forty-eight hours for that purpose if not in session. If the Congress, within twenty-one days after receipt of the latter written declaration, or, if Congress is not in session, within twenty-one days after Congress is required to assemble, determines by two-thirds vote of both Houses that the President is unable to discharge the powers and duties of his office, the Vice President shall continue to discharge the same as Acting President; otherwise, the President shall resume the powers and duties of his office.

Amendment 26

Section 1. The right of citizens of the United States, who are eighteen years of age or older, to vote shall not be denied or abridged by the United States or by any State on account of age.

Section 2. The Congress shall have power to enforce this article by appropriate legislation.

Index

B: PERSONS

Presidents
(election in which candidate)

Others

(if presidential candidate, election in which candidate)

C: SUBJECTS